CW01022402

Mastering MuseScore

Marc Sabatella

with

Thomas Bonte, Nicolas Froment, and Werner Schweer

MuseScore BVBA

Copyright © 2015 Marc Sabatella
Published by MuseScore BVBA
ISBN 1-5086-2168-3
Inquiries and feedback: mastering-musescore@musescore.com

Foreword

Marc joined the MuseScore community back when version 0.9.6 was the state of the art. His presence immediately stood out as he was challenging MuseScore's capabilities to the limits and posting about his findings in the MuseScore forums. Soon he started to dabble with the MuseScore source code, scratching his own itch as we say in open source world.

I got to know him better when we started to communicate via the online #musescore chat channel. While I helped him to learn about MuseScore's code architecture, he, on his turn, shared his knowledge on music theory. These daily and nightly conversations continued over the span of several years and resulted in countless small and large improvements in the MuseScore software. It is without question that without Marc's involvement, MuseScore would not be what it is today.

While I have personally learned a great deal from Marc, he has also helped hundreds of people through the MuseScore forum by answering their questions, whether these were beginner or more advanced questions. As a result he accumulated know-how on all the typical barriers in each stage of the MuseScore learning curve and it is now all bundled in this book.

I know MuseScore inside out and I very much enjoyed reading this book. I'm sure you will enjoy the book as much as I have.

Nicolas Froment @lasconic
MuseScore CTO

Contents

III   Other Score Elements   127

Part I

Getting Started

Chapter 1

Introduction

What Is MuseScore?

MuseScore is a free and open source application for creating and playing music scores. It runs on Windows, Mac OS, and Linux, and it has been translated into over 50 different languages. MuseScore can be used to create everything from simple lead sheets to piano music to guitar tablature to arrangements for jazz and rock bands, choirs, and full orchestras. MuseScore provides almost all of the features of the expensive proprietary notation programs, but with none of the cost, and with a user interface that emphasizes simplicity.

MuseScore is also a community of users. The support site `musescore.org` provides discussion forums, a free online Handbook, tutorial videos, and other documentation, an issue tracker, and much more. The score sharing site `musescore.com` allows people to share their scores online and to browse for new scores to enjoy. There are also companion apps available for mobile devices to make it even easier to take advantage of the scores shared on `musescore.com`.

By putting so many powerful capabilities into the hands of so many people, MuseScore is revolutionizing the field of music notation. It has been downloaded millions of times and is being used by countless individual musicians and composers as well as by schools and universities throughout the world.

What is even more impressive is that so much of this was already happening with MuseScore 1.3 and previous versions, but the MuseScore 2.0 release is a real game-changer. It represents the culmination of over four years of development effort, with thousands of suggestions and contributions from users resulting in significant improvements in virtually every aspect of the program. It is now easier than ever to create scores that look and sound their best.

Of course, you probably know most of that or you would not be interested in this book. But hopefully thinking about what you have just read gives you some sense of why we are so excited to bring you MuseScore 2.0 and to provide this opportunity to help you master it. Before we go on and start exploring the many features of MuseScore, I would like to take a moment to give you a little background on MuseScore.

History of MuseScore

The project began in the early 2000's as an offshoot of the MusE sequencer that Werner Schweer was developing for Linux. He started to try to add a notation option to MusE itself, but he soon realized that music notation was better suited to a separate application, and thus MuseScore was conceived. It continued to be developed on Linux only at first, but soon Nicolas Froment joined the team, fixing bugs and helping to port the code to Windows and Mac OS. MuseScore uses the free and open source Qt libraries to help the application run on multiple platforms with a consistent look and feel. The third core member of the team, Thomas Bonte, is responsible for the development of the `musescore.org` and `musescore.com` web sites and community. Thanks to the open source nature of the product, there are many other programmers – including this author – who have also contributed to the development of MuseScore.

MuseScore became increasingly full-featured and stable over the years, and finally the first official release – MuseScore 1.0 – was made available in February of 2011. This was followed by 1.1, 1.2, and 1.3 over the course of the next two years, mostly just fixing bugs and adding a few small improvements. Even before the release of MuseScore 1.0, however, MuseScore 2.0 was already in development. The team realized that what they were undertaking was monumental enough in scope that it would be quite some time before it was ready, so the 1.X series included very little of the work that was being done for 2.0. The work on the 2.0 version was made available via a series of experimental nightly builds, mostly used just by the developers and a few hard core early adopters interested in helping test the code.

By August of 2014, work on MuseScore 2.0 had reached a point with regard to features and stability where a beta release became feasible, and the new version started to see wider exposure. Based on the extraordinarily enthusiastic response, development focused on responding to the feedback received and the issues reported, and the product moved quickly toward release. Meanwhile, work on this book was proceeding in tandem with the development of the application itself. MuseScore 2.0 was released in March of 2015, and this book was published a couple of months later. The current version of MuseScore as of this writing is 2.0.2, which provides a number of fixes and other small improvements over the original 2.0 release.

About This Book

Although there is a free Handbook (|Help⟩⟩Online Handbook|, or `https://musescore.org/en/handbook`) available for MuseScore that covers most of its features, this book is designed to be a more comprehensive guide that should prove invaluable for those wishing to truly master MuseScore. It is divided into five main parts:

Getting Started – quick introduction to the program
Note Entry and Editing – everything you need to know about notes (the main elements in almost every score)
Other Score Elements – clefs, key and time signatures, dynamics, lyrics, articulations, etc.
Staves, Parts, and Layout – organizing the staves of your score
Working with MuseScore – playback, printing, customization, etc.

Because MuseScore provides such a wealth of free online documentation, you may be wondering why anyone would want to buy this book. One reason is simply to support the development of the software. Since MuseScore itself is free, sales of this book help to fund the team who makes it possible for everyone to enjoy MuseScore. But I hope you will also find the information in this book complete and clear enough that it helps you get even more out of MuseScore than you thought possible!

This book is available in both printed and electronic versions. Please support me and the MuseScore team by purchasing this book from official sources only (e.g., Amazon, the Kindle / iBooks stores). If you should somehow find yourself in possession of an unauthorized copy of this book and are finding it valuable, consider purchasing it legitimately, or even just making a donation to MuseScore directly via `musescore.org`.

If you have questions about MuseScore, the best place to ask is on the forums on `musescore.org`, which you can access directly from MuseScore via |Help⟩⟩Ask for Help|. If you have comments you would like to share about this book itself, you may contact us at `mastering-musescore@musescore.com`.

Acknowledgements

I would like to thank David Bolton, Nicolas Froment, Tony Mountifield, Steven Otto, Joachim Schmitz, Mark Stanton, and Isaac Weiss for their feedback on this book. Between them, they caught many errors I am very happy to have had the opportunity to correct. Also, thanks to Xavier Bertels for the beautiful cover design.

I and all MuseScore users are deeply indebted to Werner Schweer for creating this amazing software, and to Nicolas Froment and Thomas Bonte for all they have done to make MuseScore the success it is. I would also like to express my personal gratitude to them for encouraging me to write this book.

It would be impossible to adequately acknowledge everyone who has contributed to the development of MuseScore and its community. The best I can do is encourage you to join us on `musescore.org` and `musescore.com` and see for yourself just how many people are passionate about MuseScore, and if you are interested, get more involved yourself!

Chapter 2

Finding Your Way Around

MuseScore enables you to easily create beautiful sheet music. The design of the interface incorporates many concepts that should be familiar from word processing, graphic design, or other programs you may have used. A large score window is the central focus of the interface, and there are also menus, toolbars, palettes, and other windows that contain controls for creating scores. Music can be entered using the mouse, computer keyboard, an on-screen piano keyboard, or a separate MIDI keyboard or other controller. MuseScore can play back your score using a built-in synthesizer or by integrating with other programs on your computer.

The user interface is designed to present controls for all of these facilities in an intuitive and uncluttered manner. But the sheer number of features supported by MuseScore means that a quick tour is in order. In this chapter, I will introduce you to the different areas of the MuseScore user interface, so that if in subsequent chapters I refer to the *Inspector* or some other window or toolbar, you will know how to find it.

> MuseScore runs on Windows, Mac OS, and Linux, and it works similarly on all three platforms. However, there are some details of the user interface that are system-dependent. For instance, menus are arranged differently on Mac OS than other systems because of the way application menus are integrated with the Apple menu. Also, keyboard shortcuts that involve the Ctrl key replace this with Cmd on Mac OS, and shortcuts that involve Alt replace this with Option. Users of keyboard layouts other than the US-standard QWERTY layout may find a few shortcuts work differently than described as well. Keyboard shortcuts can be customized as discussed in *Shortcuts* in the chapter on *Customization*.

Start Center

The first window you will see when MuseScore starts up is the *Start Center*. You can also display this at any time using the menu command View ⟩ Start Center or the keyboard shortcut F4.

Start Center

The left side of this window displays options to create a new score and to open an existing score, as well as thumbnails of your most recent scores. See the chapters on *Creating a New Score* and *File Operations* for more information.

When you first start MuseScore, the *Start Center* includes a sample *Getting Started* score that you may find useful as you first learn MuseScore. This is no longer shown once you have started using MuseScore to create your own scores, but you can bring it back at any time if you clear your recent scores list via File ⟩ Open Recent ⟩ Clear Recent Files .

The right side of the *Start Center* window displays an *Online Community* page, drawn from content on the score sharing web site musescore.com. It allows you to find scores online that you can download and open in MuseScore.

Open or create a score, or press the Close button, to proceed to the main window.

Main Window

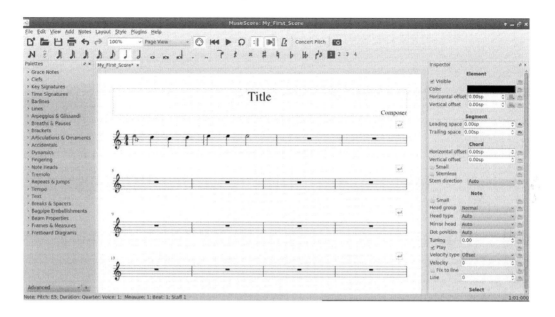

The main window in MuseScore is divided into a number of separate areas – toolbars, panes, secondary windows, etc. Most of these areas can be displayed or hidden via the View menu and/or keyboard shortcuts. You can also dock and undock some of them by simply dragging them away from their default location. In the case of the toolbars, you can also right-click an empty area of the toolbar area to customize which specific toolbars are displayed. When windows are docked within the main window, you can drag the divider between panes to resize them. See the chapter on *Customization* for more information.

Main Menu

At the top of the main window is a menu bar. This works just like other menus you are accustomed to in other programs.

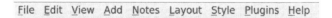

Toolbars

The toolbar area is located just below the main menu.

This toolbar area contains several distinct toolbars that can be enabled or disabled by right-clicking an empty area and checking or unchecking the corresponding options in the context menu that appears. The toolbars are:

File Operations – standard controls like open and save (see *File Operations* and *Printing and Graphic Output*)

Transport Tools – playback controls like rewind and play (see *Playback and Audio Output*)

Concert Pitch – control to transpose a score between written and sounding pitch (see *Transposition*)

Image Capture – control to capture a region of your score as an image (see *Printing and Graphic Output*)

Note Input – controls to enter notes and rests (see *Entering Notes and Rests*)

Score Window

The score window is the main document area within MuseScore. The score you are working on is displayed here.

> Any time you are working within the main window but the keyboard focus is in the *Inspector* or somewhere else other than the score window, the Esc key will return focus to the score window.

Page and Continuous View

A score can be displayed in either of two views – *Page View* or *Continuous View*. You can select between using a control in the *File Operations* toolbar. See *Navigation* for more information.

In *Page View*, you see a view of the whole page, or as much of it as will fit given your current zoom setting (also selected on the *File Operations* toolbar).

In *Continuous View*, you see a horizontally scrolling view.

Tabs

You can have several scores open at once. MuseScore displays tabs for each open score at the top of the score window. In addition, if the current score contains linked parts (see *Parts*), then a tab for each part is displayed underneath the main tab for the score.

My_First_Score ×	Prelude_and_Fugue_7_-_OpenWTC ×	Thiago* ×	Reunion* ×

Thiago*	Trumpet	Trombone	Baritone Saxophone	Guitar	Piano	Bass	Drums

You can switch between scores using the shortcut Ctrl + Tab .

Documents Side by Side & Documents Stacked

Not only can you have several scores open at once, but you can also *view* two scores at once – or, just as importantly, two different views of the same score. You can enable a side by side view using View ⟩ Documents Side By Side .

You can also enable a stacked view using View ⟩ Documents Stacked

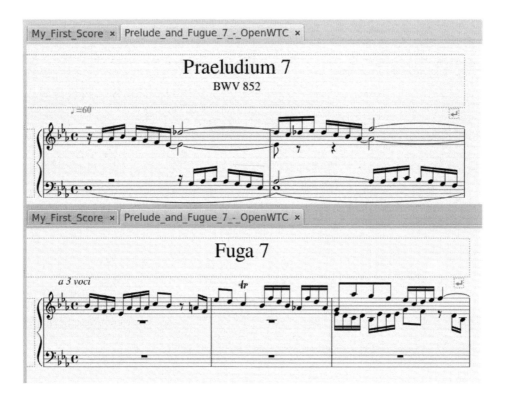

Palettes

The *Palettes* are found at the left side of the main window. The *Palettes* contain most of the markings that you will need for your score, beyond the actual notes and rests.

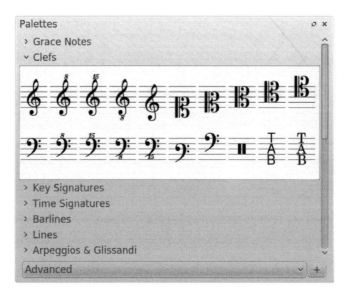

Note that the image above shows only a subset of the available palettes. Depending on your screen size and configuration, you may need to scroll to see the rest.

By default, MuseScore displays a *Basic* workspace containing only a minimal subset of the available palettes, and several of the palettes similarly contain only a subset of the available elements. If you are reading this book, however, I am assuming that you are probably interested in more than just the basics. I recommend you take a moment right now to change to the *Advanced* workspace using the control at the bottom of the *Palettes* area.

You can also customize palettes, adding new elements to existing palettes, rearranging them, or creating new palettes entirely. This is discussed further in the chapter on *Customization*.

The individual palettes within the *Palettes* window can be expanded and collapsed independently by simply clicking on their names. If you right-click the title bar of the *Palettes* window, a context menu appears with the option Single Palette. With this option disabled (the default), you can have multiple palettes open at once.

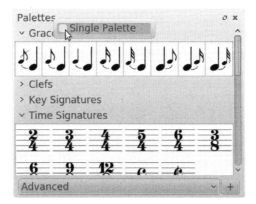

If you enable this option, then opening one palette will automatically close whichever palette was previously open.

There are generally two different ways to add items from the palette to your score. Items can be added by dragging the icon from the palette to a specific element in your score – typically a note or a measure. When using drag and drop, take care to drop when the target highlights.

However, a much more efficient way to add palette items is to first select one or more elements in your score, then double-click the palette icon. This is normally equivalent to dragging the palette item to each of the selected elements.

Certain element types have special handling to allow you to apply a palette item to a selected range as a whole rather than to each individual element. These cases will be discussed as they come up.

The *Palettes* window can be enabled and disabled using View ⟩ Palettes or the keyboard shortcut F9 . It is resizable and can be undocked if desired.

Inspector

The *Inspector* is normally displayed on the right side of the main window.

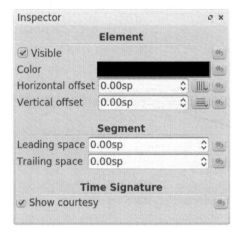

The *Inspector* displays and allows you to alter many of the properties of the elements in your score. The contents of the *Inspector* vary according to what type of element is selected.

You can enable or disable the *Inspector* using View ⟩ Inspector or the keyboard shortcut F8 . It is resizable and can be undocked if desired.

Status Bar

The status bar at the bottom of the main window displays information about the currently selected element as well as information about the current mode.

Note; Pitch: D5; Duration: Quarter; Voice: 1; Measure: 1; Beat: 2; Staff 1   Note input mode   1:02:000

Optional Windows

In addition to dialog boxes that are used for specific tasks, MuseScore provides a few more windows that you can display if you wish to access the controls they provide.

Navigator

You can enable the *Navigator* using `View` `Navigator` or the keyboard shortcut `F12`. It is displayed at the bottom of the main window and is resizable but cannot be undocked.

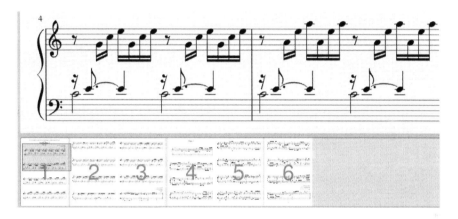

The *Navigator* gives you a thumbnail view of your entire score and shows you which portion of the score is currently in view within the score window. For more information, see *Navigation*.

Selection Filter

You can enable the *Selection Filter* using `View` `Selection Filter` or the keyboard shortcut `F6`. It is displayed on the left side of the main window and can be resized or undocked if desired.

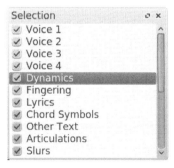

The *Selection Filter* allows you to control which element types are selected when making range selections. It is resizable and can be undocked. For more information, see *Making Selections*.

Master Palette

You can enable the *Master Palette* using View〉Master Palette or the keyboard shortcut Shift +
F9 . It is a separate window.

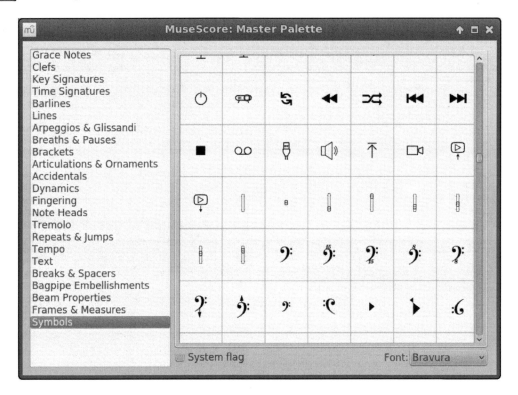

The *Master Palette* contains all of the markings supported by MuseScore and includes one
section labeled *Symbols* that contains hundreds of symbols that do not appear on any of the
standard palettes by default but can be added to your score directly from the *Master Palette*.
In addition, the *Time Signatures* and *Key Signatures* sections allow you to define custom time
and key signatures respectively. See *Key Signatures*, *Time Signatures*, and *Articulations and
Other Symbols*.

Piano Keyboard

You can enable the *Piano Keyboard* using View〉Piano Keyboard or the keyboard shortcut P .
It is displayed at the bottom of the main screen and can be resized or undocked if desired.

The *Piano Keyboard* can be used during note input as an alternative to entering notes using the mouse, the computer keyboard, or a MIDI keyboard. See *Entering Notes and Rests*. It can also display music as it is played.

Mixer

You can display the *Mixer* using [View] [Mixer] or the keyboard shortcut [F10]. It is a separate window.

You can use the *Mixer* to select specific instrument sounds for playback (see *Staves and Instruments*) as well as to control the relative volume, pan, and effects settings for the different instruments (see *Playback and Audio Output*).

Play Panel

You can display the *Play Panel* using [View] [Play Panel] or the keyboard shortcut [F11]. It is a separate window.

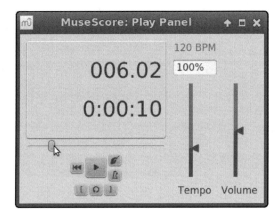

The *Play Panel* contains additional playback controls, including count-in, metronome, loop controls, etc. See *Playback and Audio Output*.

Although the *Play Panel* contains a slider marked *Tempo*, this is not the way to set the overall tempo for a score. Tempo markings should normally be placed directly on the score from the *Tempo* palette. See *Tempo Markings* in the chapter on *Text*. The *Tempo* slider in the *Play Panel* is for temporary overrides to the tempo, such as if you wish to play the score more slowly for practice purposes.

Synthesizer

You can display the *Synthesizer* using View ⟩ Synthesizer. It is a separate window.

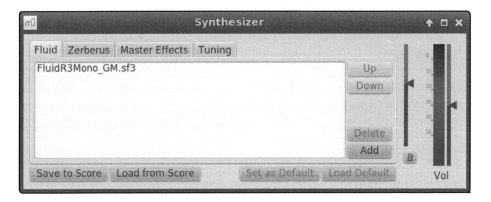

The *Synthesizer* controls the soundfonts and effects used by MuseScore for playback. See *Playback and Audio Output*.

Accessibility

MuseScore strives to be as accessible as possible. While the *Palettes* and a few other controls are not keyboard-friendly – so creating a score from scratch will be a challenge for a blind user – most of the rest of the user interface is fully accessible and provides screenreader feedback using NVDA. A blind musician can use MuseScore as a score reader and converter, with some limited ability to edit scores.

While a full discussion of the accessibility features of MuseScore is beyond the scope of this book, interested users should consult the Accessibility section of the documentation in Help ⟩ ⟩ Online Handbook for the latest information.

Chapter 3

Your First Score

In this chapter, I will walk you through the creation of a very simple score via a "paint-by-numbers" type of approach. That is, I do not provide much in the way of explaining how things work here. Instead, I simply tell you what to do, and refer you to other relevant chapters where you can learn more.

The score we are creating is for a song many of us will remember from childhood.

Mary Had a Little Lamb

Sarah Josepha Hale   Lowell Mason

For this demonstration, we will start with the empty score that MuseScore normally displays on start up. If you have already closed this and need to create a new score, go to File〉New to create one, then follow the prompts from there. See *Creating a New Score* for more information.

Entering Notes

The first thing we will do is enter the notes for the first half of the song. To do this, click somewhere within the first measure, then click the N button on the toolbar or use the keyboard shortcut N . This places MuseScore into *Note input* mode. You can then begin entering the notes as follows:

1. Click the ♩ button on the toolbar, or use the keyboard shortcut [5]
2. Type the letter name or click in the staff to enter the first note: *E*

This is what you should see:

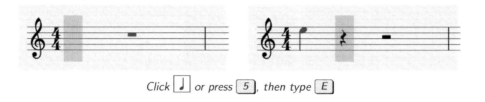

Click ♩ *or press* [5] *, then type* [E]

If you enter notes by typing the letter names – which is usually the most efficient method – MuseScore tries to guess which octave you want based on the previous notes you have entered. However, since you had not entered any notes yet, its guess in this case is not what we wanted. Press [Ctrl]+[↓] (Mac: [Cmd]+[↓]) to drop the note down an octave.

Press [Ctrl] +[↓]

From here on out, MuseScore should be able to figure out the octave correctly.

You may now continue entering the rest of the notes for the first measure: *D, C, D*. Since they are all quarter notes (crotchets), you do not need to specify this again – the duration already selected remains in effect. Just enter the notes, either by typing or by clicking in the staff.

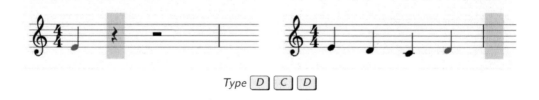

Type [D] [C] [D]

Notice that the cursor moves on to the next measure automatically.

Continue entering notes into the second measure. The first two notes are quarter notes (crotchets), so you can enter them immediately, but the last note is a half note (minim). You will need to click the ♩ button on the toolbar or use the keyboard shortcut [6] before entering the last note.

If you make a mistake at any point in this demonstration, the easiest thing to do for now is use the *Undo* command. You can use the ⟲ button on the toolbar or the standard keyboard shortcut Ctrl + Z (Mac: Cmd + Z). While in *Note input* mode, the Backspace key functions as an *Undo* command as well. For more information on how to make corrections or other changes to music you have already entered, see *Editing*.

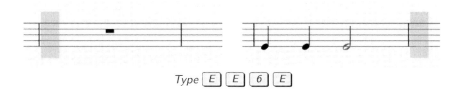

Type E E 6 E

The next measure is very similar. But since we now have the half note duration selected, we need to switch back to the quarter note.

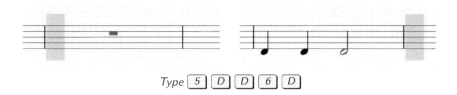

Type 5 D D 6 D

Enter the fourth measure in a similar manner.

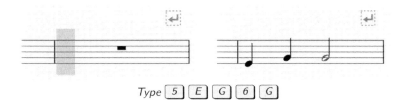

Type 5 E G 6 G

At this point, leave *Note input* mode by pressing Esc (or pressing N , or clicking the N button on the toolbar) so we can turn our attention to the lyrics.

See *Entering Notes and Rests* for much more on note input.

Entering Lyrics

Now that we have the notes for the first four measures, we will turn our attention to the lyrics. Press Esc to be sure you are no longer in *Note input* mode. Click the first note and press Ctrl +

L to enter *Lyrics edit* mode. You can then start typing the lyrics normally, using a hyphen
(-) to separate the syllables of "Ma-ry" and typing a space (Space) between words.

Type "Ma-ry had a"

If you make a mistake while entering lyrics, you may notice that Backspace returns to
its usual function of deleting the character to the left of the cursor, and *Undo* is not
active at all. But you can press Shift + Space to back up to the previous syllable.

The next three measures are entered just as easily – type "lit-tle lamb, lit-tle lamb, lit-tle
lamb."

Press Esc once you get this far to leave *Lyrics edit* mode.
See *Lyrics* for more on entering lyrics.

Completing Note Input

The next two measures are so similar to the first two that I will use this as an opportunity to
show how copy and paste works.

First, click an empty spot in the first measure to select it. A blue rectangle appears around
the measure, showing that is selected. Then Shift +click an empty spot in the second measure
to extend the selection to encompass it as well.

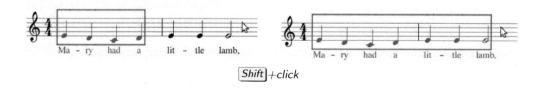

Shift +click

For more on making selections, see *Making Selections*.

Once you have selected the region, press the standard shortcut $\boxed{\text{Ctrl}}$+$\boxed{\text{C}}$ (Mac: $\boxed{\text{Cmd}}$+$\boxed{\text{C}}$) to copy the selection to the clipboard.

To paste this selection to the second line of the song, click the rest in measure five, then press the standard shortcut $\boxed{\text{Ctrl}}$+$\boxed{\text{V}}$ (Mac: $\boxed{\text{Cmd}}$+$\boxed{\text{V}}$) to paste the contents of the clipboard to that location.

Press $\boxed{\text{Ctrl}}$ + $\boxed{\text{V}}$

For more on copy and paste, see *Editing*.

If you compare what we have now to what we want, you will see it is not quite right. The second measure of the pasted selection (measure six) should contain four quarter notes, not two quarter notes and a half note. We need to change the half note into a quarter. To do this, click the half note and then click the $\boxed{\text{♩}}$ button or use the keyboard shortcut $\boxed{\text{5}}$.

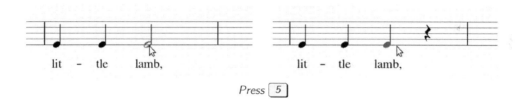

Press $\boxed{\text{5}}$

We can now continue entering the rest of the song. Click the quarter rest that appears at the end of the measure and press $\boxed{\text{N}}$ to enter *Note input* mode. You can then enter more notes.

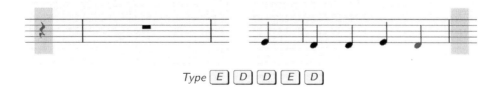

Type $\boxed{\text{E}}$ $\boxed{\text{D}}$ $\boxed{\text{D}}$ $\boxed{\text{E}}$ $\boxed{\text{D}}$

We will use a dotted half for the last note. Dots are part of the duration of a note, so we will select this before entering the note itself. Click $\boxed{\text{♩}}$ or use the keyboard shortcut $\boxed{\text{6}}$ to set the duration to half note, then click the $\boxed{\text{.}}$ or use the keyboard shortcut $\boxed{\text{.}}$ to specify that you want a dotted half note. Then enter the final note.

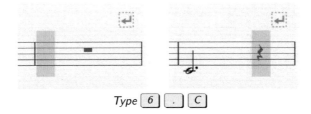

Type 6 . C

You can now press Esc to leave *Note input* mode.

Next, enter the remaining lyrics. Click the first note without lyrics (the last note of measure seven), press Ctrl + L , and type the remaining lyrics.

Press Esc again to leave *Lyrics edit* mode.

Cleanup

Our song is almost finished! We need to delete the extra measures we do not need. To do this, click the first empty measure (measure 9), then Shift +click the last measure of the piece or press Shift + Ctrl + End to select the rest of the measures. Press Ctrl + Delete (Mac: Cmd + Delete) to delete these measures from the score. Note that pressing Delete alone deletes the *contents* of selected measures, but we need to delete the measures themselves. See *Editing* and *Measure Operations* for more information.

Finally, we should enter the title and composer information. Double-click the placeholder title "My First Score" and type the actual name of this song.

Mary Had a Little Lamb

More is known about the authorship of this song than you might realize, so we will enter this information now as well. Double-click the text "Composer" and replace it with "Lowell Mason". Then go to Add ≫ Text ≫ Lyricist and enter "Sarah Josepha Hale". See *Text* for more information on the text editing and formatting capabilities of MuseScore. See Wikipedia for more information on the origin of the song!

Playback

Although we could have done this at any point to listen to the work in progress – and perhaps you did so even without being told – we can now listen to our song. Click the ▶ button on the toolbar or press Space to hear the playback. It is not very impressive to hear, of course, since this is just a simple melody. But as you enter or download more complex scores, MuseScore will play those as well, and it can create fairly realistic renditions of orchestras, jazz combos, rock bands, and much more. See *Playback and Audio Output* for more information.

Moving On

Before we leave this demonstration, you may wish to save the song. Go to File ⟩ Save or use the standard keyboard shortcut Ctrl + S , then choose a folder and specify a file name for your song. MuseScore uses the file extension *.mscz* for the scores you create.

MuseScore can, of course, create much more complex scores than this one – scores with as many instruments as you care to write for, with as many measures as you like, and with just about anything you might wish to include in terms of time signatures, key signatures, articulations, chord symbols, and many other types of markings. So let us move on now and learn about all that MuseScore can do!

Part II

Note Entry and Editing

Chapter 4

Creating a New Score

The first thing you will probably want to do with MuseScore is start making music, and the first step is creating a score. To create a new score, either click the *Create New Score* icon in the *Start Center* if that is currently being displayed, or go to File ⟩ New or use keyboard shortcut Ctrl + N (Mac: Cmd + N). This brings up the *Create New Score* wizard.

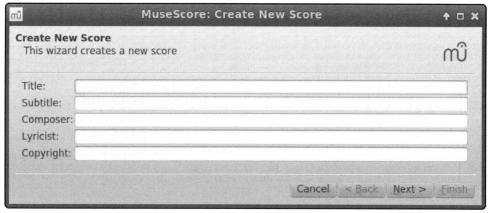

Score information

In the first screen of this wizard, you can enter title, subtitle, composer, lyricist, and copyright information for your score. By the way, if you leave any of these fields blank, you can add them later, using Add ⟩ Text for the first four fields or File ⟩ Info for copyright.

Template Selection

After entering the basic information about your score, hit Next to move to the next screen, which is where you will begin setting up your score.

Here, you can select from a collection of preconfigured scores of various types such as solo piano, concert band, SATB choir, lead sheet, rock band, as well as any custom templates you created and saved to your Templates folder (see the section on *Creating Templates* in the

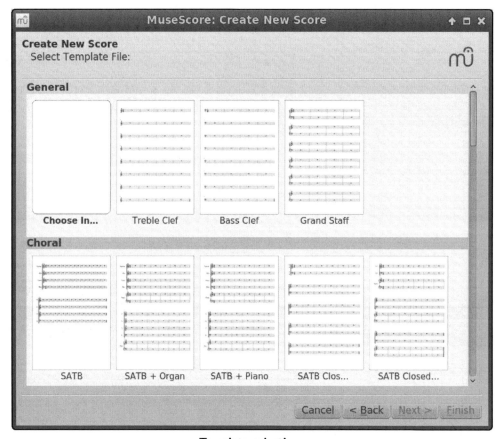

Template selection

chapter on *File Operations*). A template defines defaults for almost everything in your score. Most significantly, it defines the list of instruments included in your score, but it also defines page size and margins, staff size and spacing, fonts, and most other score settings.

If you prefer to start from scratch rather than using a template, the *Choose Instruments* option allows you to select the specific instruments you wish to write for, using default settings for page size etc.

Instrument Selection

If you select the *Choose Instruments* option in the first screen of the *Create New Score* wizard, then you are presented with the next screen, which enables you to select and order the instruments in your score.

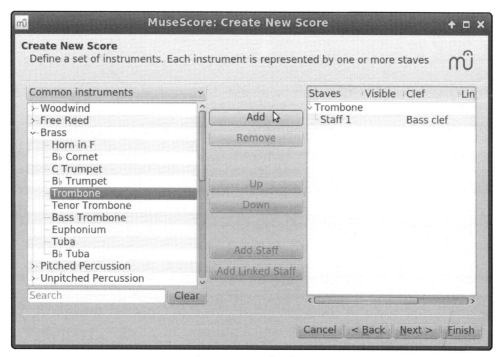

Instrument selection

Adding instruments to your score

On the left is a list of all the instruments supported by MuseScore, grouped according to family (e.g., woodwind, brass, keyboards). To add a staff for trombone, for example, click *Brass* to open that group, then double-click *Trombone*, or click *Trombone* then press Add.

By default, MuseScore shows only the most common instruments for each family. The full list of instruments supported by MuseScore is much longer. If you wish to add an instrument not on the list of *Common instruments*, you can display the full list by selecting *All instruments* from the drop-down menu at the top of the instrument list. There are also selections for jazz, orchestral, early music, and ethnic instruments, so if you are writing in one of those genres, you may try selecting it in that drop-down menu to restrict the list to just the instruments common to that genre.

You can also use the search box at the bottom of the list to find an instrument if you are not sure how it is classified. For instance, if you wish to write for dulcimer but do not know what category MuseScore has it in, just start typing that name into the search box, and MuseScore will automatically display any matching instruments in the list above.

If an instrument you wish to write for is not included in the list anywhere, do not worry. You can just add a similar instrument and later edit the properties for that staff to change the name, transposition, playable range, and any other relevant attributes to suit your needs. See the chapter on *Staves and Instruments* for more information.

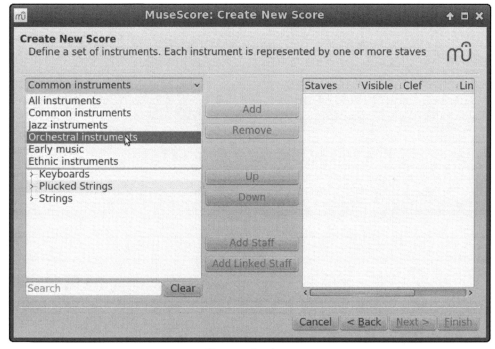

Genre selection

Modifying the list of instruments in your score

By default, MuseScore displays the instruments in the order you added them, but you can reorder them as you see fit. Simply select an instrument and press either Up or Down to move it higher or lower in the list.

You can also remove any instruments you added mistakenly, using the Remove button.

Adding a staff to an instrument in your score

Instruments like the piano are normally written on two staves, and MuseScore knows this. When you add piano as an instrument, you will see the two staves listed. Most other instruments use only a single staff by default. But if you wish to add a second (or third) staff to any given instrument, select a staff and then click Add Staff to add a new staff below the selected one.

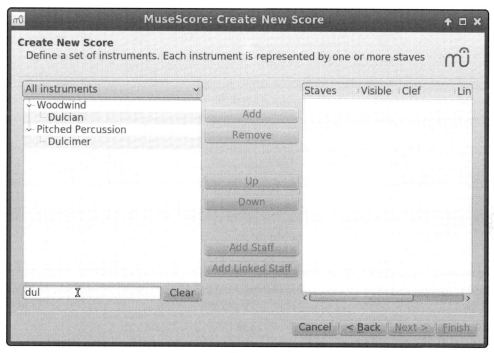

Search

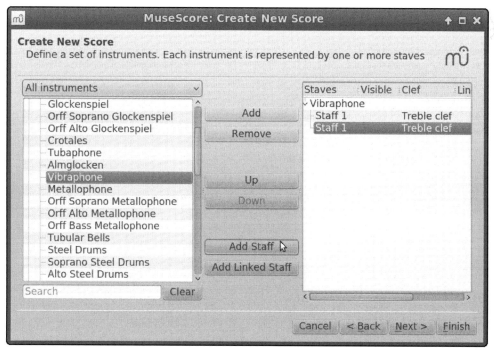

Adding a staff

Adding a linked staff to an instrument in your score

Adding a linked staff

Plucked stringed instruments like the guitar can be notated in standard notation or in tablature. You can include both types of staves in the same score, and you can link them so that entering or editing notes on one staff automatically updates the other.

To create linked staves, first add the instrument normally, then click its staff and press Add Linked Staff. A linked staff is added and defaults to the same staff type (e.g., standard notation or tablature) as the staff it is linked to. However, you can change the staff type using the drop-down menu.

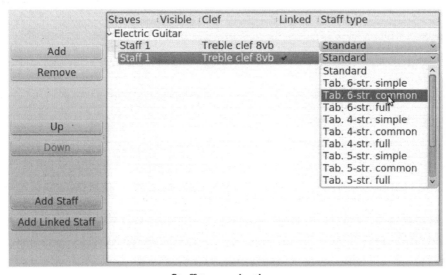

Staff type selection

It is possible to customize most aspects of an instrument definition – its transposition, its clef, its staff type, and more – after score creation. See *Staves and Instruments* for more information.

Key Signature and Tempo

Once you have selected a template or set up your instrument and staff list, press $\boxed{\text{Next}}$ to continue to the next screen of the wizard. This takes you to a screen where you can select the initial key signature and tempo marking for your score.

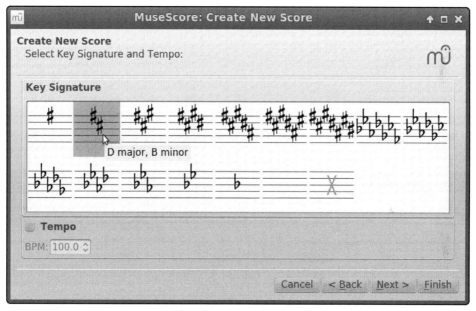

Key signature selection

The key signatures are shown as they appear in treble clef, but even if that is not the clef you are most familiar with, it should be obvious which keys are which by the number of flats or sharps. You can also hover your mouse over one of the key signatures to display a tooltip.

The *Tempo* checkbox controls whether an initial tempo marking is displayed on your score, and if enabled, you can select the initial tempo using the spin box below.

Time Signature and Measures

When you are finished with the key signature and tempo screen, the $\boxed{\text{Next}}$ button takes you to the final screen, where you can select the initial time signature and number of measures in your score.

The time signature can be specified using numbers or using the "cut time" or "common time" symbols.

The pickup measure section enables you to specify the length of a pickup (anacrusis) using time signature notation. If you want a half beat pickup, check the *Pickup Measure* box and set

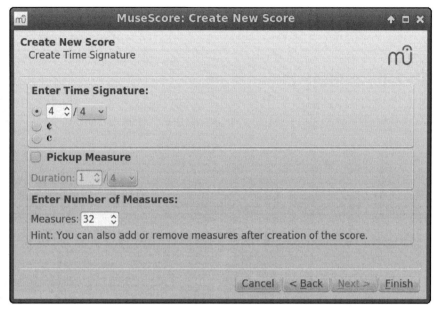

Time signature selection

the length to 1/8.

The final setting in this dialog enables you to specify the number of measures in the piece. As the hint in the dialog says, you can add or remove measures later if necessary.

When you are done with all settings, hit Finish and your score is created with the instruments, key signature, tempo, time signature, pickup, and length you specified. You are now ready to start entering notes!

Chapter 5

Entering Notes and Rests

Note entry is the most used feature of any notation program, so it is important to be comfortable with how it works. I would also recommend practicing along with the examples in this chapter. You will probably spend more time entering notes and rests than doing anything else in MuseScore, so you should understand the process as well as possible. The note entry system in MuseScore is very efficient, but if you are accustomed to other notation programs, it may take some time to adjust to the differences.

Notes and rests are added to a score via the aptly-named *Note input* mode. To enter *Note input* mode, hit the Esc key if necessary to make sure you are not in some other input or editing mode, click the score where you would like to start entering notes, and then click the N icon at the left edge of the note input toolbar.

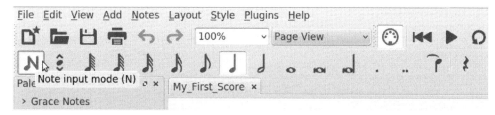

Note input toolbar

You can also use the keyboard shortcut N to enter *Note input* mode, or the menu Notes > Note Input.

You can leave *Note input* mode the same way you got in – using the toolbar icon or the keyboard shortcut. Pressing the Esc key also works to return you to *Normal* mode from *Note input* or any other mode.

Once you are in *Note input* mode, you can start entering notes and rests into your score. MuseScore provides several different methods for doing this:

- Clicking on a staff using your mouse

- Typing using your computer keyboard

- Using the built-in *Piano Keyboard*

A number of commands in MuseScore work only in *Note input* mode, or only in *Normal* mode, so it is important to know mode you are in. When you are in *Note input* mode, the toolbar icon is highlighted, as shown above. You will also see an indication in the status bar at the bottom of the screen, and a special note input cursor (a blue box) will appear to indicate where notes or rests will be entered.

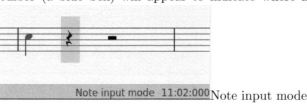

Note input mode

- Using a MIDI keyboard

These methods all work the same basic way. First you select the duration, and then you enter the notes or rests. The selected duration remains in effect until you change it, enabling you to quickly enter a whole series of notes and rests of the same duration.

Selecting Duration

As with many actions in MuseScore, you can select a duration by clicking with your mouse or by typing on your computer keyboard.

In this book, I often describe how to do things via the mouse first. But do yourself a favor and learn to use the keyboard shortcuts that I also describe where appropriate. These can be much more efficient.

Selecting duration using the mouse

To select a duration using your mouse, simply click the icon on the note input toolbar. The icon highlights to indicate it has been selected.

Selecting a note value icon

Notice that as you hover your mouse pointer over an icon, the name of the note value and the keyboard shortcut appear in a tooltip, as shown above.

To add a dot to the selected duration, click the dot icon after selecting the basic note value. The note value icon and dot icons will both remain highlighted.

Even if you are planning to enter a rest rather than a note, you will still use the duration icons with pictures of notes on them. The process of entering rests is described in *Entering Rests* below.

Also, notice that the icon for eighth note (quaver) shows a single note with a flag rather than beamed notes. You will use this same icon for all eighth notes (quavers); MuseScore handles the beaming automatically. You can customize the default beaming as explained in the section *Setting the default beaming* in the chapter on *Time Signatures*, and you can also override it on a note-by-note basis as explained in the section on *To control beaming* in the chapter on *Editing*.

Selecting the dot icon

Clicking the dot again will unselect it. Changing note values will also unselect the dot. This is normally just as you would want. For instance, after entering a dotted quarter note, the next note you enter is likely to be an eighth note, with no dot. There is also a double dot icon on the toolbar that acts the same way.

Selecting duration using the computer keyboard

To select a duration using your computer keyboard, press the key corresponding to the desired note value.

Duration shortcuts

When you press a duration shortcut key, the corresponding icon on the toolbar is automatically selected.

You can see which keys correspond to which note values by hovering your mouse pointer over an icon. But the keys are laid out in a straightforward way that is very simple to learn. The numbers 4, 5, and 6 correspond to the commonly used note values of eighth note (quaver), quarter note (crotchet), and half note (minim). Memorize that, and you can figure out anything else from there.

To add a dot to the selected duration, press the keyboard shortcut .. Like the corresponding toolbar icon, the shortcut acts as a toggle.

There is no keyboard shortcut for double dot by default, as double dots are less common and in fact are actively discouraged by some publishers. But as with many commands in MuseScore, it is possible to define your own shortcut via Edit ⟩ Preferences ⟩ Shortcuts. See the section on *Shortcuts* chapter on *Customization* for more.

Selecting duration using a MIDI keyboard

If you have a MIDI keyboard, you can configure it so that particular keys will select durations rather than enter notes. For more information on how to set this up, see the section on *Note Input* in the chapter on *Customization*.

Entering Notes

Once you have entered *Note input* mode and selected a duration, you can start entering notes. As mentioned previously, MuseScore supports several different methods for doing this. The duration you selected will remain in effect until you change it.

Entering notes using the mouse

To enter notes using your mouse, click where you want the note to appear. A note of the currently selected duration will appear at that location.

Click

The note you place will honor the current key signature and any previous accidentals in the measure. Thus, if the key signature or a previous accidental indicates that a *C* really means *C♯*, then a *C♯* will actually be added when you click a line or space corresponding to *C*. The same is true when adding notes via your computer keyboard. That is to say, when you add a note by clicking or typing, it will not appear with an accidental, but it will honor the key signature and any previous accidentals in the measure.

Click

To add accidentals, see the section *Accidentals*.

Be careful to position the mouse pointer accurately both vertically (correct staff line or space) and horizontally (correct time position), as MuseScore will attempt to add the note at the position where you click. You may find it helps to zoom in on the score a little more than you might otherwise to make it easier to place the pointer precisely. You can zoom by holding Ctrl (Mac: Cmd) while using the mouse scroll wheel or by using the drop-down menu in the toolbar.

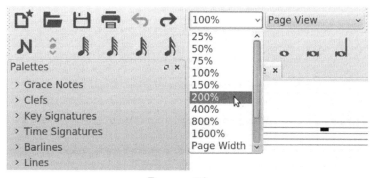

Zoom settings

Regardless of the zoom setting, it can be difficult to add notes that are several ledger lines above or below a given staff, as MuseScore may think you are trying to add a note to a different staff. To work around this, enter the note anywhere you can, then move the note up or down as appropriate. MuseScore provides a variety of keyboard commands that can move the most recently entered note. Perhaps the most useful in this context are Ctrl + ↑ and Ctrl + ↓ (Mac: Cmd + ↑ and Cmd + ↓), which move the note up or down an octave. So to enter a note an octave below middle *C*, you could first enter the middle *C* and then press Ctrl + ↓ .

Press Ctrl + ↓

Other useful shortcuts include Alt + Shift + ↑ and Alt + Shift + ↓ , which change the pitch of the most recently entered note diatonically by step (e.g., from *C* to *D* in the key of *C*, skipping *C*♯). See the chapter on *Editing* for more information on altering the pitch of a note once it has been entered.

Entering notes using the computer keyboard

To enter notes using your computer keyboard, simply press the letter name A - G corresponding to the pitch you want. The note will be entered at the cursor position and the cursor will then move to the right, just as when typing ordinary text. For example, by typing C , you can enter a *C*:

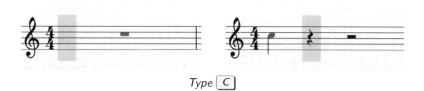

Type C

You may notice some notes you enter are colored red or dark yellow (a dull green). This is how MuseScore informs you that the notes you have entered are outside the actual range of the instrument (red), or at least difficult for amateurs to produce (dark yellow).

See the chapter *Staves and Instruments* for information on customizing when these warnings are displayed.

Keyboard input can be very efficient – you can enter notes as fast as you can type. Remember, after selecting the duration, you can then enter a whole series of notes that all have that same duration. The example below shows how you would enter the first few notes of *Mary Had A Little Lamb* once you are in *Note input* mode.

When entering notes by typing their letter names, MuseScore chooses the closest octave for each note. This makes entering melodies consisting of steps and small leaps easy, but it means there is an extra step required to enter larger leaps. For instance, in the example above, after entering the *E* in the last measure, typing G entered the *G* above that, since it is closest. Small leaps are more common than large ones, so this is usually a good thing. But if you want to leap down to the G below the *E*, you will need to lower its pitch an octave using Ctrl + ↓ .

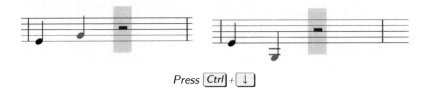

Press Ctrl + ↓

See *Editing* for more information on commands to alter pitches

If you move your mouse around the score while in *Note input* mode, you will see that a "shadow" note head reflecting the note value you have selected follows the mouse pointer. For instance, when you select a half note (minim) as the duration, MuseScore displays the appropriate note head as you move the mouse pointer.

However, I recommend moving the mouse pointer out of the way – even off the page – while entering notes using the computer keyboard, MIDI, or the *Piano Keyboard*. The note input cursor, not the mouse pointer, is what will determine where notes are entered using these forms of input. The shadow note just gets in the way when not using the mouse.

Entering notes using the Piano Keyboard

To use the *Piano Keyboard*, first enable it if necessary via View ⟩ Piano Keyboard (keyboard shortcut P).

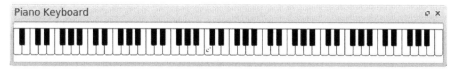

Piano Keyboard

After selecting a duration you can simply click a note on the piano keyboard to enter it. One advantage to this method is that you can easily enter notes in any octave with no extra steps required. Another is that you can enter notes with accidentals directly by simply playing a note that would require one. MuseScore automatically figures out which notes need accidentals, and it will guess the proper spelling based on the key.

See the section on *Accidentals* for more information.

You can resize the *Piano Keyboard* by using Ctrl (Mac: Cmd) plus the mouse scroll wheel.

Entering notes using a MIDI keyboard

To enter notes using a MIDI keyboard, first make sure it is plugged in to your computer. Restart MuseScore after plugging in the keyboard in order for MuseScore to recognize it.

Once your MIDI keyboard is connected and recognized, you can use it just like the *Piano Keyboard* – select a duration, then and play the keys corresponding to the notes you want. Note that you cannot simply play in rhythm and have MuseScore figure out the note values. You still have to tell MuseScore the duration of each note before entering it. But in addition to the advantages MIDI input shares with the *Piano Keyboard* (entering notes in any octave, entering notes with accidentals), a MIDI keyboard enables you to enter a whole chord at once (see *Chords* below). You can also configure particular keys to select duration or perform other tasks that would normally require you to click or type. For more information, see the section on *Note Input* in the chapter on *Customization*.

Accidentals

Accidentals include all sharps, flats, naturals, double sharps, double flats, and microtonal adjustment symbols placed in front of individual notes (as opposed to flats and sharps that are part of the key signature). An ordinary accidental has the effect of changing the pitch of a note from what would be expected according to the key signature and/or any previous accidentals in the measure. There are also courtesy accidentals that simply serve as a reminder of the pitch after a previous change; these do not actually alter the pitch. MuseScore supports both types of accidental.

As mentioned above, when entering notes using the mouse or computer keyboard, accidentals are never added at first. So if you wish to add an accidental to a note, you need to add it after entering the note. Although accidentals are added automatically as needed when entering notes via the *Piano Keyboard* or a MIDI keyboard, you may need to correct the spelling sometimes. This can be done by pressing the J key, as we will see shortly.

Ordinary accidentals

To add an ordinary accidental to the most recently added note, you can click the appropriate icon on the note input toolbar.

You can also use the ↑ or ↓ keys to raise or lower the pitch, which causes MuseScore to calculate and add the necessary accidental for you.

In general, the ↑ key spells accidentals with sharps whereas ↓ spells with flats. However, MuseScore will always prefer a spelling that is in the key. So for instance, you are not able to enter an A♭ in the key of E by entering an A then pressing ↓ – it will automatically be respelled as G♯ because that is in the key. You can enter the A♭ directly using the toolbar, but you can also change a G♯ into an A♭ by pressing J to change the spelling of the note. See *Changing pitch* in the chapter on *Editing* for more information.

You can also use the icons in the *Accidentals* palette, which gives you access to various microtonal accidentals as well.

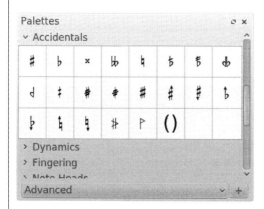

As with most palette icons, you apply one either by double-clicking it or by dragging from the palette to any desired note in the score. Adding an accidental via the palette has the same effect as adding one via the toolbar.

After adding an accidental, it remains in effect for notes you enter in the rest of the measure, in accordance with standard rules of notation. You only need to enter an accidental where you actually want one to appear in your score.

So if your score is in *C* major, and you enter an *F♯* followed by an *F* on that same line or space later in the measure, it is automatically understood to be an *F♯*. It will be displayed with no accidental because the previous accidental remains in effect. If you wish to enter an *F♮*, enter the *F* (which will be understood at first to be *F♯*) and then use the $\boxed{♮}$ icon on the toolbar to explicitly change it to *F♮*.

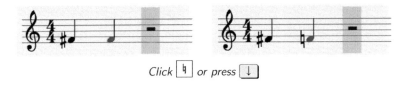

Click $\boxed{♮}$ or press $\boxed{↓}$

Courtesy accidentals

The rules of notation say that an accidental lasts only until the end of the current measure, so a note altered by an accidental in one measure returns to normal in the next. However, it is considered good practice to add "courtesy" (aka "cautionary" or "reminder") accidentals where there is any chance of confusion. For example, in the following passage, the *F♯* carries through to the end of the first measure but is canceled by the barline, so the *F* in the second measure is *F♮*.

It would be easy for a human musician to miss this when reading, however. The standard recommendation is to add an explicit courtesy natural sign on the *F* in the second measure even though it is not technically required. Courtesy accidentals can be added using the appropriate icon on the toolbar or on the palette. So in this case, you would click the $\boxed{♮}$ icon after entering the *F* in the second measure to add an explicit accidental.

Click $\boxed{♮}$

This natural sign has no actual effect on the music – that *F* was already an *F♮* because the barline cancels the previous sharp. But the courtesy accidental greatly reduces the likelihood of reading errors. The $\boxed{↑}$ and $\boxed{↓}$ keys cannot be used to create courtesy accidentals. But you can define keyboard shortcuts for the toolbar accidentals as described in *Shortcuts* in the chapter on *Customization*.

Some people like to use parentheses around courtesy accidentals to avoid possible confusion. If you wish to add parentheses around an accidental, you can apply them from the *Accidentals* palette, but you need to leave *Note input* mode to do it or else the parentheses will be added to the note rather than the accidental. Once you are back in *Normal* mode, click the accidental and then double-click the parentheses icon in the palette.

Double-click [()]

The difference in effect between using the arrow keys for accidentals versus using the toolbar or palette icons can sometimes be confusing, but it need not be if you keep this distinction in mind:

The arrow keys always change the pitch of a note, whether that produces an explicit accidental or not. The toolbar and palette icons always add an explicit accidental to a note, whether that changes the pitch of the note or not. For this reason, I normally think of the arrow keys as the best way to create regular accidentals, and I use the icons only for courtesy accidentals. But you can use these commands however you like as you long as you keep the basic distinction in mind: arrow keys always change pitch, icons always add explicit accidentals.

Chords

A chord is normally defined as multiple notes that share a single stem. Internally, MuseScore treats all notes as chords – a single note is just a chord of one note. This will become more relevant when we look at the various properties you can set in the *Inspector*, where some properties belong to the note and others to the chord.

In this section, when I use the word "chord," I am describing how to add multiple notes that share a single stem. By the way, it is also possible to have multiple notes that sound at the same time but do not share a stem. This is described below in the section *Multiple Voices*.

To create a chord in MuseScore using any of the available input methods except MIDI, start by adding the first note normally. You can then enter additional notes onto that same chord as described below. For MIDI input, you can actually enter the whole chord at once.

Entering chords using the mouse

To add notes to a chord using your mouse, simply position your mouse pointer and then click.

Click

When building chords using this method, you can add notes in any order.

Entering chords using the computer keyboard

To add notes to a chord using your computer keyboard, hold [Shift] while typing the letter name for note to add it to the current chord.

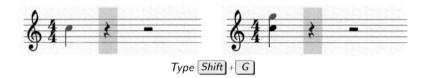

Type [Shift] + [G]

When you press [Shift] plus a letter, MuseScore normally builds the chord from the bottom up. You may need to use [Ctrl]+[↓] – or occasionally [Ctrl]+[↑] – after adding a note, to change the octave.

MuseScore provides other useful keyboard shortcuts that can be used to build chords. Instead of specifying additional notes by letter name, you can build chords by interval. [Alt] plus a number adds the corresponding interval above the chord. So you could also create the above examples by typing [C] [Alt]+[5] (since *G* is a fifth above *C*).

> MuseScore also has commands to build a chord top down rather than bottom up, but there are no keyboard shortcuts defined for these commands by default. In previous releases of MuseScore, [Shift] plus a number would perform this function, but these shortcuts conflict with the note duration shortcuts on keyboards that require [Shift] just to access the numbers. If these keys are available on your keyboard, they make a natural choice for these commands (*Enter second below* et al). See *Shortcuts* in the chapter on *Customization* for information on how to customize your keyboard shortcuts.

Another shortcut that comes in handy when entering chords is [R], for repeat. When used in *Note input* mode, this repeats the current note or chord. For example, you might type [G] [Alt]+[3] [Alt]+[3] [Alt]+[3] to enter a *G* dominant seventh chord, but after that you can simply press [R] to repeat the entire chord.

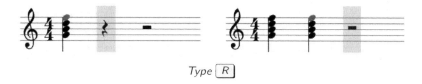

Type R

Entering chords using the Piano Keyboard

You can add a note to a chord using the *Piano Keyboard* by pressing Shift while clicking the note you would like to add.

Entering chords using a MIDI keyboard

To enter chords using a MIDI keyboard, simply play the chord. As long as you hold all the notes at the same time, they will be entered as a single chord.

Ties

Like many other elements in MuseScore, ties can be created by clicking or by typing. The process is similar either way:

1. Enter first note normally
2. Select duration for second note
3. Enter the tie

You can enter the tie by clicking the ? icon on the toolbar or by typing the keyboard shortcut + . Either way, a new note is entered at the same pitch as the first and the two are tied automatically.

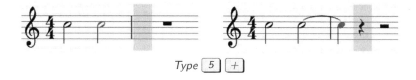

Type 5 +

MuseScore creates ties across barlines automatically where necessary. For instance, say you are on beat 4 of a 4/4 measure with the half note (minim) selected as the duration. If you try to enter a note, MuseScore will automatically enter a quarter note (crotchet) on beat 4 tied to another on beat 1 of the next measure.

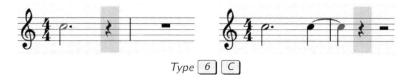

Type 6 C

In order to tie a whole chord, you need to enter the two chords individually, exit *Note input* mode, and then add the tie. See *Tying chords* in the chapter on *Editing* for more information.

> A tie is used to connect two notes of the same pitch, to denote that the duration of the first is to be extended by that of the second. Do not confuse ties with slurs, which look similar but which connect multiple notes of different pitches, to indicate that they are to be played smoothly. See *Slurs* in the chapter on *Articulations and Other Symbols* for more information.

Entering Rests

Rests are entered much like notes: first you select the duration, then you enter the rests. You select the duration exactly as you do for notes, and in fact, once you have selected a duration, you can enter any number of notes and rests as long as they all have the same duration. However, while entering rests via the computer keyboard works much like entering notes, entering rests using the mouse works a little differently.

Entering rests using the computer keyboard

To enter rests using your computer keyboard, first select the duration as usual, then use the shortcut 0 to enter a rest at the current cursor position. This is just like how you enter notes, except instead of typing a letter A - G , you use the number 0 .

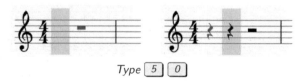

Type 5   0

Entering rests using the mouse

To enter rests using your mouse, after selecting the duration you must also press the ♩ icon on the toolbar before clicking in the score. This icon will be highlighted along with the duration and will remain highlighted and in effect until you toggle it off or change durations.

Notice that the icon displays a picture of a quarter (crotchet) rest, but do not be fooled – you will use this same icon to enter any type of rest. The duration icons tell you the value of the rest you are about to enter. The mouse pointer also shows you an image of the rest that will be entered. Clicking in the score enters a rest of the currently selected duration.

Click

Entering rests using a MIDI keyboard

To enter rests using a MIDI keyboard, see *Note Input* in the chapter on *Customization* for more information. Basically, you will configure a key of your choice to enter a rest rather than the note it would normally add.

> Measures start off by default with a full measure rest, so you do not need to enter whole rests for empty measures. As you enter notes into a measure, they "steal" time from that default rest, so that full measure rest is replaced by rests representing the amount of time left in the measure. This happens automatically, but you still normally need to enter rests manually when you want them anywhere else within a measure.

Tuplets

A tuplet is a grouping of notes that divides the beat into a different number of equal divisions than is usual for the time signature. This includes a division of the beat into three or five equal parts in a simple meter like 4/4, or a division of the beat into two or four equal parts in a compound meter like 6/8. You can even have tuplets nested within other tuplets. MuseScore supports almost any kind of tuplet you can think of.

Creating triplets

You can enter basic triplets as follows:

1. Select the duration representing the total length of the triplet

2. Press Ctrl + 3 (Mac: Cmd + 3) or use Notes ⟩ Tuplet ⟩ Triplet to divide that length into thirds

3. Enter notes or rests normally

So to create an eighth note triplet – three eighth notes (quavers) in the space of one beat – you would first select the quarter note (crotchet) as the total duration by clicking ♩ or pressing 5 , then create the triplet by pressing Ctrl + 3 .

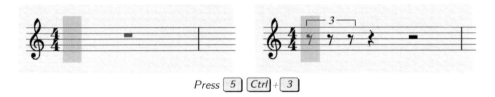

Press 5 Ctrl + 3

Then you can enter the notes.

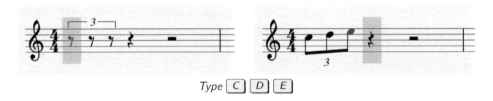

Type C D E

Or, for quarter note triplets – three quarter notes (crotchets) in the space of two beats – you would first select the half note (minim) as the duration by clicking ♩ or pressing 6 , then create the triplet by pressing Ctrl + 3 .

Press 6 Ctrl + 3

Once you have created a tuplet, you can enter other arrangements of notes within it. For example, a common variation on the triplet is a quarter note taking the space of the first two eighths followed by an eighth. To enter this, create the triplet normally with 5 Ctrl + 3 , then enter a quarter note followed by an eighth by typing 5 C 4 D .

Type 5 C 4 D

Creating other tuplets

The same process applies for other more complex tuplets: first select the duration corresponding to the total length of the tuplet, then press $\boxed{\text{Ctrl}}$ (Mac: $\boxed{\text{Cmd}}$) plus the key corresponding to the number of equal parts you want that duration divided into, or use the $\boxed{\text{Notes}} \rangle \boxed{\text{Tuplets}}$ menu.

So to enter a tuplet consisting of four quarter notes in the space of three beats, first select the dotted half as the duration, then press $\boxed{\text{Ctrl}} + \boxed{4}$.

Press $\boxed{6}$ $\boxed{.}$ $\boxed{\text{Ctrl}} + \boxed{4}$

As shown in the example at the top of this section, you can create nested tuplets (tuplets within tuplets). The inner tuplet is entered the same way as the outer: select total duration, then $\boxed{\text{Ctrl}}$ plus the number of equal units into which you wish to divide that duration.

Press $\boxed{\text{Ctrl}} + \boxed{3}$

If you need the duration divided into more than nine equal parts, or to create other more complex tuplets, you can use $\boxed{\text{Notes}} \rangle \boxed{\text{Tuplets}} \rangle \boxed{\text{Other}}$ to bring up a dialog box with more options.

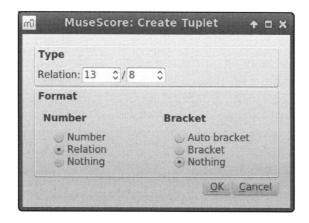

As you can see, this dialog lets you control whether the tuplet is displayed with a simple number with a ratio, or with no numeric indication, and also whether a bracket is used or not. The example below was created using the settings shown above.

The meaning of the various options in this dialog is as follows:

- **Number**

    Number – display tuplet with a number (eg, *3*)
    Relation – display tuplet with a ratio (eg, *3:2*)
    Nothing – display tuplet with no number or ratio

- **Bracket**

    Auto bracket – display tuplet with no bracket for simple beamed tuplets, with bracket for
        more complex tuplets
    Bracket – display tuplet with bracket
    Nothing – display tuplet with no bracket

The appearance of tuplets can also be customized as described in *Changing Appearance and
Behavior* in the chapter *Editing*.

Multiple Voices

When you want to have two different rhythms at the same time in the same staff, use multiple
voices. Do not be fooled by the name – this is not something that applies only to vocal music. In
fact, it is at least as common in piano and guitar music. For example, in the following excerpt,
notice how the notes with stems up form one distinct part with its own rhythm, while the notes
with stems down form another.

To accomplish this in MuseScore, you need to enter the notes as separate voices.

Note entry in multiple voices

MuseScore supports up to four voices per staff, numbered 1–4. By default, all notes you enter
are in voice 1, and stem direction is handled automatically according to the usual conventions
of music notation. But MuseScore automatically adjusts stem directions for any measure that
contains notes in multiple voices: voices 1 and 3 point up, 2 and 4 point down. So the previous
example would be created by entering the upstem notes in voice 1 and the downstem notes in
voice 2.

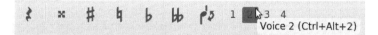

To enter notes into a specific voice, click the appropriate voice icon on the note input toolbar after entering *Note input* mode but before entering the notes, or use the keyboard shortcut Ctrl +Alt (Mac: Cmd+Alt) plus the number. The icon stays highlighted as shown above, and the note input cursor changes color accordingly.

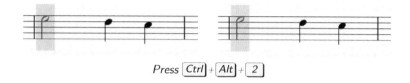

Press Ctrl + Alt + 2

The general procedure for entering notes in multiple voices is as follows:

1. Press N if necessary to enter *Note input* mode
2. Enter the notes for voice 1
3. Navigate back to start point
4. Press Ctrl+Alt+ 2 to change to voice 2
5. Enter the notes for voice 2

The stem and rest positions adjust automatically for voice 1 as soon you start entering notes into voice 2.

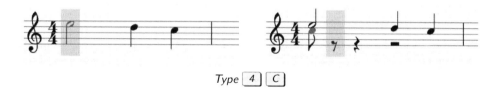

Type 4 C

Layout with multiple voices

MuseScore handles most potential collisions between notes and rests in different voices correctly, adjusting positions of elements according to standard conventions of music notation.

Automatic handling of collisions between voices

Depending on what is going on in the music, it might be necessary to override the default positions of notes, stems, or rests. For more information on how to do this, see *Changing Appearance and Behavior* in the chapter on *Editing*.

This is especially likely when using more than two voices in the same staff. As mentioned above, MuseScore supports four voices per staff. They all work the same way: while in *Note input* mode, navigate to the desired location, change to the desired voice, and start entering notes. Voice 3 defaults to stems up, voice 4 to stems down. Of course, this means that it may be hard to distinguish voices 1 and 3 because they both have the same direction, and the same for voices 2 and 4. This is an inherent difficulty with music notation, and it is up to you to figure out how you want the music to look. Sometimes you can solve these problems by deliberately pointing stems in the "wrong" direction for the voice. Other times you may choose to nudge a note slightly to the left or right to avoid colliding with another note in a different voice.

It is usually best to deal with these issues after initial note entry.

Hiding and deleting unneeded rests

In most cases, multiple voices are used consistently throughout the measure. Even if a voice rests for part of a measure, as in the first measure of the above example, it is usually best to show the rests. Occasionally you may encounter situations where this is unnecessary, however. In these cases, the best thing to do is to enter the part with the rests but then hide them. Rests, like notes and indeed most score elements, can be hidden after entry by pressing ⊻ or by unchecking *Visible* in the *Inspector* (see *Changing Appearance and Behavior* in the chapter on *Editing*). Invisible elements remain in a grayed-out state when viewing your score on your computer screen, so you can still work with them. But they will not print or appear when exporting your score to PDF or any other graphic format. You can also delete rests in voices other than 1, but this leaves "holes" in the score that can cause problems if you wish to later edit the measure, so I recommend hiding the rests instead.

In the example below, the eighth notes on beat 4 in the following are the only things that you need to see in voice 2, so you can safely hide the leading rests in that voice.

Grace Notes

Grace notes are small notes attached to a main note that are played as ornaments. MuseScore supports a variety of grace note types, including acciaccaturas (a grace note with a slash through the stem, intended to be played very fast) and appoggiaturas (a grace note without the slash, intended to take half the value of the main note). Grace notes are normally placed before the main note to which they apply, but MuseScore also supports grace notes placed after the main note (used for trill endings, for example).

> MuseScore respects the difference between acciaccaturas and appoggiaturas during playback, so use the proper type.

Entering grace notes

Grace notes are added using the *Grace Notes* palette.

If you do not see all of the grace notes shown here and miss them, be sure to select the *Advanced* workspace in the menu at the bottom of the palettes.

To add a grace note, first enter the main note to which the grace note should be attached, then double-click one of the icons on the *Grace Note* palette (or drag it from the palette to the note). This creates a grace note of the same pitch as the main note.

Double-click

Once you have added the grace note, you can use the arrow keys to move it up or down.

Press ↓

This process is the same regardless of the type of grace note being added.

You can also use the keyboard shortcut ⃤ / ⃤ to enter an acciaccatura. Shortcuts for the other grace notes are not defined by default, but you can define them yourself as described in *Shortcuts* in the chapter on *Customization*.

To add the slur often used to connect a grace note to the main, press the keyboard shortcut ⃤ S ⃤ after entering the grace note. See *Slurs* in the chapter on *Articulations and Other Symbols* for more information.

Multiple grace notes

To add multiple grace notes to the same main note, you can add grace notes to the main note one at a time. Subsequent grace notes are added the same way as the first: via drag and drop, by double-clicking a palette icon, or using keyboard shortcut.

Double-click

You can form chords of grace notes in the same manner as for regular notes – press ⃤ Shift ⃤ plus a letter to add the specified pitch or ⃤ Alt ⃤ plus a number to add the specified interval.

Press ⃤ Shift ⃤ + ⃤ 6 ⃤

Cross-Staff Notation

In piano music, we sometimes see a group of notes on one staff that logically belong to another. This is commonly done to avoid ledger lines or to show which hand should play which notes in an independent musical voice.

To create this cross-staff notation in MuseScore, enter the notes on the staff they that they logically belong to, but then press Ctrl+Shift+↑ or Ctrl+Shift+↓ (Mac: Cmd+Shift+↑ or Cmd+Shift+↓) to move the notes to the staff above or below, respectively.

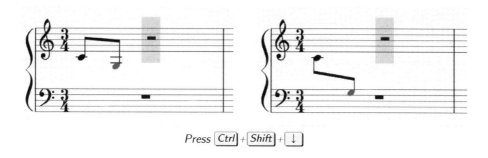

Press Ctrl + Shift + ↓

If you wish to move a small number of notes, doing this one note at a time in *Note input* mode is fine. But to move an entire passage to another staff, you are probably better off entering the notes normally first, then leaving *Note input* mode and selecting and moving them all at once, as described in the chapters *Making Selections* and *Editing*.

When using cross-staff notation with beamed notes, you may wish to adjust the position of the beam. For more information on how to do this, see *Changing Appearance and Behavior* in the chapter *Editing*.

Shortcuts

Note entry using the keyboard can be extremely efficient if you take advantage of the shortcuts. Here is a list of the shortcuts we have covered in this chapter.

- 1 - 9 – select duration

- [A] - [G] – enter pitch
- [↑] – raise pitch a semitone
- [↓] – lower pitch a semitone
- [Ctrl]+[↑] – raise pitch an octave
- [Ctrl]+[↓] – lower pitch an octave
- [Alt]+[Shift]+[↑] – raise pitch a step diatonically
- [Alt]+[Shift]+[↓] – lower pitch a step diatonically
- [J] – change enharmonic spelling
- [Shift] plus letter ([A] - [G]) – add note to chord
- [Alt] plus number ([1] - [9]) – add interval above to chord
- [+] – create tie
- [Ctrl]+[2] - [Ctrl]+[9] – create tuplet
- [Ctrl]+[Alt]+[1] - [Ctrl]+[Alt]+[4] – switch to specified voice
- [/] – add acciaccatura (grace note)
- [Ctrl]+[Shift]+[↑] – move note or rest to previous staff of instrument
- [Ctrl]+[Shift]+[↓] – move note or rest to next staff of instrument

Remember, on Mac OS, you need to substitute [Cmd] for [Ctrl] and [Option] for [Alt].

Chapter 6

Navigation

MuseScore provides many ways of moving around your score. Most of these work in both *Note input* mode as well as *Normal* mode, although there are a few differences that I will discuss as we come to them.

Page Navigation

MuseScore can handle scores that are arbitrarily large – hundreds of measures or more. Clearly, these will not normally fit on screen all at once. And even for scores of a single page, unless you reduce the zoom level, the entire page will not usually fit. So you will need ways of moving the page within the visible window and of moving from page to page. In this section, I will present a number of different navigation controls provided by MuseScore.

> During playback, the score normally scrolls automatically to follow along. You can disable this by pressing the ▶❙ (*Pan score during playback*) button. This allows you to keep the score focused in one location or to scroll manually instead.

Zoom settings

MuseScore normally displays your score at 100% scale, which should approximate the actual size at which your score will print (although this may depend in part on your monitor resolution). You can zoom in or out using the drop-down menu on the toolbar.

You can also use the Ctrl key with your mouse wheel (or equivalent touch gesture) to zoom the score in and out, or keyboard shortcuts Ctrl + + and Ctrl + - (Mac: Cmd + + and Cmd + -). To quickly reset to 100%, you can use the shortcut Ctrl + 0 (Mac: Cmd + 0).

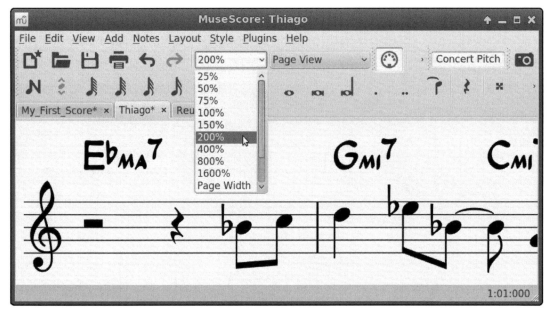

Zoom settings

Scrolling through your score

The easiest way to scroll through your score is using your mouse wheel. Up and down motions scroll the score vertically; to scroll horizontally, use the mouse wheel in conjunction with `Shift`.

If you just need to move the score by a small amount, you might find it simpler to reposition the score by dragging it. Just click on an empty area of the page and drag in any direction.

Drag down

Dragging is one of the few navigation operations that does not work in *Note input* mode. That is because clicking on the page in order to drag it will result in a note being entered!

Paging through your score

MuseScore responds to the page navigation keys on most keyboards as follows:

- Home – go to beginning to score
- End – go to end of score
- PgUp – go to previous page
- PgDn – go to next page

Some keyboards lack these keys, but they usually provide an equivalent shortcut. Consult the documentation for your keyboard to learn more.

The Find command

If there is a specific place in the score you wish to view, you can go directly to any given measure number, page number, or rehearsal letter using the menu command Edit ⟩ Find or the keyboard shortcut Ctrl + F (Mac: Cmd + F). This will display a search box at the bottom of the screen.

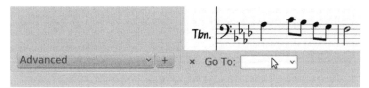

The Find command

Into this box, you can type a measure number (e.g., "43"), a page number preceded by the letter "P" (e.g., "p7"), or a rehearsal letter (e.g., "H"), and MuseScore will reposition to that location.

Navigator

If your score is more than a page or two long, you might find it useful to work with a thumbnail view of it. MuseScore provides such a tool, called the *Navigator*. To enable (or disable) the *Navigator*, go to View ⟩ Navigator or use the keyboard shortcut F12. The *Navigator* includes a thumbnail of each page in your score and displays a blue rectangle that represents the portion of the score is currently in view.

As the name implies, this is not just a picture of the score – you can use it to navigate through your score. Simply drag the blue rectangle around and the score will move with it.

You can resize the navigator pane by dragging its upper border.

Page and Continuous View

By default, MuseScore starts in *Page View*, which displays your music on screen the way it will appear on a printed page.

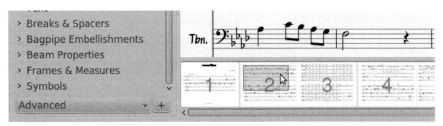

The Navigator

Sometimes the line breaks can be disorienting, especially if you are entering notes and finding things wrapping around from line to line as you enter them. It can be more convenient to do note input in *Continuous View*, which presents your score in one long horizontal strip. To switch views, use the drop-down menu in the toolbar.

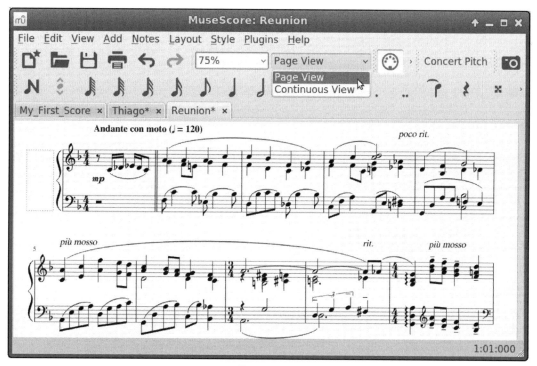

Page View

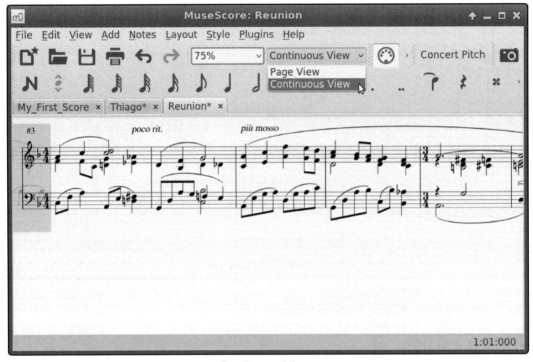

Continuous View

Cursor Navigation

The controls discussed above allow you to position the score within the window. MuseScore also provides commands to move a cursor through the score, whether note by note, measure by measure, or staff by staff. These commands can be invaluable in editing, in making selections, and even in simply browsing your score.

Cursor types

Before we continue, I would like to clarify what I mean by "cursor" here.

You have probably already noticed that while you are in *Note input* mode, MuseScore uses a blue box as a cursor to highlight the position at which the next note will be entered. You may have also noticed that as you enter notes and rests, the most recently entered note or rest is colored blue. This is actually indicating the note is "selected," in the same way that this means for copy and paste or other commands that work on selections. And indeed, this is what allows commands like ↑, which raises the pitch of the most recently entered note, to work. MuseScore is not actually keeping track of what note you entered most recently and remembering this as you move the cursor. This command – like most commands in MuseScore – operates on a selection, regardless of how that selection was made. We will learn how to take advantage of this in the chapter *Editing*.

So, immediately after entering a note or rest, the note or rest you just entered is selected, but the note input cursor moves on to the next position at which you can enter a note. As you enter music, the note input cursor thus stays one step ahead of the selection. When you use any of the navigation commands discussed in this chapter while in *Note input* mode, both the note input cursor and the selection move together in sync.

Although the examples thus far have shown the selected note and the note input cursor in blue, in fact the color depends on what voice you are in. See *Multiple Voices* in the chapter on *Entering Notes and Rests* for more information on voices.

When not in *Note input* mode, there is no cursor in the usual sense. However, a note, rest, or other element might be selected. And the currently-selected element – which is colored blue (or according to its voice) – serves as a cursor of sorts. In particular, when not in *Note input* mode, the navigation commands discussed in this section actually change what element is selected. So as you use the navigation commands, the effect of watching the selection change is pretty much the same as if there were an actual cursor. I use the term "cursor" for convenience, so I can say that (for example) the → moves the cursor right, rather than saying that it "changes the selection from whatever note is currently selected to the next note to the right."

Because the "cursor" in *Normal* mode is really just a selection, you can move it anywhere you like by simply clicking in the score. But this will not work in *Note input* mode. Clicking while in *Note input* mode will add a note where you click! Use only the keyboard for navigation while in *Note input* mode.

Horizontal navigation

Horizontal navigation commands move the cursor through a single staff, moving forward or backward in time position.

The $\boxed{\rightarrow}$ and $\boxed{\leftarrow}$ keys move the cursor note by note:

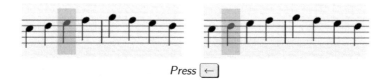

Press $\boxed{\leftarrow}$

$\boxed{Ctrl}$ + $\boxed{\rightarrow}$ and $\boxed{Ctrl}$ + $\boxed{\leftarrow}$ (Mac: $\boxed{Cmd}$ + $\boxed{\rightarrow}$ and $\boxed{Cmd}$ + $\boxed{\leftarrow}$) move the cursor measure by measure:

Press $\boxed{Ctrl}$ + $\boxed{\rightarrow}$

Both of these commands ignore clefs, key signatures, and other elements – they only navigate through notes and rests. Should you wish to navigate through other elements as well, use the commands $\boxed{Ctrl}$ + $\boxed{Alt}$ + $\boxed{Shift}$ + $\boxed{\rightarrow}$ and $\boxed{Ctrl}$ + $\boxed{Alt}$ + $\boxed{Shift}$ + $\boxed{\leftarrow}$ (Mac: $\boxed{Cmd}$ + $\boxed{Option}$ + $\boxed{Shift}$ + $\boxed{\rightarrow}$ and $\boxed{Cmd}$ + $\boxed{Option}$ + $\boxed{Shift}$ + $\boxed{\leftarrow}$).

Press $\boxed{Ctrl}$ + $\boxed{Alt}$ + $\boxed{Shift}$ + $\boxed{\leftarrow}$

These commands can be invaluable if you are visually impaired and are using MuseScore with a screenreader. By navigating in this fashion, and with the screenreader reading the contents of the status bar, you can read a score element by element and gain a complete understanding of it. If these are commands you would plan to use a lot, you might consider customizing the keyboard shortcuts as described in *Shortcuts* in the chapter on *Customization*.

Vertical navigation

Vertical navigation commands move the cursor through the notes heard at a single point in time, moving through notes of a chord, between voices, or to different staves.

[Alt] + [↑] and [Alt] + [↓] move the cursor up and down through the individual notes of a chord.

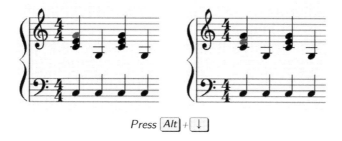

Press [Alt] + [↓]

If you run off either end of the chord in a multi-staff score, [Alt] + [↑] and [Alt] + [↓] will move to the previous or next voice or staff.

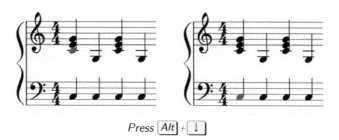

Press [Alt] + [↓]

[Ctrl] + [Alt] + [↑] and [Ctrl] + [Alt] + [↓] (Mac: [Cmd] + [Option] + [↑] and [Cmd] + [Option] + [↓]) move the cursor up and down to the top and bottom notes of a chord.

There is also a command to move to the voice or staff without first moving through the notes of the current chord, but there is no shortcut set up for it by default. If you decide this is a useful command, you can create a shortcut for it as described in *Shortcuts* in the chapter *Customization*.

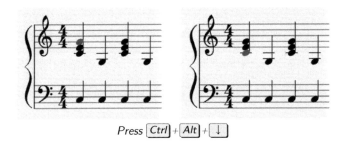

Press Ctrl + Alt + ↓

Shortcuts

We have learned a lot of keyboard shortcuts in this chapter; here is a summary.

- Ctrl + + – zoom in
- Ctrl + - – zoom out
- Home – go to beginning to score
- End – go to end of score
- PgUp – go to previous page
- PgDn – go to next page
- Ctrl + F – go to measure, page, or rehearsal mark
- ← – move cursor to previous note/rest
- → – move cursor to next note/rest
- Ctrl + ← – move cursor to previous measure
- Ctrl + → – move cursor to next measure
- Ctrl + Alt + Shift + ← – move cursor to previous element
- Ctrl + Alt + Shift + → – move cursor to next element
- Alt + ↑ – move cursor up to next higher note in chord, previous voice, or previous staff
- Alt + ↓ – move cursor down to next lower note in chord, next voice, or next staff
- Ctrl + Alt + ↑ – move cursor to top note of chord
- Ctrl + Alt + ↓ – move cursor to bottom note of chord

Remember, on Mac OS, you need to substitute `Cmd` for `Ctrl` and `Option` for `Alt`.

Chapter 7

Making Selections

MuseScore provides a number of operations such as copy and paste, transposition, and deletion that work on individual elements, complete measures (bars), or other selected elements or ranges of music. In this chapter, we will learn how to make selections. In the next chapter (*Editing*), we will learn about some of the things you can do once you make a selection.

Selections in MuseScore fall into three basic categories:

Single – a single element, such as one note
List – multiple elements, possibly of different types
Range – a region of music that includes everything from a given start time position to a given end time position, possibly including the contents of multiple consecutive staves

---

Single selections are actually just list selections that happen to contain only one element. But certain operations – like changing the duration of a note – only work with single selections. Also, as noted in the chapter on *Navigation*, the "cursor" in *Normal* mode is really just a selection consisting of a single note or other element. So it can be convenient to describe it as a separate selection type.

An important note about selections: list and range selections are relevant mostly in *Normal* mode. While in *Note input* mode, single selection is done automatically during navigation and note entry. In the other edit modes we will learn about later (e.g., the *Text edit mode* discussed in the chapter on *Text*), the selection is reset to just the element being edited.

Single Selection

A single selection is made by simply clicking on an element. Just about any type of element can be selected in this fashion. Once selected, an element will turn blue (or the color corresponding to the voice of the element).

Click

Navigation commands move the current selection to a different single element, as described in the chapter on *Navigation*.

List Selection

A list selection is literally a list of single selections. Each selected element will be displayed in blue, or the color corresponding to the voice of the element. There are a number of ways of creating list selections.

The most direct way to build a list selection is to select each element individually. Just as in many other applications, MuseScore allows you to select multiple elements one by one by holding Ctrl (Mac: Cmd) while clicking them. This allows a group of elements to be selected even if they are not adjacent.

Ctrl+click

You can also select a group of adjacent elements by dragging a rectangle around them while holding Shift. If you select a group of notes and rests this way, MuseScore will create a range selection (see below), but selecting other element types will create a list selection.

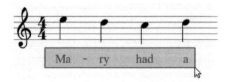

These methods are useful for selecting just a handful of elements, or elements that are in close proximity. But MuseScore also provides some very powerful controls for making larger list selections based on the type of an element – note, rest, clef, rehearsal mark, etc. These controls are accessed by right-clicking an element and then clicking Select to bring up a menu of selection options.

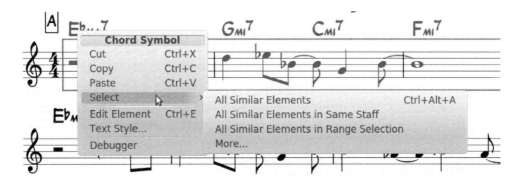

The options in this menu allow you to create list selections of similar items as follows:

All Similar Elements – this selects all elements of the same type in the entire score

All Similar Elements in Same Staff – this selects all elements of the same type in the current staff (relevant for scores consisting of multiple staves – see the chapter on *Staves and Instruments*)

All Similar Elements in Range Selection – this selects all elements of the same type within the current range selection (if one exists)

More – this opens a dialog with additional options

The Select ⟩ More option brings up a dialog that allows you to control the selection further.

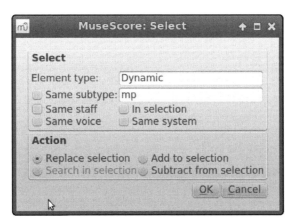

This dialog displays the type of the element and gives you a number of options for making a new selection or modifying an existing one. The dialog is divided into two parts. The top part lets you specify which other similar elements you wish to specify.

Same subtype – this specifies all elements of the same subtype (e.g., for *Dynamics*, all *mp* markings)

Same staff – this specifies all elements of the same type in the current staff

In selection – this specifies all elements of the same type within the current range selection

Same voice – this specifies all elements of the same type in the same voice (see *Multiple Voices* in the chapter on *Entering Notes and Rests*)

Same system – this specifies all elements of the same type in the same system (one "line" of music, but including all staves for scores consisting of multiple staves)

The bottom part of the dialog lets you control what is done with the elements you have specified.

Replace selection – make a new list selection that includes the specified elements only
Add to selection – add specified elements to existing list selection, or create a new list selection if one does not exist
Search in selection – this option is not currently implemented
Subtract from selection – subtract specified elements from existing selection; if current selection is a range selection, it is converted into a list selection

These options collectively allow you to build quite complex list selections. For instance, you could first use the *Same system* option to select all articulations in current system, but then right-click an staccato marking in voice 1 and use the *Same voice* and *Subtract from selection* options in this dialog to exclude the staccato markings in voice 1 from the selection, leaving only the articulations in voices 2-4 and articulations other than staccato in voice 1 selected. You could then right-click a slur and use the add to selection options to add all of the slurs in the entire score to the selection. This is not something most people will need very often, of course, but when you need it, this can be a powerful tool.

Range Selection

A range selection is easily differentiated from a list (or single) selection in MuseScore in that when you select a region, a blue rectangle appears around it. As with single and list selections, it is also the case that all elements within the region turn blue (or the colors corresponding to their voices) to indicate that they have been selected.

There are a number of ways of selecting ranges in MuseScore, both using the mouse and the keyboard.

Using the mouse

A single measure in a single staff can be selected by clicking an empty spot within it.

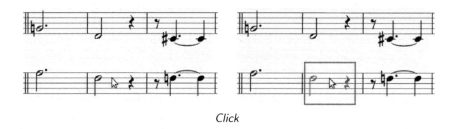

Click

Sometimes zooming in on the score can make it easier to find an empty spot to click within a crowded measure.

A range of notes or measures can be selected by dragging while holding [Shift]. You may recall this method can also be used to create list selections. The rule is that if the drag rectangle includes notes, then the selection automatically becomes a range selection.

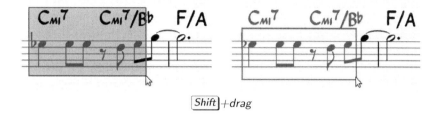

[Shift]+*drag*

A range of notes or measures can also be selected by clicking the first to select it and then clicking the last while holding [Shift] to extend the selection to the entire range from the first to the last.

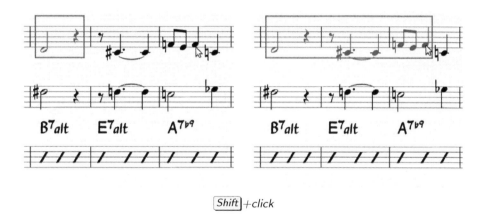

[Shift]+*click*

This method can also be used to select a range across multiple staves.

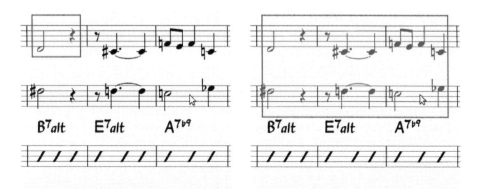

[Shift]+*click*

You can use a single Shift +click to select a range consisting of a single chord, if nothing is currently selected.

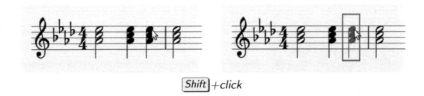

Shift +click

Using the keyboard

You can also use keyboard shortcuts for selection. These work as in most applications: holding Shift while using navigation keys such as → will select while moving the cursor. So you can click any note, press and hold Shift, and then use the navigation commands discussed in the chapter *Navigation* to extend the selection as you move the cursor.

Here is a full list of the selection shortcuts:

- Shift + ← – extend selection to the previous note or rest
- Shift + → – extension selection to the next note or rest
- Shift + Ctrl + ← – extend selection to the previous measure
- Shift + Ctrl + → – extend selection to the next measure
- Shift + Home – extend selection to the beginning of the system (line)
- Shift + End – extend selection to the end of the system
- Shift + Ctrl + Home – extend selection to the beginning of the score
- Shift + Ctrl + End – extend selection to the end of the score
- Shift + ↑ – extend selection to previous staff
- Shift + ↓ – extend selection to next staff

Remember, on Mac OS, you need to substitute Cmd for Ctrl and Option for Alt.

In the example below, I am extending the selection to the end of the system using Shift + End.

Press Shift + End

Here, I am extending the selection to the next staff using ⟨Shift⟩+⟨↓⟩.

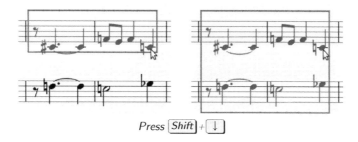

Press ⟨Shift⟩+⟨↓⟩

Selecting notes or rests in a range

As mentioned previously, a range selection contains all elements within the range, not just notes and rests. Since certain operations may require a list selection containing notes or rests only, MuseScore makes it easy to easily convert a range selection into a list selection of notes or rests. In addition to the ⟨Select⟩⟩⟨All Similar Elements in Range Selection⟩ command seen above, which you can access by right-clicking a note or rest within a range selection, you can also simply press the ⟨Notes⟩ or ⟨Rests⟩ button within the *Inspector*. See *Individual note and rest properties* in the chapter on *Editing* for more information.

Selection Filter

A range selection normally includes all elements between the start and end position. However, MuseScore does allow you to exclude elements from a range selection by type using the *Selection Filter*.

> Actually, it is not quite true that a range selection normally includes all elements between the start and end position. It excludes elements that are attached to the system as a whole as opposed to any particular staff. This includes tempo text, rehearsal marks, and voltas. You will notice that these elements are not highlighted when you make a range selection.

To display the *Selection Filter*, go to ⟨View⟩⟩⟨Selection Filter⟩ or use the keyboard shortcut ⟨F6⟩.

By default, all of the items listed in the *Selection Filter* are checked, which means that the corresponding element types will be included in range selections. By unchecking any of the items in the filter, the corresponding element types will be excluded from range selections. This applies to the current range selection as well as any other range selections you make until you change the filter settings.

For example, you might wish to exclude chord symbols from a range selection, so that you can delete the notes but keep the chord symbols. To do this, uncheck *Chord Symbols* in the

Selection Filter

Selection Filter. Any range selections you make will exclude chord symbols. You will be able to tell this because the chord symbols will not be highlighted in blue.

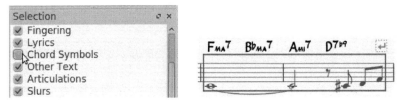

Make range selection

Keep in mind that while a range selection can include all sorts of elements, it is at its heart defined by the *notes* between the start and end time positions. You can exclude individual voices from a selection (see *Multiple Voices* in the chapter in *Entering Notes and Rests* for more on voices), but you must take care in doing so. If you exclude *Voice 1*, then any measure that does not contain multiple voices will not be selectable, because there will be no notes to select.

Chapter 8

Editing

When you want to make changes to notes or rests you have already entered – such as to fix mistakes – there are a number of ways you can go about this. Many things can be done while still in *Note input* mode, while others are best done in *Normal* mode (the mode you are in when you first start MuseScore or when you leave *Note input* or any other mode). It is not always obvious which changes can be done in which mode, so I recommend reading through this chapter carefully and working through the examples if you have the time.

Basic Concepts

Before I discuss the specific editing techniques available in the different modes, there are a couple of general observations that I would like to make.

Undo

When it comes to fixing mistakes, the *Undo* command is often the simplest solution. MuseScore, like most programs, keeps a history of changes you make and allows you to undo them one by one. So immediately after entering a note or rest, or performing almost any other operation, you can undo it using Edit ⟩ Undo , the toolbar icon ↶ , or the keyboard shortcut Ctrl + Z (Mac: Cmd + Z). While in *Note input* mode, the Backspace key (Mac: Delete) also works to undo.

Press Ctrl + Z or Backspace

Replace versus insert

There is one crucial concept to understand about how MuseScore works when it comes to making changes. Once you enter a note or rest into a score, its position in time – which measure and beat it occurs on – remains fixed, unless you explicitly change it or replace it with something else. That is not to say you cannot change the time position of notes; just that you usually need to do it explicitly (via cut and paste) rather than expecting notes to change time positions on their own just because you make a change somewhere else.

This means that all note and rest entry is done in what a word processor might call "replace mode" or "overtype mode," as opposed to "insert mode." That is, when you enter a note or rest of a given duration, it always replaces whatever was at that location. So in that sense, making changes while in *Note input* mode is exactly like entering notes and rests in the first place. It is just a matter of positioning the cursor where you want to make your change, then entering new notes and rests to replace what was there before. You do not need to first delete anything; just enter the new content. MuseScore ensures that your measures always contains the correct number of beats and that notes not replaced are kept at their original time position.

An example will hopefully make this clear. In the score below, I have a half rest and a half note, with the *Note input* cursor positioned on the rest. If I elect to enter a quarter note at that point, the second half note does not move earlier or later in time. It stays right where I originally put it – on beat 3. A quarter rest is automatically inserted after the quarter note I enter, to make sure that half note stays on beat 3.

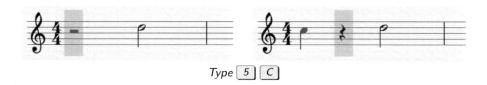

On the other hand, if I had entered a dotted half note instead of a quarter note on beat 1, there would be no way to keep the half note on beat 3. The last beat of the new dotted half note *replaces* the first beat of the original half, leaving one beat of the original half note on beat 4.

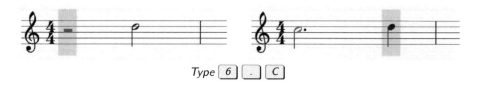

In this respect, the way MuseScore works is similar to at least one popular notation program, but different from some others. People who come to MuseScore expecting note entry to work like a word processor in "insert" mode often have trouble adjusting at first. If you find yourself in that category, please be patient. Once you become accustomed to how note entry and editing in MuseScore works, you should come to find it quite natural and efficient.

Making Changes in Note Input Mode

As mentioned above, one way to make changes in note entry mode is to navigate to the location where you wish to make the change, then simply enter new notes and rests. The new ones replace the old. Enter as many new notes or rests as you like, hit Esc when you are done, and everything should work out with no need to delete anything first or to do anything special to insert new notes or rests.

In the following example, I am replacing the first two quarter notes with four eighth notes, leaving the last two quarter notes right where they were – on beats 3 and 4.

Type 4 C B C D

In addition to simply re-entering new notes to replace the old ones, you can also perform a variety of operations to modify the selected note or rest. As explained in the chapter on *Navigation*, the most recently entered note is automatically selected, but when you move the cursor, the selection follows. So immediately after entering a note, you can modify it, or you can navigate to any other note and modify it in the same way.

Changing pitch

We have already seen some of the commands that change the pitch of the selection note, in the chapter on *Entering Notes and Rests*. ↑ and ↓ raise or lower pitch a half step, while Ctrl+ ↑ and Ctrl+↓ (Mac: Cmd+↑ and Cmd+↓) raise or lower pitch an octave.

Two additional commands that alter the pitch of the selected note are Alt+Shift+↑ and Alt+Shift+↓, which raise or lower the pitch diatonically (staying within the key). So with *G* selected, Alt+Shift+↑ will raise it to either *A* or *A♭* depending on which is in the key.

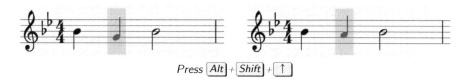

Press Alt+Shift+↑

There is one other command that is worth mentioning in this context, even though it technically does not change pitch. Pressing J will change the *enharmonic spelling* of a note while keeping the pitch the same.

Press J

Adding and removing notes

We have already seen some of the commands for adding and deleting notes, in the chapter on *Entering Notes and Rests*. The commands we have seen to add notes to the selected chord are [Shift] plus a letter [A] - [G] (adds note above chord) and [Alt] plus a number (adds interval above to chord). There is also [/] to add a grace note.

To remove the selected note from the chord it belongs to, use [Delete].

Press [Delete]

The same command will turn a note into a rest if the note is not part of a chord.

Press [Delete]

Again, as suggested above in *Replace versus insert*, deleting a note does not cause subsequent notes to move earlier in time. To make that happen, you need to leave *Note input* mode and use cut and paste as described in the section *Making Changes in Normal Mode*.

Changing duration

To change the duration of a note, you have three basic choices. One is to leave *Note input* mode and make the change as described in the section *Making Changes in Normal Mode*. Another is to simply replace the note – select the duration, re-enter the pitch. However, there are a pair of commands that can alter the duration of a note while still in *Note input* mode, without the need to re-enter the pitch. These are [Q] and [W], which change the duration of note to the next shorter or longer (respectively) note value.

Press [Q]

> One advantage of using the [Q] and [W] keys to change duration is that, unlike re-entering the notes, these commands preserve lyrics, articulations, and other markings attached to the note.

Changing time position

Changing the time position of a note – or an entire passage – is something that would normally be done outside of *Note input* mode, using cut and paste. However, there are a pair of commands that can be useful for small corrections within *Note input* mode. [Shift]+[←] and [Shift]+[→] will exchange the selected note with the previous or next note, thus effectively moving it earlier or later in time.

Press [Shift] + [→]

Repitch mode

MuseScore provides a special sub-mode within *Note input* mode in which you can quickly replace the pitches of existing notes while leaving their durations unchanged. To enable this sub-mode – which I will refer to as *Repitch* mode – make sure you are in *Note input* mode with the cursor positioned where you want to start replacing pitches, then click the [⇕] icon in the note input toolbar. You can also use the keyboard shortcut [Ctrl]+[Shift]+[I] (Mac: [Cmd]+[Shift]+[I]). The icon will highlight to indicate you are in *Repitch* mode.

Repitch mode

Once you have entered *Repitch* mode, you can then simply type the new pitches; no need to select durations. The existing notes will be replaced with the new pitches but the durations of the original notes will be left intact.

Press [F] [E] [F] [G] [F] [A] [C]

Making Changes in Normal Mode

When you are not in *Note input* mode, there is no note input cursor. But remember – the commands discussed in the previous section *Making Changes in Note Input Mode* are actually working on the current selection. In *Note input* mode, the selection is always a single note or rest, but in *Normal* mode, you can have single, list, or range selections. Most of the commands covered in the previous section actually will work on any type of selection. There are also new commands you can take advantage of that only work in *Normal* mode (in most cases because they require range selections).

So first, let me list the commands we have learned for *Note input* mode that will operate on any type of selection in *Normal* mode as well:

- ↑ – raise pitch a semitone
- ↓ – lower pitch a semitone
- Ctrl + ↑ – raise pitch an octave
- Ctrl + ↓ – lower pitch an octave
- Alt + Shift + ↑ – raise pitch a step diatonically
- Alt + Shift + ↓ – lower pitch a step diatonically
- J – change enharmonic spelling
- Shift plus letter (A - G) – add note to chord
- Alt plus number (1 - 9) – add interval above to chord
- + – create tie
- Delete – delete note
- Ctrl + 2 - Ctrl + 9 – create tuplet
- / – add acciaccatura (grace note)
- Ctrl + Shift + ↑ – move note or rest to previous staff of instrument
- Ctrl + Shift + ↓ – move note or rest to next staff of instrument

Remember, on Mac OS, you need to substitute Cmd for Ctrl and Option for Alt.

The fact that these commands work on range selections can be very powerful. For example, the commands that add notes to chords can be used to add notes to an entire selection, such as to double it in octaves.

Press Alt + 8

Using the tuplet command on a range selection allows you to quickly create extended passages of tuplets.

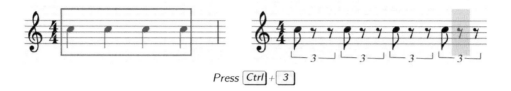

Press Ctrl + 3

The commands to create cross-staff notation work with range selections as well.

Press Ctrl+Shift+↑

You can also delete the contents of a selection, replacing everything with rests. The command for this is Delete . MuseScore tries to be smart about choosing these rests. It does not simply replace each note with a corresponding rest, but instead uses larger durations where appropriate. If the region includes an entire measure, then the contents are replaced by a full measure rest.

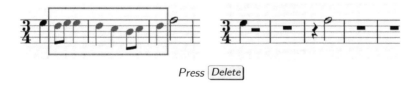

Press Delete

To actually delete the measures themselves, the command is Ctrl + Delete (Mac: Cmd + Delete). See the chapter on *Measure Operations* for more information.

Changing pitch using the mouse

In *Normal* mode, you can click and drag a note up or down to change its pitch.

Drag down

This does not work in *Note input* mode because the click necessary to initiate the drag would add a note instead.

Respell pitches

If you have a range of notes where the spelling of the notes does not fit the key correctly – perhaps because the score was imported from a MIDI file with no key information, or the spellings resulted from transposition or copy and paste – then MuseScore can try to correct the spelling automatically. Select the range of notes you would like corrected and go to Notes ⟩ ⟩ Respell Pitches. MuseScore will respell pitches according to a simple but reasonably effective analysis of the music. It may not produce exactly the results you prefer, but if there were a large number of errors to begin with, this may at least reduce the number you need to correct by hand.

Notes ⟩ Respell Pitches

Changing the duration of a note or rest

Changing duration of a note or rest is only possible for a single selection. But in addition to the Q and W commands to shorter or lengthen a note as in *Note input* mode, you can also set the duration directly using the note value icons on the note input toolbar or corresponding keyboard shortcuts. This includes the simple note values like ♩ (6) as well as the commands to add dots.

Press .

Tying chords

Ties between chords (as opposed to between single notes) can only be created in *Normal* mode.

    1. Enter the chords individually (not tied)
    2. Leave *Note input* mode
    3. Select the first chord
    4. Press the 🎵 button or the shortcut +

  By the way, an easy way to select a chord is to click it while holding Shift , as shown in *Range Selection* in the chapter on *Making Selections*.

Press +

Moving notes between voices

MuseScore provides two different methods of moving notes from one voice to another.

Exchanging the contents of two voices

MuseScore can exchange the complete contents of two voices for an entire measure or range of measures. To do this, select the range, then go to Edit ⟩ Voices and choose the appropriate pair of voices to exchange.

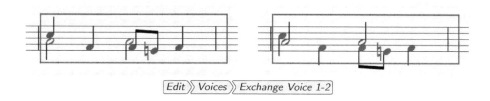

Edit ⟩ Voices ⟩ Exchange Voice 1-2

Moving notes to another voice

In some cases, it may work to move individual notes by simply using the voice change icons or keyboard shortcuts while *not* in *Note input* mode. This will only work if the the note can be moved without requiring any changes to the durations of any existing notes in the destination voice. That is, it will work if the destination voice contains rests or nothing at all for the duration of the note being moved. It will also work if the destination voice contains notes that exactly match in time position and duration, in which case they will be combined into chords.

In the following example, I have selected the notes of voice 2 (using the *Selection Filter*) and am moving them into voice 1. The notes that can be moved are moved and are replaced by rests in the original voice; the notes that cannot be moved are left alone.

Press Ctrl+Alt+1

You can then hide or delete the rests and adjust stem directions if you wish.

MuseScore also provides an *Implode* command that can be used to combine several voices into one. See *Implode* in the chapter on *Other Editing Tools* for more information.

Copy, Cut, and Paste

MuseScore supports the standard clipboard operations of copy, cut, and paste. These work as they do in most other programs.

Duplicating a selection using copy and paste

First, select a range and use Edit ⟩ Copy or Ctrl + C (Mac: Cmd + C) to copy the selection to the clipboard.

Next, click or navigate to where you would like to paste the selection, and use Edit ⟩ Paste or Ctrl + V (Mac: Cmd + V) to paste it.

Press Ctrl + V

By default, a copy and paste operation on a range selection copies all notes in the region as well as most items attached to those notes, such as articulations and dynamics. But you can suppress certain types of elements from being included in the selection – and hence, from both the copy and the paste – by using the *Selection Filter* described in *Selection Filter* in the chapter on *Making Selections*.

You can also use copy and paste in a limited fashion for list selections. Only a few element types are supported. But if you select a list of lyrics, articulations, chord symbols, and/or figured bass elements that are attached to one set of notes, you can copy and paste these to another set of notes, and MuseScore will do its best to match up the pasted elements to the correct notes.

For example, you can select the lyrics for a group of notes.

You can then paste them to a different set of notes.

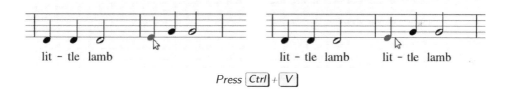

For lyrics and most other elements that can be pasted in this fashion, MuseScore looks at the notes themselves to decide how to match things up. But when pasting chord symbols in this fashion, MuseScore uses their beat positions rather than the notes to match things up, so you can paste a list chord symbols to a passage with very different rhythms and they will still line up correctly.

Duplicating a selection using the Repeat command

Copy and paste can be especially useful when copying a passage to a different staff, or to a different part of the score. But if you simply want to repeat a passage immediately after the original, MuseScore provides an easier way of doing this. Simply select the region and then press R .

Press R

Moving a selection with cut and paste

As with most other programs, Edit ⟩ Cut or Ctrl + X (Mac: Cmd + X) works the same way as copy except that the original selection is deleted. The effect of cut and paste is that of *moving* the selection, then, rather than *duplicating* it. This is an especially significant operation in MuseScore because this is how you can move a passage earlier or later in time.

For example, say you were trying to enter a C major scale in quarter notes but accidentally repeated the E.

While your first instinct in trying to fix this might be to delete the first E, remember that MuseScore never moves notes as a result of that kind of editing operation. Deleting the E would simply replace it with a rest, leaving the other notes right where they were.

Press Delete

So instead, the way to move the rest of the scale earlier is cut and paste. First, select the region you want moved and cut it.

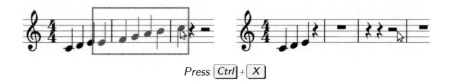

Press Ctrl + X

Then click the place you want to move the selection to and paste it.

Press Ctrl + V

Manual Adjustments

While MuseScore usually does a great job of placing the elements in your score automatically, there may be times when you wish to take more control. In many of these cases, the best way of going about this is by going to the Style menu and changing the settings that control the defaults for various types of elements. Still, there may be times when you want fine-tune the positioning for individual elements. Certain types of adjustments are specific to particular types of element – time signatures, for example, have different controls than slurs. However, there are other adjustments that are common to most element types, and those are what we will discuss here.

Dragging with the mouse

Many elements can be dragged with the mouse. This includes most items that can be attached to notes, such as articulations, dynamics, and accidentals.

Drag

To constrain a drag operation to be vertical only, press and hold Shift while dragging; to constrain a drag horizontally, press and hold Ctrl (Mac: Cmd).

Whether constrained in direction or not, dragging operations normally allow you to drag an element by any amount you like. To make it easier to align elements, you can select the ⦀ (*Enable snap to horizontal grid*) and/or ☰ (*Enable snap to vertical grid*) options in the *Inspector*.

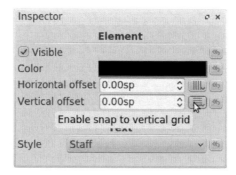

No actual grid will appear, but drag operations will nonetheless "snap" to an imaginary grid. The origin of the grid is the default position for the element, and the grid lines are spaced at half the distance of the staff lines.

MuseScore uses the size of a staff space – referred to as a *spatium* and abbreviated *sp* – as a unit of measurement throughout the program. Using this rather than something like millimeters or inches allows everything to scale smoothly if you change the size of the music. See *Music Size* in the chapter on *Page Layout* for more information.

You can also drag multiple items at once by making a list selection (see *List Selection* in the chapter on *Making Selections*) and pressing and holding Ctrl (Mac: Cmd) when initiating the drag operation.

Drag

Since Ctrl is also the command to constrain a drag horizontally, you will only be able to drag horizontally at first when dragging multiple elements. But if you release the Ctrl key after initiating the drag, you will then be able to drag freely.

For notes specifically, dragging works only in the vertical direction, and it actually changes the pitches of notes. To fine-tune the horizontal position of notes on the page, the *Inspector* (see *Using the Inspector* below) will normally be the best method.

Nudging with the keyboard

Most elements can be nudged left, right, up, or down using the arrow keys. The arrow keys by themselves move elements in fine increments ($0.1sp$). To move in full $1sp$ increments, press and hold Ctrl (Mac: Cmd) while nudging.

Press Ctrl + ↑

For text elements such as in the example above, you can simply click on the text and then begin nudging. For most other items, however, you need to double-click them first to put them into *Edit* mode before you can nudge them.

You can use this method to move notes, but what we think of as a "note" is actually represented in MuseScore as separate elements for the note head, stem, flag, beam, dots, etc. These can be manipulated individually in MuseScore, which is sometimes desirable, but if you just wish to move the entire "note," what you really want is to move the *chord*. MuseScore uses that term even for single notes to refer to the collection of elements that includes note heads, stems, flags, beams, dots, etc. To act on a chord as a unit, use the *Chord* section of the *Inspector* (see below).

Using the Inspector

The *Inspector* contains a number of different settings, depending on the type of element selected. The available options also depend on whether the selection is homogeneous (containing only elements of the same type) or not. For non-homogeneous selections – including both list and range selections that contain multiple element types – the only controls provided are for color and visibility.

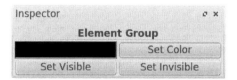

For homogeneous selections, other options become available depending on the type of the element(s) selected.

Visibility

To use the visibility commands for non-homogeneous selections, simply click Set Invisible or Set Visible as appropriate. You can also use the keyboard shortcut V to toggle the visibility of selected elements. Note that invisible elements will normally continue to display on screen, but grayed out.

Press V

These will not print or export to PDF or other graphic formats. If you would rather not see grayed out invisible elements on screen either, you can turn off the View ⟫ Show Invisible option.

For homogeneous selections, there is a single *Visible* option that you can check or uncheck.

Color

To use the color command, start by clicking the black rectangle. A standard color picker dialog will appear.

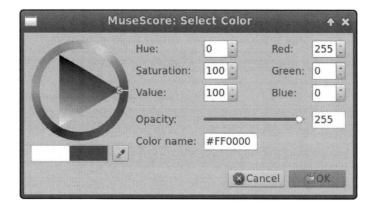

Once you have selected a color in this dialog, press OK. The color will now be displayed in the *Inspector*, but it is not applied yet if the selection is non-homogeneous. To confirm the application of the color to all selected elements, press Set Color. This extra step is not necessary for homogeneous selections.

Position

For single or homogeneous selections, two additional options become available: *Horizontal offset* and *Verical offset*. These controls provide very precise control over the position of selected elements. You can click in a spinbox and then use the arrow keys on your keyboard, or use the arrow icons with the spinboxes, to change the value in 0.5*sp* increments. For even greater precision, you can type values directly into the spinboxes.

Press ↑ ↑ ↑

Next to these spinboxes are the ▥ and ☰ buttons to enable snapping to a grid (see *Dragging with the mouse* above). Next to these are the ↩ reset buttons. Pressing either of these restores the corresponding setting to the default.

Flipping direction

Many elements in a score can be placed in one of two vertical orientations. For instance, stems can point up or down; ties can curve up or down; fermatas can be placed above or below the staff. MuseScore allows you to flip most of these elements between the two vertical directions using either the *Inspector* or the context menu. In addition, the keyboard shortcut X serves to flip most of these elements.

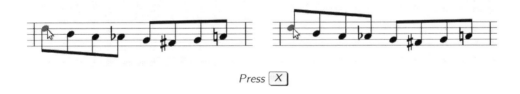

Press X

Changing shape

The shape of certain elements can be modified by double-clicking them to put them into *Edit* mode and adjusting the handles that appear. Handles can be adjusted by dragging or using the keyboard; and just as for nudging, you can get fine adjustments using the cursor keys alone, or adjust in 1*sp* increments by pressing and holding Ctrl (Mac: Cmd) while nudging.

Examples will be presented when we cover the specific element types than can be edited in this fashion.

Reset

Most manual adjustments to most elements can be reset by selecting them and pressing Ctrl + R (Mac: Cmd + R) or using the equivalent menu command Layout ⟩ Reset.

Changing Appearance and Behavior

In addition to the general adjustments described above, there are many controls available for customizing the appearance and behavior of different element types. In this section, I will present the customizations available for notes and rests; customizations available for other element types can be found in the chapters discussing those elements.

Most of the time, these sort of manual adjustments should not be necessary. So if you are reading this for the first time, you may wish to just skip over this section and the corresponding sections in other chapters, and perhaps return later as you find the need for more control.

Global note and rest settings

MuseScore provides a number of global controls over the appearance and behavior of notes and rests. In addition to the settings described below, see also the chapters on *Measure Operations* and *Page Layout* for more settings and commands that affect notes, particularly with regard to spacing.

- Layout ⟩⟩ Page Settings

  Staff space – size of space between staff lines, which scales everything else accordingly

- Style ⟩⟩ General ⟩⟩ Score

  Musical symbols font – font used for notes, rests, and other score symbols

- Style ⟩⟩ General ⟩⟩ Notes

  Shorten stems – progressively shorten stems that extend above or below the staff
  Progression – amount to shorten stem for each step
  Shortest stem – minimum length when shortening stems
  Accidental note distance – distance from accidental to note
  Accidental distance – distance between accidentals
  Dot size – size of dots
  Note dot distance – distance from note to dot
  Dot dot distance – distance between dots
  Stem thickness – thickness of stem
  Ledger line thickness – thickness of ledger lines
  Ledger line length – length of ledger lines (not counting width of note head)

- Style ⟩⟩ General ⟩⟩ Beams

  Beam thickness – thickness of beams
  Beam distance – distance between beams
  Broken beam minimum length – minimum length for the broken beams that appear in mixed groups
  Flatten all beams – force all beams to be horizontal

- Style ⟩⟩ General ⟩⟩ Slurs/Ties

  Line thickness at end – thickness of end of tie or slur

Line thickness middle – thickness at middle of tie or slur

Dotted line thickness – thickness of dotted line ties or slurs

Minimum tie length – minimum default length of tie (extra space will added between notes to enforce this)

- Style 》 General 》 Sizes

Small staff size – relative size for staves marked *Small* in *Staff Properties* (see *Staves and Instruments*)

Small note size – relative size for notes and chords marked *Small* in *Inspector* (see below)

Grace note size – relative size for grace notes

- Style 》 General 》 Tuplets

Maximum slope – maximum default angle for tuplet bracket

Vertical distance from stem – vertical distance from stem to tuplet bracket

Vertical distance from note head – vertical distance from note head to tuplet bracket

Avoid the staves – avoid placing tuplet number within staff

Distance before the stem of the first note – horizontal distance from left end of tuplet bracket to stem of first note

Distance before the head of the first note – horizontal distance from left end of tuplet bracket to head of first note

Distance after the stem of the last note – horizontal distance from stem of last note to right end of tuplet bracket

Distance after the head of the last note – horizontal distance from head of last note to right end of tuplet bracket

Individual note and rest properties

Since notes and rests are usually the most important elements in a score, there are an especially large number of customizations possible for them. Most are found in the *Inspector*, although a few are accessed via the context menu that pops up when you right-click an element.

As I have mentioned before, MuseScore actually treats all notes as being part of chords, so even a single note is considered to belong to a chord. One of the times this distinction is important to keep in mind is when setting properties for a note using the *Inspector*. Properties that affect a whole chord – like stem direction – are found in the *Chord* section of the *Inspector*. Properties that affect individual notes within a chord – like note head – are found in the *Note* section.

Chord properties

These properties affect the chord as a whole, including all note heads, stem, dots, hooks, and beams if appropriate.

- *Inspector*

Horizontal offset – position for the chord as a whole

Vertical offset – position for the chord as a whole

When you select a range, you are actually selecting the notes, rests, stems, flags, and all other elements in that range, and therefore, the *Inspector* will only show you the controls that it normally shows for mixed selections. However, at the bottom of the *Inspector* are buttons Notes and Rests than will change the range selection into a list selection containing only notes or rests, respectively. Thus, if you wish to use the *Inspector* on all notes in a range, you can select the range and then press the Notes button to change the selection to a list selection, which will then enable the controls that are only available for notes.

Small – size of chord as a whole
Stemless – suppress the stem for chord
Stem direction – direction of stem (*Up, Down,* or *Auto*)

Note properties

These properties affect an individual note within a chord.

- *Inspector*

  Small – size of note and elements attached to notes such as accidentals, dots, and ties
  Head group – overall style of note head (*Normal, Cross, Slash,* etc.)
  Head type – duration type to use for note head (*Whole, Half, Quarter,* etc.)
  Mirror head – horizontal position of note head relative to stem (*Left, Right, Auto*)
  Dot position – vertical position of dots (*Top, Bottom, Auto*)
  Tuning – pitch deviation in cents from equal temperament
  Play – enable/disable playback of this note
  Velocity type – override note playback MIDI velocity (volume) using relative (offset) or absolute (user) value
  Velocity – relative or absolute value for MIDI velocity (volume on a scale of 1-127)
  Fix to line – display note on fixed line regardless of clef or transposition
  Line – line to use with *Fix to line* option

You can use the keyboard shortcut Shift + X to toggle the mirror property of a note.

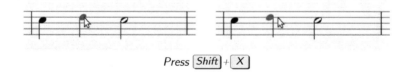

Press Shift + X

Rest properties

- *Inspector*

  Small – size

Accidental properties

- *Inspector*

  Small – size

Tie properties

- *Inspector*

  Line type – Continuous, Dotted, Dashed

You can use the X command to flip the direction of a tie.

Press X

Stem properties

- *Edit* **mode** – the length of a stem can be adjusted by double-clicking it and adjusting the handle (see below)

You can flip the stem of a chord using the X command after selecting the stem, the chord, or any note in the chord.

Press X

To adjust the length of a stem, double-click it to put it in *Edit* mode, then move the handle. You can drag it with the mouse or use the keyboard cursor keys, with or without Ctrl (Mac: Cmd), to get coarser or finer adjustments.

Drag

Beam properties

- *Inspector*

  Local relayout – space notes within this beam independently of rhythm in other voices or on other staves

  Direction – *Up*, *Down*, or *Auto*

  Grow left – increase or decrease feathered beam spacing on left side

  Grow right – increase or decrease feathered beam spacing on right side

  Horizontal – force beam to be horizontal

  User position – enable/disable manual adjustments in fields below

  Position – manual adjustments to beam position

- *Edit* **mode** – you can adjust the size, shape, and position of a beam by double-clicking it and adjusting the handles (see below)

- *Beam Properties* **palette** – override the default beaming (see *To control beaming* below)

Beams can be flipped above or below the notes using the ⎡X⎤ command or the *Direction* property in the *Inspector*.

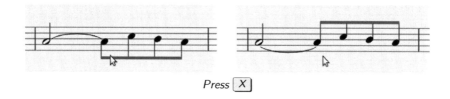

Press ⎡X⎤

To fine-tune the position of the beam, double-click it to put it in *Edit* mode, then move the handles. You can drag with the mouse or use the keyboard cursor keys, with or without ⎡Ctrl⎤ (Mac: ⎡Cmd⎤) to get coarser or finer adjustments. The left handle controls the vertical position of the beam; the right handle controls the angle.

Drag

Tuplet properties

- *Inspector*

  Direction – *Up*, *Down*, or *Auto*

  Number type – *Number*, *Relation*, or *Nothing*

  Bracket type – *Automatic*, *Bracket*, or *Nothing*

- Style 》 Text 》 Tuplet – font settings for number (see *Text*)

- **Edit mode** – you can edit the size, shape, and position of a tuplet bracket by double-clicking it and adjusting the handles

Brackets can be flipped above or below the notes using the X command or the *Direction* property in the *Inspector*.

To fine-tune the position of the bracket, double-click it to put it in *Edit* mode, then move the handles. You can drag with the mouse or use the keyboard cursor keys, with or without Ctrl (Mac: Cmd) to get coarser or finer adjustments. The two handles provide independent control over the end points of the bracket, allowing adjustment both vertically and horizontally.

Drag

You can also simply drag the entire bracket if desired.

Common Tasks

To control beaming

MuseScore normally decides how to beam notes according to the time signature, using standard engraving rules. For example, in 4/4 time, eighth notes are automatically beamed in groups of four by default. If you wish to change the defaults – say, to have eighth notes automatically beamed in groups of two, or in groups of eight – then see *Setting the default beaming* in the chapter *Time Signatures*. If you wish to override the defaults just for a specific passage, however, you can use the *Beam Properties* palette.

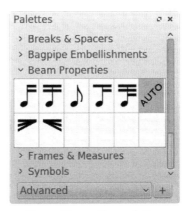

Beam Properties palette

These properties are applied to notes (chords, technically), not to the beams themselves. To use this palette, either drag an icon to the note you wish to affect, or click the note and then double-click a palette icon. The icons on this palette are defined as follows:

Beam start ⏸ – begin a new beam with this note
Beam middle ⏸ – continue the previous beam through this note
No beam ♪ – do not beam this note
Beam 16th sub ⏸ – create single sub-beam between groups at this note
Beam 32nd sub ⏸ – create double sub-beam between groups at this note
Auto ⏸ – restore default beaming for this note
Feathered beam, slower ◤ – feather beams converging to right
Feathered beam, faster ◥ – feather beams converging to left

For example, to break a beam, click the note after the desired break and then double-click the ⏸ (*Beam start*) icon.

Double-click ⏸

To join a beam, select the note after the current break and then double-click the ⏸ (*Beam middle*) icon.

Double-click ⏸

You can perform these actions while still in *Note input* mode, so you can override the beaming as you enter notes (recall that the note just entered is automatically selected). Or, if you are in *Normal* mode, you can apply a beam property to a whole selected passage at once.

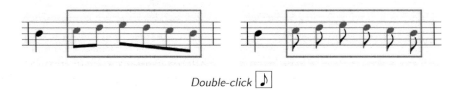

Double-click ♪

You can also extend beams over rests using these same properties.

Double-click

To customize note heads

MuseScore supports a number of different note heads that can be useful for a variety of purposes, from percussion notation to slash notation to shape music notation to early music to ghost notes to spoken word. You can select these alternate note heads using the *Head group* drop-down menu in the *Inspector*, or you can apply them using the *Note Heads* palette.

Note Heads palette

These note heads are applied in the same way as other palette elements – either drag one directly to a note, or else select the note (or multiple notes) and double-click the palette icon.

To merge unisons

Occasionally you may wish to allow two notes in different voices to share a note head even though they have different rhythm values (e.g., eighth and half) and thus cannot normally be shared. This is common in guitar music, for example. To achieve this effect in MuseScore, set one of the notes to use the same *Head type* as the other using the *Inspector*, or simply mark one note invisible by pressing V .

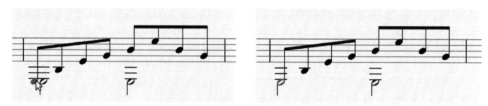

Set Head type to Half

Shortcuts

We have learned a lot of keyboard shortcuts in this chapter; here is a summary.

- ↑ – raise pitch a semitone
- ↓ – lower pitch a semitone
- Ctrl + ↑ – raise pitch an octave
- Ctrl + ↓ – lower pitch an octave
- Alt + Shift + ↑ – raise pitch a step diatonically
- Alt + Shift + ↓ – lower pitch a step diatonically
- J – change enharmonic spelling
- Shift plus letter (A - G) – add note to chord
- Alt plus number (1 - 9) – add interval above to chord
- + – create tie (*Normal* mode only: tie chord)
- Delete – delete note
- Ctrl + 2 - Ctrl + 9 – create tuplet
- / – add acciaccatura (grace note)
- Ctrl + Shift + ↑ – move note or rest to previous staff of instrument
- Ctrl + Shift + ↓ – move note or rest to next staff of instrument
- Q – change to next shorter duration (single selection only)
- W – change to next longer duration (single selection only)
- 1 - 9 – change duration (*Normal* mode only)
- Ctrl + Alt + 1 - Ctrl + Alt + 4 – move to specified voice *Normal* mode only
- Shift + ← – exchange with previous note (*Note input* mode only)

- Shift + → – exchange with next note (*Note input* mode only)
- Ctrl + Shift + I – toggle *Repitch* mode (*Note input* mode only)
- Ctrl + C – copy selection to clipboard
- Ctrl + X – cut selection to clipboard
- Ctrl + V – paste clipboard
- R – repeat selection
- V – toggle visibility
- X – flip
- Shift + X – mirror note head

Remember, on Mac OS, you need to substitute Cmd for Ctrl and Option for Alt.

Chapter 9

Measure Operations

MuseScore understands, and indeed relies heavily on, the division of music into measures (also known as "bars"). In addition to adding and removing measures, there are many operations that can be performed on measures and properties associated with measures that you can control.

Adding and Removing Measures

Measures can be added or removed anywhere in the score.

Appending measures to the end of the score

To add measures to the end of your score, choose either Add〉Measures and then either Append One Measure (shortcut Ctrl + B , or Cmd + B on Mac) or Append Measures (Alt + Shift + B). If you choose Append One Measure , it will be added immediately.

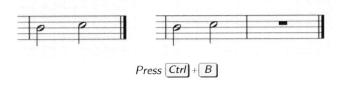

Press Ctrl + B

If you choose Append Measures , you will be prompted to enter the number of measures you wish to append.

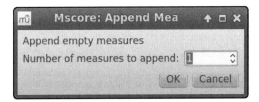

111

Inserting measures at any point in the score

To insert measures anywhere else in your score, select anything in the measure you want to insert in front of, then choose [Add]>[Measures] and select either [Insert One Measure] ([Ins]) or [Insert Measures] ([Ctrl]+[Ins]). If you choose [Insert One Measure], it will be added immediately.

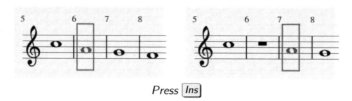

Press [Ins]

If you choose [Insert Measures], you will be prompted to enter the number of measures you wish to insert. The dialog is similar to the corresponding dialog for the append operation.

Deleting measures

We have already seen that the [Delete] key will delete the contents of a selected range. To completely remove a measure or range of measures from your score – as opposed to simply erasing their contents – first select the region, then select [Edit]>[Measure]>[Delete Selected Measures] or use the keyboard shortcut [Ctrl]+[Delete] (Mac: [Cmd]+[Delete]).

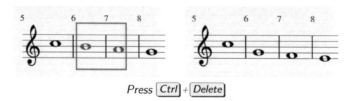

Press [Ctrl]+[Delete]

Barlines

MuseScore supports a variety of barline types, including double bars, repeat signs, dotted barlines, barlines through staves, partial barlines, and more.

Double bars, repeat bars, and other barline styles

The basic barline styles available are found in the *Barlines* palette. If you do not see all the options seen here and miss some of them, be sure to switch to the *Advanced* workspace using the control at the bottom of the palette window.

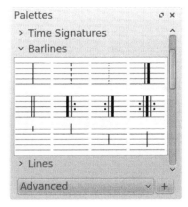

To apply one of these barline styles, either select the barline to which you wish to apply it and then double-click the palette icon, or else drag the palette icon to the measure or barline. This will apply the style to all staves simultaneously.

As shown in the example above, when dragging an element to a measure, release when the measure highlights.

Most of the barline styles apply to the right barline of a measure, but the start repeat barline applies to the left barline.

If you wish to apply a barline style to one staff only, then press and hold Ctrl (Mac: Cmd) while dragging the barline icon to the measure or barline, or select the barline and then press and hold Ctrl (Mac: Cmd) while double-clicking the palette icon.

Press and hold Ctrl

Extending barlines through staves

To extend barlines through adjacent staves, double-click the barline on any measure on the top staff to enter *Edit* mode, then drag the lower handle down to the bottom staff. When you release, this change will be applied to all barlines for this staff.

If you wish to extend just a single barline, then press and hold Ctrl (Mac: Cmd) while dragging the handle.

Ctrl+drag

Changing barline length

Barlines normally extend from the top staff line to the bottom (or from just above to just below for single-line staves like those used for percussion instruments). To change the length of a barline, double-click it to enter *Edit* mode, then press and hold Shift while dragging one of the handles. When you release, this change will be applied to all barlines for this staff.

Shift+drag

If you wish to change the length of just a single barline, then press and hold Ctrl (Mac: Cmd) as well as Shift.

Ctrl + Shift +drag

Mid-measure barlines

A barline that does not truly end the measure but divides it visually can be inserted at any point within a measure. Either click the note or rest before which you wish the barline to appear and then double-click the desired barline icon in the palette, or else drag the icon to the note.

Measure Numbering

By default, MuseScore displays measure numbers automatically at the beginning of every system. You can control the numbering using options in the `Style` ⟩ `General` ⟩ `Header, Footer, Numbers`, `Style` ⟩ `Text` ⟩ `Measure Number`, and `Measure Properties` dialogs as discussed below.

Controlling which measures are numbered

The options to control which measures are numbered are found toward the bottom of the dialog `Style` ⟩ `General` ⟩ `Header, Footer, Numbers`.

The options in this dialog are as follows:

Measure numbers – select whether measure numbers are displayed at all
Show first – select whether to show numbers on first measure
All Staves – select whether to show number on all staves or just the topmost staff
Every system – specify that numbers should be shown on first measure of each system
Interval – specify that numbers should be shown at a regular interval

For example, setting the *All staves* option, disabling *Show first*, and setting *Interval* to "1" will cause measure numbers to display on every measure of every staff, except the first measure.

Controlling the position and font of measure numbers

The default appearance of measure numbers is controlled by the settings in Style ⟩⟩ Text ⟩ ⟩ Measure Number . For more information on text styles, see *Text Formatting* in the chapter on *Text*.

You can also manually position any given measure number as discussed in *Manual Adjustments* in the chapter on *Editing*.

Overriding the numbering of specific measures

Measures are normally numbered consecutively starting with "1". However, MuseScore allows you to override this numbering for a given measure by right-clicking it and selecting Measure Properties from the resulting context menu. The relevant properties are found toward the bottom of the dialog.

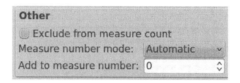

The *Exclude from measure count* and *Add to measure number* options can be used to alter the numbering, so that certain measures or numbers are skipped. The *Measure number mode* defaults to *Automatic*, which means that the global style settings will determine whether a number is displayed for this measure. The *Always Hide* option can be used to suppress the measure number for a measure with a rehearsal mark. The *Always Show* option can be used to show measure numbers only for specific measures. Combined with a text style (see the chapter on *Text*) that makes measure numbers larger and places a frame around them, this would allow measure numbers to be used as a substitute for rehearsal markings.

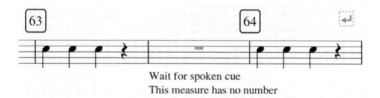

Wait for spoken cue
This measure has no number

Multimeasure Rests

In scores for multiple instruments, it is common for an instrument to rest for several measures at a time. In the score itself, this would normally be shown using ordinary measure rests, since other instruments would presumably still be playing.

In the individual parts for the instruments, however, it is customary to show multiple measures of rest with a special symbol that indicates the number of measures to rest.

MuseScore normally handles this automatically when you generate individual parts from a full score. The full score will display normal measure rests, and the parts for the individual instruments will display multimeasure rests. For more information on scores and parts, see the chapter *Parts*.

Toggling display of multimeasure rests

To toggle the display of multimeasure rests manually, you can toggle the *Create multimeasure rests* option in Style ⟩ General ⟩ Score.

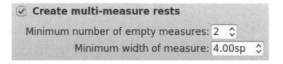

You can also use the keyboard shortcut M.

Press M

Breaking a multimeasure rest

Sometimes when a part rests for many measures, you may need to break the multimeasure rest into smaller pieces. This might be so you can show a key or time signature change, tempo change, rehearsal mark, double bar, segno, coda, or other significant event. MuseScore handles most of these cases automatically.

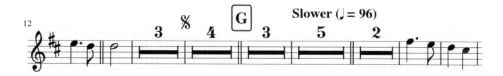

If you need a measure to break a rest even though it does not contain any of the types of elements that automatically break a rest, you can force it to break by right-clicking the measure and selecting [Measure Properties], then checking the *Break multimeasure rest* option.

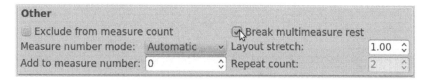

Of course, in order to be able to right-click the measure, you may need to first turn multimeasure rests off, then turn them back on after setting the *Break multimeasure rest* property.

Right-click, [Measure Properties], set Break multimeasure rest, press [M]

Splitting and Joining Measures

MuseScore allows you to divide and combine measures. These commands have a variety of uses, some of which will be seen below. But first, I will explain how the split and join commands work.

To split a measure into two parts, select the note before which you wish to split the measure, then use [Edit ⟩ Measure ⟩ Split Measure]. The result is that the measure is split into two measures. Each measure will have its *Actual* duration (see the chapter on *Time Signatures*) set appropriately for the number of beats it contains.

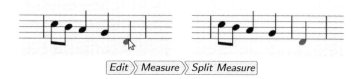

[Edit ⟩ Measure ⟩ Split Measure]

To join measures, select the measures you wish to join, then Edit ⟩ Measure ⟩ Join Measures.
The selected measures will be replaced by one measure with an appropriate *Actual* duration.

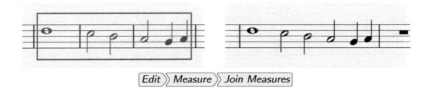

Edit ⟩ Measure ⟩ Join Measures

The split command can be used to allow a measure to be broken into two parts with the
first part at the end of one system and the second part at the beginning of the next (common
in hymns).

The join command can be useful to create the effect of unmetered music.

Note that these commands currently are disabled for scores with linked parts, so wait
until you are done making these sorts of changes before generating parts.

Changing Appearance and Behavior

The most important controls for altering the appearance and behavior of measures have already
been discussed (see in particular the sections on *Measure Numbering* and *Multimeasure Rests*),
but there are a number of additional options that can occasionally be useful.

Global measure settings

- Style >> General >> Score

  Minimum number of empty measures – threshold for creating multimeasure rests
  Minimum width of measure – minimum width to render multimeasure rests

- Style >> General >> Measure

  Minimum measure width – minimum width to render measures
  Spacing – spacing factor; larger values result in more spacing between notes
  Barline to note distance – distance from barline to first note of measure if there are no grace notes or accidentals
  Barline to grace note distance – distance from barline to grace note
  Barline to accidental distance – distance from barline to accidental
  Note to barline distance – distance from last note of measure to barline
  Minimum note distance – minimum distance between notes
  Multimeasure rest margin – distance between barlines and the horizontal bar indicating a multimeasure rest
  Staff line thickness – thickness of staff lines

- Style >> General >> Barlines

  Show repeat bar tips – use "winged" repeat signs
  Barline at start of single staff – display barlines at start of system when it contains only one staff
  Barline at start of multiple staves – display barlines at start of system when it contains multiple staves
  Scale barlines to staff size – display thinner barlines on small staves
  Barline thickness – thickness of normal barlines
  Final barline thickness – thickness of additional line in end or repeat barline
  Final barline distance – distance between lines in end or repeat barline
  Double barline thickness – thickness of lines in double barline
  Double barline distance – distance between lines in double barline

Individual measure properties

If you right-click a measure, you can display the *Measure Properties* dialog. Several of the settings in this dialog have been discussed already, but others have not. A few will be discussed in other chapters.

Staves

visible – controls whether this measure is visible for each individual staff

stemless – controls whether notes in this measure are displayed without stems for each individual staff

Measure Duration

Actual – actual duration for this measure (see *Time Signatures*)

Other

Exclude from measure count – exclude this measure from the numbering

Measure number mode – select from *Automatic, Always Show,* or *Always Hide*

Add to measure number – add the specified amount to the measure number

Break multimeasure rest – break multimeasure rest starting with this measure

Layout stretch – increase or decrease the width of this measure (see *Page Layout*)

Repeat count – number of times to repeat this measure (see *Repeats*)

Note at the bottom of the dialog there are also controls to let you move from measure to measure without needing to close and reopen the dialog. This can be useful if you want to apply some particular settings to several measures in a row.

Individual barline properties

The *Inspector* allows you to control a few properties for barlines.

Style – *Normal, Dashed barline, Dotted barline, Double barline, Final barline, End repeat, Start repeat, End-start repeat*

Spanned staves –number of staves spanned by this barline

Span from – top staff line spanned

Span to – bottom staff line spanned

Span preset – selection of common span settings (*Staff default, Tick 1, Tick 2, Short 1, Short 2*)

Common Tasks

To make a measure narrower or wider

MuseScore uses the concept of "stretch" to alter the width of a measure from its default value. The stretch factor for a measure is shown in the *Measure Properties* dialog as discussed above, but there is a simpler way to increase or decrease the stretch for a selected measure or range. To increase the width of the selected measures, use Layout ⟩⟩ Increase stretch or the keyboard shortcut } . To decrease the width, use Layout ⟩⟩ Decrease stretch or the keyboard shortcut { . The stretch is changed in 10% increments; you can use either command multiple times to stretch measures by larger amounts.

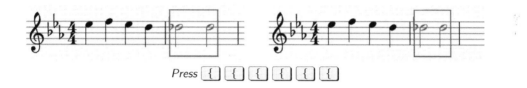

To change the number of measures on a system

MuseScore does not have a single direct command to place a specific number of measures on any given system, because there is no single way this can be achieved. Instead, MuseScore provides a variety of commands to suit different needs.

If you wish to enforce a certain number of measures per system for the entire score, there is the Edit ⟩⟩ Tools ⟩⟩ Add/Remove Line Breaks command discussed in *Page Layout*.

Edit ⟩⟩ Tools ⟩⟩ Add/Remove Line Breaks , *Break lines every 4 measures*

However, MuseScore will not put more measures on a system than can fit given your current settings for staff size and note spacing. So if you wish to fit more measures per system throughout your score, you will need to reduce the staff size or measure spacing. To reduce staff size, use the *Staff space* option in the Layout ⟩ Page Settings dialog, as discussed in the chapter *Page Layout*. To reduce the note spacing, you can either use the *Spacing* option in Style ⟩ General ⟩ Measure discussed above, or you can select your entire score and reduce the stretch using { .

Reduce Staff space

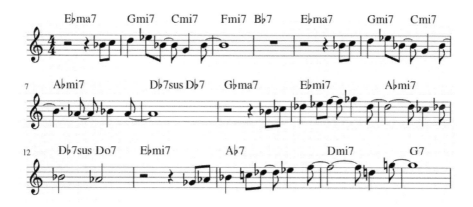

To fit more measures on a given system than MuseScore does by default given your current staff size and note spacing, you need to decrease stretch for that system alone. So select the measures you wish to appear on a single system and press ⎡ { ⎤ as many times as needed to allow the measures to fit.

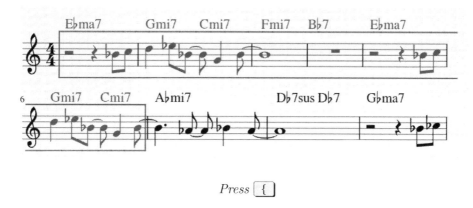

Press ⎡ { ⎤

To fit fewer measures on a given system than MuseScore does by default, the simplest thing to do is add a line break. You can either add one from the *Breaks & Spacers* palette to the desired last measure of the system, or click the barline and then press ⎡Enter⎤.

Add line break

Part III

Other Score Elements

Chapter 10

Clefs

MuseScore supports a large variety of different clefs, and you can change clefs anywhere within a score. In addition to the standard treble and bass clefs, you can use the alto, tenor, or other C clefs, a percussion clef, tablature clefs, and some special versions of treble and bass clefs that are transposed by an octave or two or shifted to different places on the staff.

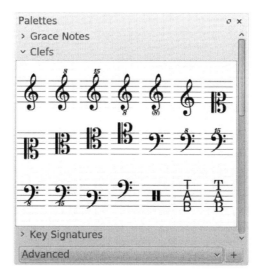

If your palette does not contain all of these clefs and you miss them, be sure to select the *Advanced* workspace using the control at the bottom of the palette.

As with most palette items, clefs can be applied by dragging the palette icon to an element in your score or by clicking the score element then double-clicking the palette icon.

Initial Clef

When you first choose instruments to add to your score, MuseScore automatically chooses the most common clef used to notate music for each instrument. This is true both when initially creating your score as described in *Creating a New Score* as well as when adding instruments later as described in *Staves and Instruments*. For example, when creating a score for violin, viola, and cello, MuseScore automatically adds the appropriate treble, alto, and bass clefs.

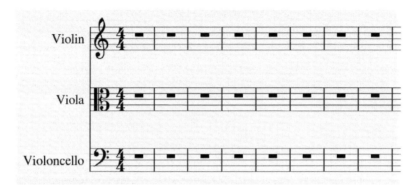

If you wish to change the clef used for a given instrument, you can use the *Clefs* palette to select a different one. You can drop the new clef directly on top of the old, or you can drop it anywhere in the first measure once you see the entire measure highlight.

You can also select the original clef or the first measure, and then double-click the palette icon for the new clef.

For instruments like the bass clarinet or baritone saxophone that transpose by large intervals, you can use different clefs depending on whether you are viewing the score in *Concert Pitch* mode or not (see *Transposition*). Any change to the initial clef with *Concert Pitch* turned on will only be in effect while *Concert Pitch* is on, and the same is true for any change made while *Concert Pitch* is turned off.

For example, the default clef for the tenor saxophone is treble. However, because this instrument sounds over an octave lower than written, this could result in many ledger lines below the staff in *Concert Pitch* mode. In order to avoid this, MuseScore automatically changes a tenor saxophone staff to an octave-transposing version of the treble clef when you switch to *Concert Pitch.* The little "8" that appears below the clef indicates that all notes sound an octave lower than written.

Enable Concert Pitch

If you prefer to use, for example, the bass clef for tenor saxophone in *Concert Pitch* mode, simply change the clef while *Concert Pitch* is turned on. When you turn *Concert Pitch* back off, the original treble clef will still be in place, but every time you return to *Concert Pitch* mode, the staff will appear in bass clef.

Clef Changes

If you need to change clefs for a staff in the middle of a score – say, from bass to treble in the bottom staff of a piano score – you can do this by dragging the clef to the first measure to which you wish the change to apply and releasing when the measure highlights.

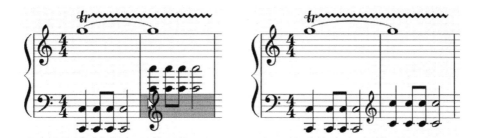

Notice that the pitches of any notes already entered do not change; MuseScore automatically displays the notes as appropriate for the new clef.

You can also select a single measure and then double-click a clef in the palette to apply the change to that measure. If you select a range that is anything but a single measure, the clef change is applied at the beginning of the range and the original clef is restored at the end.

You can change clefs mid-measure by dropping the clef directly onto the note before which you want the clef to appear.

You can also add a mid-measure clef change by clicking the first note you wish to apply it to and then double-clicking the palette icon for the clef. Or, anywhere there is already a clef but you but wish to change it to a different clef, you can click the existing clef and then double-click the palette icon for the new one, or drag and drop the palette icon directly onto the existing clef.

MuseScore handles the details of clef layout automatically. A clef change that is applied to a measure is displayed before the barline; a clef change added anywhere but at the beginning of a system is displayed a little smaller than usual; a clef change at the beginning of a system is announced by a "courtesy" clef change at the end of the previous system. For information on how to change how clefs are displayed, see *Changing Appearance and Behavior* below.

To remove a clef change that was added by any of these methods, click the clef and press Delete .

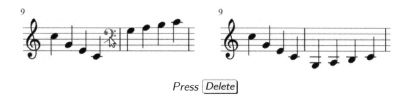

Press Delete

Changing Appearance and Behavior

In addition to the general manual adjustments available for most element types (see *Manual Adjustments* in the chapter on *Editing*), MuseScore provides a number of options to control various defaults for all clefs as well as properties for individual clef changes.

Global clef settings

The settings that affect the default appearance and behavior of clefs are found in the Style menu as well as in the *Staff Properties* dialog accessed via the context menu.

- Style ⟩⟩ General ⟩⟩ Clefs

   Default TAB clef – choose between standard and serif styles for tablature clefs

- Style ⟩⟩ General ⟩⟩ Measure

   Clef left margin – set default distance before clef at start of system
   Clef/Key right margin – set default distance after clef / key signature / time signature at start of system
   Clef to barline distance – set default distance before clef change appearing at end of measure

- Style ⟩⟩ General ⟩⟩ Page

   Create clef for all systems – display clef at the start of each system
   Create courtesy clefs – display courtesy clef change at end of the previous system when a clef change occurs at the start of a system

- Style ⟩⟩ General ⟩⟩ Sizes

   Small clef size – relative size of smaller clefs used for mid-system clef changes

- Staff Properties

   Show clef – display clefs for this staff

Individual clef properties

Clefs have only a few properties that can be set using the *Inspector* and/or context menu.

- *Inspector*

    Leading space – amount of extra space to add before this clef on all staves of system
    Trailing space – amount of extra space to add after this clef on all staves of system
    Show courtesy – control display of courtesy clef for this clef change

- **Context menu**

    Hide/Show Courtesy Clef – control display of courtesy clef for this clef change

Common Tasks

To suppress courtesy clef changes

If a clef change occurs at the beginning of a system, it is customary to show a courtesy clef at the end of the previous system. MuseScore does this for you automatically, as we saw previously. However, there are cases where you might not want this. Examples include theory or exercise worksheets. In these cases, courtesy clefs might be unnecessary and distracting.

If you wish to suppress the display of one particular courtesy clef, click the "main" clef at the start of the next system and turn off the *Show courtesy* option in the *Inspector*. You can also right-click the courtesy clef itself and choose Hide Courtesy Clef from the context menu. The courtesy clef will be removed.

You might also want to suppress the courtesy clef between movements of a work or between songs in a larger collection. MuseScore provides other features specially designed to meets the needs of these cases, however. See *Section breaks* in the chapter on *Page Layout* and *Creating Albums* in the chapter on *File Operations* for more information on these features.

If you know you will not want courtesy clefs to appear anywhere in your score, you can tell MuseScore not to generate them in the first place by turning off the *Create courtesy clefs* option in [Style 〉 General 〉 Page].

To suppress clefs at the start of each system

MuseScore normally displays a clef at the start of each system, as standard music notation practice demands. However, for certain types of music, it is not uncommon to omit clefs after the first system. To get this result in MuseScore, go to [Style 〉 General 〉 Page] and turn off the *Create clef for all systems* option.

In the example above, I also disabled the *Create key signature for all systems* option in that same dialog (see *Key Signatures*), and enabled the *Barline at start of single system* option (see *Measure Operations*) to emulate the look of certain jazz fakebooks.

If you would like to suppress even the clef on the first system, you can do this by right-clicking the staff, going to Staff Properties, and turning off the *Show clef* option. This can be useful to generate completely blank manuscript paper.

Note that I also made the rests and barlines invisible.

Shortcuts

There are a few predefined keyboard shortcuts that can used to enter clefs directly while in *Note input* mode. These are two-character sequences, entered by pressing the keys in succession.

- Ctrl + Y Ctrl + 1 – treble clef
- Ctrl + Y Ctrl + 2 – bass clef

Chapter 11

Key Signatures

MuseScore supports the standard key signatures used in Western music, from the key of C major / A minor with no flats or sharps up through the keys with seven flats or seven sharps. You can change keys anywhere within a piece, and MuseScore automatically handles transposition of key signatures when writing for transposing instruments like clarinets or trumpets. You can also create an open (atonal) key signature that does not transpose, and you can even define your own custom key signatures.

Key signatures are added through the *Key Signatures* palette.

You can also bring up the key signature portion of the *Master Palette* using the keyboard shortcut Shift + K .

Note that this window normally shows controls that can be used in creating custom key signatures (see *To create a custom key signature* below), but I have hidden these in the image above as they are not relevant here.

Initial Key Signature

As we have already seen, you can select the initial key signature for a piece in the *Create New Score* wizard (see *Creating a New Score*). This key signature is automatically applied to all staves in your score, except for unpitched percussion or other instruments that traditionally do not use key signatures.

For transposing instruments like clarinets and trumpets, the key signature is automatically transposed (see the chapter on *Transposition*).

If you decide you wish to change the initial key signature, you can add a new one from the palette. Select the original key signature in the score, the first measure, or any note in the measure, and then double-click the desired key signature in the *Key Signatures* palette. You can also drag a key signature from the palette onto the first measure or onto the initial key signature.

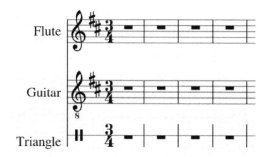

Key signatures on pitched and unpitched staves

Key signatures on transposing and non-transposing staves

When adding a key signature to your score, it is always added at concert pitch (see the chapter on *Transposition*). This means that in a score for clarinet and piano, adding a *D* major key signature actually adds an *E* major key signature to the clarinet staff, unless you are in *Concert Pitch* mode.

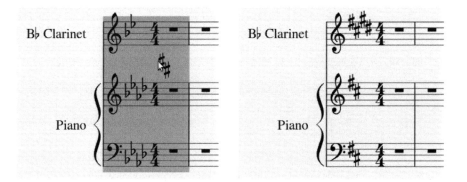

Aside from this automatic transposition, adding a key signature to your score applies the same key signature to all staves. If you are literally creating polytonal music and wish to change the key signature for one staff only other than for reasons for transposition, press and hold the [Ctrl] key (Mac: [Cmd]) while dragging the key signature to your score.

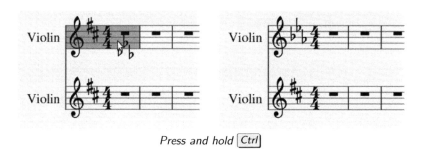

Press and hold [Ctrl]

Key Signature Changes

You can change key signatures at any measure within a piece. Simply drag a key signature from the palette to the measure you wish the key signature to appear in.

Notice that MuseScore preserves the pitch of any existing notes and automatically corrects the spelling to fit the new key signature. In the above case, the E did not originally need a natural sign, but after the key change, it does, so one is added for you. The key signature change itself tells us that the following C is a C♮, so the natural sign that was there is removed, but it would not be a bad idea to add a courtesy accidental to make this explicit (see *Accidentals* in the chapter on *Entering Notes and Rests*).

You can also select a single measure and then double-click a key signature in the palette to apply the change to that measure. If you select a range that is anything but a single measure, the key change is applied at the beginning of the range and the original key is restored at the end.

As with changes to the initial key signature, you can apply mid-score key signature changes to individual staves to create polytonal music by pressing and holding Ctrl (Mac: Cmd) while dragging.

Key signature changes are removed by clicking them and pressing Delete.

Press Delete

Changing Appearance and Behavior

As usual, there are default settings that apply to all key signatures, properties for individual key signatures, manual adjustments, and other things you can do to change the appearance and behavior of key signatures.

Global key signature settings

- Style ⟩ General ⟩ Accidentals

♮ **in key signatures**

Only for a change to C Maj / A min – only show naturals when changing to a key
    signature with no flats or sharps

Before key signature if changing to fewer sharps or flats – always show naturals when an
    accidental no longer applies; display naturals before the new key signature

*After key signature if changing to fewer sharps or flats. Before if changing between
    sharps and flats* – always show naturals when an accidental no longer applies; display
    naturals after the new key signature when changing to fewer sharps or flats, before
    when changing between flats and sharps

- [Style ⟩⟩ General ⟩⟩ Measure]

    Key signature left margin – distance to left of key signature
    Clef/Key right margin – distance to right of clef, key signature, and time signature at
        beginning of measure

- [Style ⟩⟩ General ⟩⟩ Page]

    Create key signatures for all systems – display key signature at the start of each system
    Create courtesy key signatures – display courtesy key signature at the end of the previous
        system when a key change occurs at the start of a system

Individual key signature properties

Aside from the standard properties shared by all elements (e.g., visibility, horizontal offset), key
signatures have only a single property that can be set using the *Inspector* and/or context menu.

- *Inspector*

    Show courtesy – control display of courtesy key signature for this key change

- **Context menu**

    Hide/Show Courtesy Key Signature – control display of courtesy key signature for this
        key change

- ***Edit* mode** – the position of a key signature can be adjusted by double-clicking it and
    using the cursor keys

Common Tasks

To control the display of courtesy key signatures

As with clef changes, it is traditional to show a courtesy key signature change at the end of the
previous system if a key signature changes occurs at the beginning of a line, and MuseScore
inserts this automatically.

If you wish to suppress the display of one particular courtesy key signature, click the "main" key signature at the start of the next system and turn off the *Show courtesy* option in the *Inspector*. You can also right-click the key signature and choose Hide Courtesy Key Signature from the context menu. The courtesy key signature will be removed.

You might also want to suppress the courtesy key signature between movements of a work or between songs in a larger collection. MuseScore provides other features specially designed to meets the needs of these cases, however. See *Section breaks* in the chapter on *Page Layout* and *Creating Albums* in the chapter on *File Operations* for more information on these features.

If you know you will not want courtesy key signatures to appear anywhere in your score, you can tell MuseScore not to generate them in the first place by turning off the *Create courtesy key signatures* option in Style 〉 General 〉 Page .

To control the display of key signatures at the start of each system

As with clefs, MuseScore normally generates key signatures at the start of each system. Some editors, however, choose to omit both clefs and key signatures after the first system. We have already seen how to suppress the generation of clefs. Key signatures are suppressed the same way: go to Style 〉 General 〉 Page and turn off the *Create key signatures for all systems* option.

You can completely suppress the display of all key signatures – including on the first system – by right-clicking the staff, going to Staff Properties , selecting Advanced Style Properties , and turning off the *Show key signatures* option. This can be useful to generate completely blank manuscript paper.

To control the display of naturals in key signatures

When changing from a key with several sharps to a key with fewer sharps, some editors prefer to place natural signs in the first occurrence of the new key signature to show which sharps are no longer in effect. The same is true when changing from a key with several flats to a key with fewer flats, or from a key with sharps to a key with flats or vice versa. MuseScore can do this automatically if you enable the appropriate option in Style 〉 General 〉 Accidentals .

Style 〉 General 〉 Accidentals , *Before key signature if changing to fewer sharps or flats*

To add an open (atonal) key signature

Music that is not clearly in any key at all is often written with no key signature. This is subtly different from a key signature of *C* major / *A* minor in that no key signature at all means it should remain that way even if the music is transposed. This can be an issue when writing atonal music for transposing instruments like the *B♭* clarinet. If you create the score with a key of *C* major / *A* minor, it will be displayed with two sharps (*D* major / *B* minor) when *Concert Pitch* is turned off, when you may prefer to have the music displayed with no key signature whether transposed or not.

To add an atonal key signature, use the special *Open* key signature icon on the palette.

To create a custom key signature

MuseScore allows you to design your own key signatures, which can be useful for certain styles of music. To begin, press [Shift] + [K] to display the key signature portion of the *Master Palette*, or go to [View] ⟩ [Master Palette] ⟩ [Key Signatures]. You can create your own key signatures using the controls on the right side of this window. Simply drag accidentals to the staff. You can include any combination of sharps, flats, or other accidentals, including the microtonal accidentals.

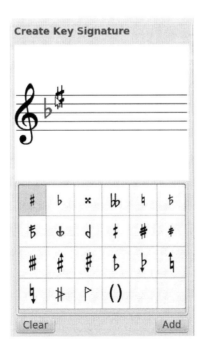

When you are done, you can press the $\boxed{\text{Add}}$ button to add this key signature to the master palette. If you will be using this same key signature often, you may wish to add it to your main *Key Signatures* palette as described in *Palettes* in the chapter on *Customization*.

Note that custom key signatures are for display only – they do not affect the playback pitch of notes upon playback. Also, they do not transpose.

Chapter 12

Time Signatures

MuseScore supports the standard forms of time signatures used in Western music, from simple meters like 4/4 to uncommon ones like 7/16 to additive time signatures like 2+2+2+3/8. You can change time signatures anywhere within a piece.

The most common time signatures are added through the *Time Signatures* palette.

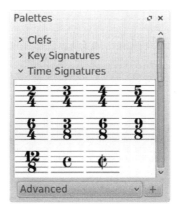

You can also bring up the time signature portion of the *Master Palette* using the keyboard shortcut Shift + T .

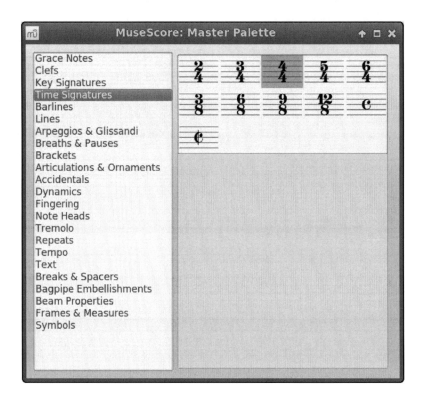

Note that this window normally shows controls that can be used in creating time signatures (see *Custom Time Signatures* below), but I have hidden them in the image above as they are not relevant here.

Initial Time Signature

As we have already seen, you can select the initial time signature for a piece in the *Create New Score* wizard (see *Creating a New Score*). This time signature is automatically applied to all staves in your score, except for tablature staff types that normally do not use time signatures.

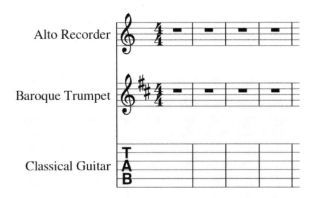

If you decide you wish to change the initial time signature, you can add a new one from the palette. Click the original time signature in the score, the first measure, or any note in the measure, and then double-click the desired time signature in the *Time Signatures* palette. You can also drag a time signature from the palette onto the first measure or onto the initial time signature.

Time Signature Changes

You can change time signature anywhere within a piece. Simply drag an icon from the *Time Signatures* palette to the measure you wish the change to appear before. When you do this, any music already present will automatically reflow across measures.

The change affects all measures up to the next time signature change or section break (see *Line, Page, and Section Breaks* in the chapter on *Page Layout* for more information on section breaks).

You can also select a single measure and then double-click a time signature in the palette to apply the change to that measure. If you select a range that is anything but a single measure, the time signature change is applied at the beginning of the range and the original time signature is restored at the end.

Custom Time Signatures

By default, the *Time Signatures* palette shows only a selection of the most commonly used possibilities. If you wish to use a more unusual meter, press ⎡Shift⎤+⎡T⎤ to display the time signature portion of the *Master Palette*, or go to ⎡View⟫ Master Palette ⟫ Time Signatures⎤. You can create your own time signatures using the controls on the right side of this window.

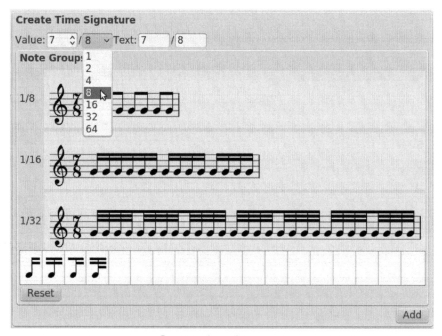

Custom time signature

For most time signatures, you can simply fill in the *Value* fields for the top and bottom numbers you desire. Then click the ⎡Add⎤ button at the bottom of the dialog to add it to the *Master Palette*.

If you expect to use one of these custom time signatures often, you can add it to your main *Time Signatures* palette for easier access in the future as described in *Palettes* in the chapter on *Customization*.

You can create additive time signatures – meters of the form 2+2+2+3/8 – as well. To do this, fill in the *Value* fields as appropriate for the total length of the measure (e.g., 9/8), but use the *Text* fields to display this however you like.

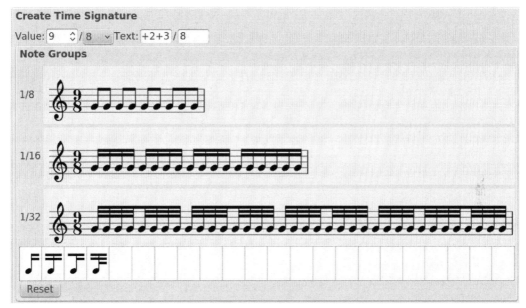

Additive time signature

The controls toward the bottom of this dialog allow you to customize the default beaming, so that a time signature of 2+2+2+3/8 is actually beamed that way. For more information, see *Setting the default beaming* below.

Changing Appearance and Behavior

A time signature influences many aspects of how MuseScore organizes and lays out music. A time signature normally applies to all staves in a score, controlling how many beats are in each measure as well as how notes within a measure should be beamed by default. For example, in 4/4, eighth notes (quavers) are normally beamed in groups of four, but in 6/8 they are beamed in groups of three.

MuseScore allows all of this to be customized. You can have different time signatures displayed in different staves (6/8 for some, 3/4 for others); you can force seven eighth notes into a 6/8 measure; and you can tell MuseScore to beam in three groups of two, or one group of four and one group of two, etc.

Global time signature settings

The default settings that affect time signatures throughout the score are as follows:

- Style ⟩⟩ General ⟩⟩ Measure

    Time signature left margin – distance to left of time signature

Clef/Key right margin – distance to right of clef, key signature, and time signature at beginning of measure

- [Style ⟩ General ⟩ Page]

Create courtesy time signatures – display courtesy time signature at the end of the previous system when a meter change occurs at the start of a system

Individual time signature properties

Most of the relevant properties for time signatures are found in the *Time Signature Properties* and *Measure Properties* dialog, accessed via the context (right-click) menu.

- *Inspector*

  Show courtesy – control display of courtesy time signature for this meter change

- **Context menu**

  Hide/Show Courtesy Time Signature – control display of courtesy time signature for this meter change

- *Edit* **mode** – the position of a time signature can be adjusted by double-clicking it and using the cursor keys

- *Time Signature Properties*

  Actual value – default duration of all measures with this time signature
  Appearance – alternate *Text* or symbols to display

- *Measure Properties*

  Actual – actual duration of this measure

In addition, the *Time Signature Properties* dialog contains controls to set the default beaming for measures with this time signature. For more information, see *Setting the default beaming* below.

Common Tasks

To control the display of courtesy time signatures

As with clef and key changes, it is traditional to show a courtesy time signature change at the end of the previous system if a time signature changes occurs at the beginning of a line, and MuseScore inserts this automatically.

If you wish to suppress the display of one particular courtesy time signature, click the "main" time signature at the start of the next system and turn off the *Show courtesy* option in the *Inspector*. You can also right-click the time signature and choose [Hide Courtesy Time Signature] from the context menu. The courtesy time signature will be removed.

> You might also want to suppress the courtesy time signature between movements of a work, or between songs in a larger collection. MuseScore provides other features specially designed to meets the needs of these cases, however. See *Section breaks* in the chapter on *Page Layout* and *Creating Albums* in the chapter on *File Operations* for more information on these features.

If you know you will not want courtesy time signatures to appear anywhere in your score, you can tell MuseScore not to generate them in the first place by turning off the *Create courtesy time signatures* option in [Style ⟩ General ⟩ Page].

To change actual duration of a measure

Sometimes a situation arises where we need to put a different number of beats in a measure than the time signature normally dictates. The pickup measure you learned to create as part of the *Create New Score* wizard is one example of this. If you forget to do this when creating your score, you can turn the first measure into a pickup by using the *Measure Properties* dialog to change the *Actual* time signature for the measure to be different from the *Nominal* time signature.

To do this, first right-click the measure and select [Measure Properties] from the context menu. In the dialog that appears, change the *Actual* field to reflect the number of beats you want to have in the measure. In the case of pickup measures, it is also traditional to exclude them from the measure numbering, so you would probably want to check the *Exclude from measure count* box in this same dialog.

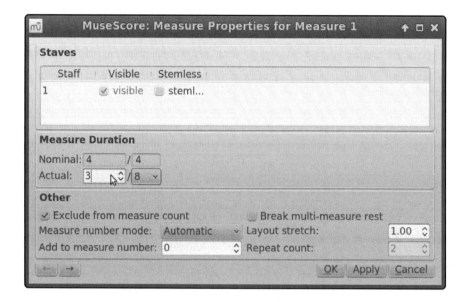

The result is the following:

Measures in which the nominal and actual durations differ will not normally display full measure rests even when empty. Instead, MuseScore will display ordinary rests that add up to the actual duration of the measure. However, if you wish to force MuseScore to use a full measure rest, you can convert ordinary rests into a full measure rest by selecting the measure and pressing [Ctrl]+[Shift]+[Delete] (Mac: [Cmd]+[Shift]+[Delete]).

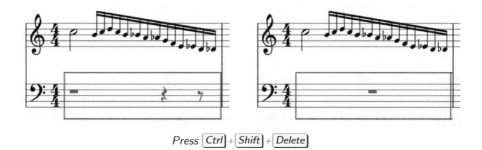

Press Ctrl + Shift + Delete

To create a local time signature

MuseScore supports scores with different time signatures in different staves. The barlines will still all align, and the duration of the measures in these staves will actually be the same as measured in real time, but MuseScore will display notes in the measures as appropriate for the time signature of that staff. To create a local time signature for a specific staff, press and hold Ctrl (Mac: Cmd) while dragging the time signature to that staff.

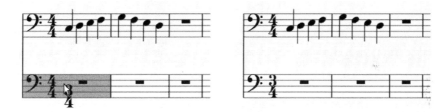

Press and hold Ctrl

In order for this feature to work, the measure to which you add the local time signature must be empty, and you must not have already created linked parts (see the chapter on *Parts*).

Once you have set up the time signatures the way you like, you can then enter notes and they will be interpreted as appropriate for the time signature applied to that staff.

Both sets of measures – top staff and bottom staff – are intended to take the same amount of real time, as should be clear from the layout. But there are four (shorter) beats per measure on the top staff, and three (longer) beats per measure on the bottom staff.

If you wish to create music in which the beat has the same duration in real time but there are different numbers of beats per measure in different staves – and hence the barlines do not align – you can create this effect by changing the *Appearance* property of the time signature in one staff, hiding the barlines in one staff, and adding new mid-measure barlines (see the chapter on *Measure Operations* for more information).

Setting the default beaming

Earlier, in the section *To control beaming* in the chapter *Editing*, we saw how to override the default beaming for specific notes. But if you would prefer different defaults, it is easier to change them at the source – the properties for the time signature.

To change the beaming properties for all staves in a score simultaneously, the easiest way is to create a new custom time signature (see *Custom Time Signatures*) and add that to your score. To change the beaming properties for one staff only, you can right-click the time signature for that staff and select ⌐Time Signature Properties⌐ from the context menu. Either way, the same basic *Note Groups* controls appear.

You can change the beam behavior for any note by dragging the appropriate icon from the toolbar at the bottom.

Drag 🎵 *icon*

You can also simply click any note to break or join the beam.

Click

When you are done, existing notes that are set to *Auto* beaming will immediately adopt the new defaults, and new notes you enter will also use these defaults.

Chapter 13

Text

MuseScore allows you to place a variety of different types of text into your score. It provides a styling facility so that the different types of text can each have their own default font and positioning settings, and it lets you customize these defaults. It also provides a way to override the default text style for individual elements.

In this chapter, we will look at some of the basic types of text elements you can add to your score. After showing examples of how to add different types of text to your score, we will look at the text editing and formatting capabilities that are common to almost all text types. Note that dynamics, lyrics, chord symbols, figured bass, and repeat text are unique enough that they will each get a chapter unto themselves.

Staff Text

The most common type of text you will probably create in MuseScore is staff text. This is text that is attached to a specific note or rest on a particular staff in a score. Staff text is used for instructions meant for the musician(s) reading that staff, such as to tell a violin player to play pizzicato. By default, staff text displays above the staff, although templates and styles for scores that use chord symbols may place it below instead.

Creating staff text

To create staff text, click the note or rest to which you would like to attach the text, then press `Ctrl`+`T` (Mac: `Cmd`+`T`) or use the equivalent menu item `Add` ⟩ `Text` ⟩ `Staff Text`. A blue cursor will appear, allowing you to start typing your text.

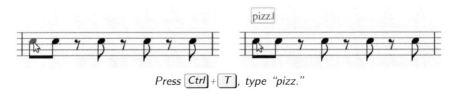

Press `Ctrl`+`T`, type "pizz."

When you are done typing your text, press $\boxed{\text{Esc}}$ or click somewhere outside the editing box.

You can also use the *Text* palette to add staff text to your score. This works like other palette elements – either drag it to your score, or else click a note or rest then double-click the palette element.

The potential advantage of this palette approach becomes clear when combined with the ability to customize the palettes. Once you have created a text marking and set all of its properties the way you like them, you can add that marking to the palette to make it easier to reuse that same marking in the future. See *Palettes* in the chapter on *Customization* for more information.

Playback: changing instrument sound

Because staff text is typically used to give instructions to players, it is often desirable for these same instructions to be followed during computer playback. While MuseScore cannot anticipate everything you might possibly wish to use staff text for, it does provide a way to select from a number of the most common options.

To set the playback behavior for a particular staff text element you have created, right-click it and choose $\boxed{\text{Staff Text Properties}}$ from the resulting context menu to display the *Staff Text Properties* dialog.

The *Change Channel* tab of this dialog allows you to change the sound of the instrument, for instruments that are already defined to have more than one sound (e.g., open and muted trumpet, arco and pizzicato strings). MuseScore allows you to change sounds for the four voices of a staff independently. To change the sound, you must first click the icon for the specific voice(s) you wish to change, then select the new sound from the drop-down menu.

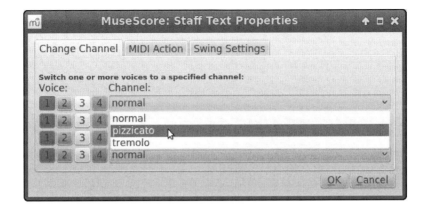

The options available will depend on the specific instrument configured for the staff. If there are no options listed other than *Normal*, it means the instrument configured for that staff does not have any other sounds defined. However, you will still be able to change sounds for this staff by adding an instrument change text instead of a regular staff text. For more information, see *Changing instrument for a staff mid-score* in the chapter on *Staves and Instruments*.

For more information on the other settings available in the *Staff Text Properties* dialog, see *Playback: swing* below.

System Text

System text is very much like staff text, except that it automatically applies to all staves in a system in a score containing multiple instruments. System text will appear above the top staff only in the score itself, but the text will also appear at that same point in all generated parts (see *Parts*). This is useful for instructions that apply to all players, such as a stylistic notation like "Joyously" or "Swing". Note however that there is a separate category of text for tempo markings; see *Tempo Markings* below.

Creating system text

System text is created much like staff text: select a note or rest to apply it to and then press the keyboard shortcut or use the corresponding menu item. The shortcut for system text is Ctrl+Shift+T (Mac: Cmd+Shift+T), and the menu item is Add ⟩ Text ⟩ System Text. You can also add the appropriate element from the *Text* palette.

Regardless of which staff you add the system text to, the text will appear above the top staff in the score.

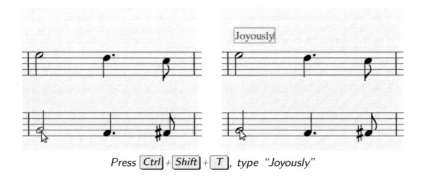

Press ⌈Ctrl⌉ + ⌈Shift⌉ + ⌈T⌉, type "Joyously"

Playback: swing

System text can have playback properties applied just as staff text can. The steps are the same: right-click the marking, choose *Staff Text Properties*, and make settings for the desired behavior. It generally does not make sense to change the playback sound for all staves at once, but the *Swing Settings* do make sense to apply to all staves, so we will look at those settings here.

By default, MuseScore plays eighth notes (quavers) straight – all the same length. This is of course the way eighth notes were traditionally intended to be played. but in jazz and some other styles, it is customary to "swing" the eighths by imparting something of a triplet feel to them, where the first eighth note of each pair is longer than the second. In some styles, we may wish to swing sixteenths instead of eighths. MuseScore can play swing eighth or sixteenth notes and even gives you fine control over the ratio of the lengths of the first to the second note in each pair.

To set up swing playback in MuseScore, add a system text, right-click it, and go to
⌈System Text Properties⟩⟩ Swing Settings⌉.

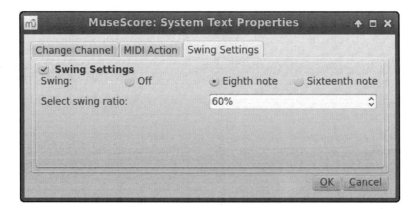

The settings in the dialog allow you to customize the swing playback associated with this text.

Swing Settings – enable / disable the swing controls (if disabled, there is no change to the swing settings)

Swing – Off, Eighth note, Sixteenth note
Select swing ratio – specify percentage of time taken by the first note of each pair (50% = straight, 66% = triplet feel)

Note there is an element labeled *Swing* on the *Text* palette already, so you can add this marking easily with no need to change the settings if the default type and degree of swing works for you. However, if you wish to have a passage where the eighth notes are straight, you will need to add a text and customize the swing settings using *Staff Text Properties*. To do this, enable the *Swing Settings* but set the *Swing* to *Off*. Disabling *Swing Settings* does not set eighth notes to straight; it simply means no change to swing settings. That allows system texts like "Joyously" to be used without changing the swing settings.

> Although I have presented the swing settings as applied to system text, you can actually apply them to staff text as well. This allows you to have some staves swing and others straight, or even have different swing ratios for different staves. For example, you might want the drums to play with a more pronounced swing eighth feel than the horns in a big band arrangement.

Tempo Markings

Tempo markings are used to tell both musicians and the playback facility in MuseScore how fast you want your piece played. Tempo markings are a special type of system text – they appear above the top staff in a score and also on all generated parts. But tempo markings also have the ability to affect the tempo in playback, and they have a different text style (see *Text style* below), displaying in larger bold face type by default.

Creating a tempo marking

To create a tempo marking, click the note or rest where you want the tempo to take effect (the first note of the piece for the initial tempo marking) and then go to Add 〉 Text 〉 Tempo Marking or use the keyboard shortcut Alt + T . This enters a default marking that you can then edit.

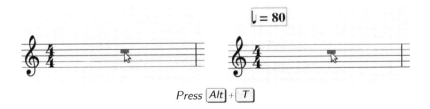

Press Alt + T

The default text includes a symbol representing the beat value – e.g., a quarter note (crotchet) in 4/4 time, or a dotted quarter note in 6/8 – and an indication of the number of beats per minute. If you wish to change the note used for the beat value, you can press ⌈F2⌉ to bring up the *Special Characters* palette (see *Entering special characters* below). So if you have music in 6/8 time but would rather give the tempo in eighth notes than in dotted quarters, simply replace the default symbols (the quarter note and dot are separate characters) with an eighth note. To change the BPM value, simply replace the it in the text.

You can also add tempo markings from the *Tempo* palette.

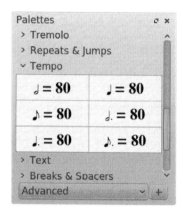

You do not need to use these symbols or numeric values at all, however. You can edit the text and replace it with anything you like.

Playback

MuseScore uses the beat and beats-per-minute (BPM) values in a tempo marking to determine the playback tempo automatically. If you have edited the text to remove this information, or if you wish to MuseScore to play the score at a different tempo from that specified by the text, you can set the actual tempo for the marking using the *Inspector*.

1. Click the tempo marking
2. Press ⌈F8⌉ if necessary to bring up the *Inspector*
3. Uncheck the *Follow Text* option
4. Enter the desired value in the *Tempo* field

Note that regardless of the time signature, the *Tempo* value in the *Inspector* needs to be expressed in terms of quarter notes (crotchets). For example, in order to set a tempo of 120 dotted quarters per minute in 6/8 time, you need to set the *Tempo* to 180 in the *Inspector*, because 120 dotted quarters works out to 180 quarter notes. Luckily, MuseScore can help you calculate this value as follows:

1. Create the tempo marking with the desired beat duration and BPM value
2. Press Esc to complete editing
3. Double-click the tempo marking you just created
4. Press F8 if necessary to bring up the Inspector
5. Turn off the *Follow Text* option
6. Replace the text in the tempo marking

By entering the tempo marking with the correct beat duration and BPM value initially, MuseScore calculates the corresponding *Tempo* value in quarter notes for you. When you turn off the *Follow Text* option, this value is locked in – it will no longer change automatically as you edit the text. You can adjust the value directly via the *Inspector* if you wish.

Rehearsal Marks

A rehearsal mark is a letter or number displayed above the staff – usually in a box – that serves as a sort of "bookmark" allowing musicians to quickly find a particular place in the music.

Like tempo markings, rehearsal marks are also a special type of system text. Like all system text, they are normally displayed above the top staff only in a score, but they display on all the individual parts. Rehearsal marks also have their own text style (see *Text style* below), so they can display with a box while other system text elements do not.

Creating a rehearsal mark

To create a rehearsal mark, click the note or rest to which you wish to attach the mark and press Ctrl + M (Mac: Cmd + M) or use Add ⟩ Text ⟩ Rehearsal Mark. This displays a cursor, and you can then type your text.

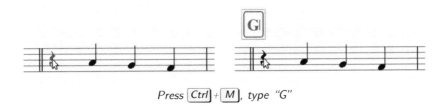

Press Ctrl + M , type "G"

You can also add rehearsal marks from the *Text* palette. Although there is only a single rehearsal marking ("B1") in the palette, adding a rehearsal mark from the palette automatically sets the text to whatever is next in sequence after the previous rehearsal mark.

MuseScore automatically detects the sequence to use. If the previous rehearsal mark is a single capital letter, MuseScore inserts the next capital letter in sequence, and the same for lower case. If the previous rehearsal mark ends in a number, MuseScore inserts one with the next number in sequence. And if the previous rehearsal mark is a number matching the measure number of the measure it is attached to, MuseScore inserts one with the measure number of the measure you are adding it to.

Resequencing rehearsal marks

In the course of editing a score, it is not uncommon that rehearsal marks may become out of sequence. You might decide to insert a new rehearsal mark between "G" and "H", or delete the section at letter "J", or just decide to use more or fewer rehearsal marks. MuseScore provides a simple command to automatically resequence rehearsal marks according to the same algorithm described above.

To use this facility, select the range of measures for which you wish to resequence rehearsal marks (if you select nothing, MuseScore will do the entire score), and go to Edit 〉 Tools 〉 Resequence Rehearsal Marks. All rehearsal marks in the selected range will be resequenced based on the first mark in the range.

Title, Subtitle, Composer, Lyricist

As described in the chapter *Creating a New Score*, you are prompted to enter a title, subtitle, and names of the composer and lyricist when you first create your score. However, if you do not enter this information at that time, or if you have deleted it, you can easily add it using the items on the Add 〉 Text sub-menu: Title, Subtitle, Composer, and Lyricist. The text is automatically placed in a frame at the top of the first page of your score.

You can also right-click within the existing frame and add the text from the Add sub-menu within the context menu that appears.

Header and Footer

MuseScore provides a header and footer facility to allow for page numbers, copyright notices, and other text to be displayed on every page. To access the header and footer controls, go to Style 〉 General 〉 Header, Footer, Numbers.

Header Text		
☐ Show first ☑ Odd/Even		
Page Left	Middle	Right
Odd		
Even		

☑ Footer Text		
☑ Show first ☐ Odd/Even		
Page Left	Middle	Right
Odd Even	Cp	
$p	$:copyright:	
Even		

The options in this dialog allow you to control the display and content of headers and footers separately. First be sure to enable or disable the *Header Text* and *Footer Text* options as appropriate, then set the content of the header and footer as follows:

Show first – displays header or footer on first page
Odd/Even – use different settings for odd and even pages
Left – text to display against left margin
Middle text to display centered
Right – text to display against right margin

The individual text fields can contain ordinary text or special symbols to automatically incorporate meta data such as the current page number.

$p – page number, except on first page
$N – page number, if there is more than one page
$P – page number, on all pages
$n – number of pages
$f – file name
$F – file path+name
$d – current date
$D – creation date
$m – last modification time
$M – last modification date
$C – copyright, on first page only
$c – copyright, on all pages
$$ – the $ sign itself
$:(tag): – meta data tag

The meta data tag allows you to insert information from the fields in the File ⟩ Info dialog. You can use these fields however you like, although the names of the fields should be suggestive of their intended purpose.

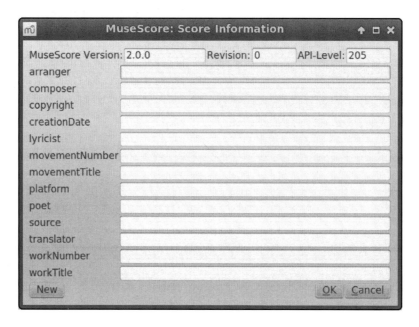

You can also use the New button to define your own custom meta data tags, and you may use these in the header and footer as well.

> You do not need to memorize these special symbols and meta data tags. Hovering your mouse pointer over one of the text fields in the Style ⟩ General ⟩ Header, Footer, Numbers dialog will display a list for you as a reminder.

Frame Text

When you want to add a block of text in between systems of a score, frame text can be used.

Creating frame text

To create a new frame for text, select the first measure of the system above which you want the text to appear, then go to Add ⟩ Frames ⟩ Insert Text Frame. This inserts a text frame and allows you to start typing.

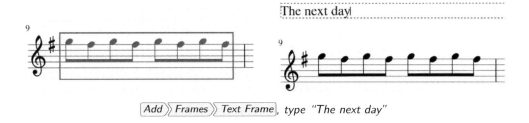

Add ⟫ Frames ⟫ Text Frame , *type "The next day"*

Another way to add a text frame is using the *Frames & Measures* palette.

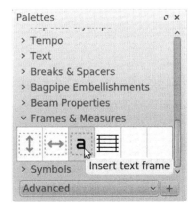

Frame text can also be added to any horizontal or vertical frame. Just right-click the frame and select Add ⟫ Text . See the chapter on *Page Layout* for more on frames.

Editing Text

Most text items can be edited after they are initially created by double-clicking them. This puts MuseScore into *Text edit* mode, which is the same mode that is used to type the text in the first place.

Double-click

Text edit mode works like many other text editors in terms of keyboard shortcuts and so forth, but there are a few special techniques you should be aware of as well.

Navigation and selection

Most keyboard shortcuts works as you might expect from other applications.

- ⟦→⟧ – move forward one character
- ⟦←⟧ – move backward one character
- ⟦Ctrl⟧+⟦→⟧ – move forward one word
- ⟦Ctrl⟧+⟦←⟧ – move backward one word
- ⟦↑⟧ – move up one line
- ⟦↓⟧ – move down one line
- ⟦Home⟧ – move to beginning of text
- ⟦End⟧ – move to end of text

Holding ⟦Shift⟧ while navigating using any of the above keys selects while moving the cursor. Other editing keys also work in the ways you would expect.

- ⟦Enter⟧ – starts a new line
- ⟦Backspace⟧ (Mac: ⟦Delete⟧)– remove character to left of cursor
- ⟦Delete⟧ (Mac: ⟦Fn⟧+⟦Delete⟧) – remove character to right of cursor
- ⟦Ctrl⟧+⟦A⟧ – select all
- ⟦Ctrl⟧+⟦C⟧ – copy
- ⟦Ctrl⟧+⟦X⟧ – cut
- ⟦Ctrl⟧+⟦V⟧ – paste

You can also position the cursor and select text using the mouse.

Entering special characters

It is not uncommon to want to include musical or other symbols within text, so MuseScore provides a way to access the symbols it provides. While typing text, either press ⟦F2⟧ or else press the ⟦@⟧ (*Insert Special Characters*) button in the text toolbar at the bottom of the screen (see *Text toolbar*, below). A dialog will appear showing a number of common symbols used in musical scores.

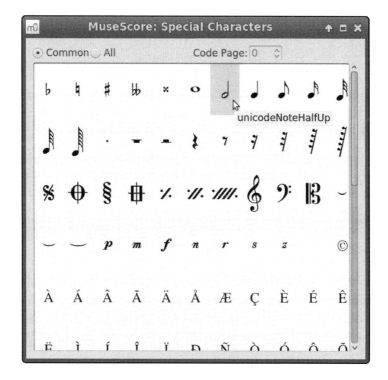

Double-click on a symbol to insert it into the score at the cursor position. The dialog remains up so you can insert multiple symbols. The buttons at the top of the dialog let you choose between a set of common symbols provided by MuseScore or a full listing of all symbols provided by the current font. There are potentially very many of these, so they are organized by *Code page*.

There are a few musical symbols for which keyboard shortcuts exist.

Accidentals		
♭	Ctrl + Shift + B
♯	Ctrl + Shift + #
♮	Ctrl + Shift + H

Dynamics		
f	Ctrl + Shift + F
m	Ctrl + Shift + M
n	Ctrl + Shift + N
p	Ctrl + Shift + P
r	Ctrl + Shift + R
s	Ctrl + Shift + S
z	Ctrl + Shift + Z

Text Formatting

In addition to the standard sorts of settings and properties that are provided for other markings, MuseScore provides a powerful text formatting facility that allows you to control the default position and font characteristics of each type of text marking separately and to override the formatting of any given text element, including the ability to change formatting within a single text element.

The key to controlling the formatting of text in MuseScore is the *Text style* facility. When you create a text element of a given type (e.g., staff text, tempo marking, rehearsal mark), it is assigned the corresponding text style. The formatting of text with any given text style is controlled by the settings for that style in [Style ⟩⟩ Text]. For instance, if you create staff text, it is given a style of *Staff*, and the formatting of all text with this style is controlled by [Style ⟩⟩ Text ⟩ ⟩ Staff]. Any changes made in this dialog will automatically affect all text with *Staff* style. This includes existing staff text as well as staff text yet to be created.

You can change the text style assigned to a text element if you like. For instance, you can create staff text but assign it the *Rehearsal Mark* style instead of the *Staff* style. It will still behave like staff text – it will display only on the staff it is attached to, and it will give you access to *Staff Text Properties* such as the ability to change instrument sounds – but it will appear using the same formatting as rehearsal marks.

You can also define your own text styles and assign them to text elements. For example, you can define a *Below Staff* text style for text you wish to display below the staff rather than above, or an *Italics Tempo* text style for tempo markings you wish to display in italics rather than bold. This makes it easy to maintain consistent formatting for related elements throughout your score.

For any given element, you can also override the font and position specified by its text style using *Text properties*, and you can use the *Text toolbar* to change formatting within a single element.

Text style

The text style for any given element type controls the default position and size of elements of that type. Changes to the text style affect existing elements of that type (unless you have already overridden their style settings) as well as elements yet to be created.

Customizing settings for a text style

To customize the settings for a text style, start by going to [Style ⟩⟩ Text] and then selecting the desired style from the list at left.

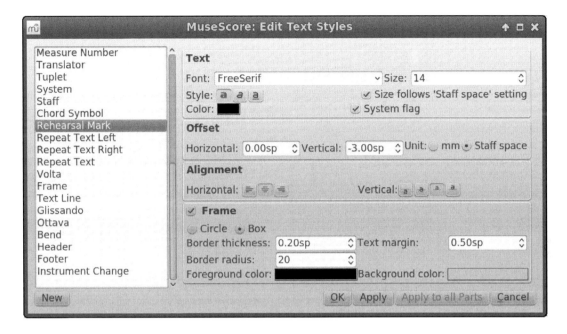

The names of the styles should be mostly self-explanatory. For example, *Title* is the default style applied to titles, *Staff* is the default style applied to staff text, etc.

Each text style defines a group of settings controlling the font, position, and other attributes. The individual settings for each style are:

Text

Font – select the font family to be used

Size – set the font size in points

Style – enable bold, italic, and/or underline

Size follows 'Staff space' setting – controls whether font size scales automatically with staff size

Color – font color

System flag – controls whether text should be attached to top staff of system and all parts, or attached to a specific staff and part only

Offset

Horizontal – horizontal position relative to reference point

Vertical – vertical position relative to reference point

Unit – units for offset (*mm* or *Staff space*)

Alignment

Horizontal – align left edge, center, or right edge to reference point

Vertical – align top, center, baseline, or bottom of text to reference point

Frame – select whether text should be enclosed in a frame and set attributes for the frame if so

Circle – circular frame

Box – rectangular frame

Border thickness – width of border

Text margin – margin between text and border

Border radius – percentage to round corners for *Box* frames

Foreground color – color of border
Background color – color of background

Creating a new text style

To create your own custom text style, go to Style ⟩⟩ Text , and in the left column, select the style upon which you wish to base your new style. Then press the New button.

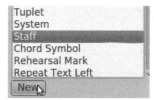 

Upon hitting OK , a new text style will be created with the specified name and with settings inherited from the original style you based your style on. You can then customize the settings for this newly added style just as you would any other style. For example, to create a "Staff Below" style, you could set the vertical offset to 6.0*sp*.

Applying a text style to selected elements

When you create a text element, it is automatically assigned the corresponding text style and displayed accordingly. However, you can assign a different style to any given text element or group of selected text elements. To do this, simply choose the desired text style using the *Inspector*.

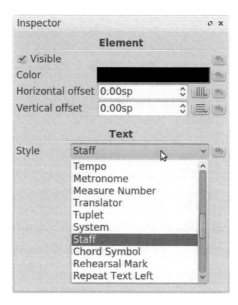

Text properties

Creating new text styles is a simple process and is very useful when you have multiple elements that you want to have the same formatting. Sometimes, however, you just want to override the formatting for one single element, such as to make one particular staff text bold.

To change the text formatting for a single element, right-click it and select Text Properties from the context menu. A dialog is displayed that contains the same settings as the text style dialog, but this dialog affects only the selected text element.

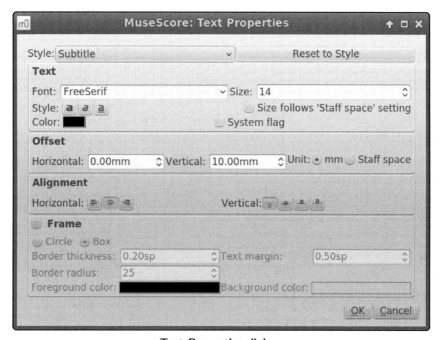

Text Properties dialog

You can set the various attributes in this dialog just as you would when customizing a text style. You can also apply a different style, or if you have altered settings in this dialog, you can reset them to the style defaults. Settings made in this dialog apply to the selected text element only.

Text toolbar

When you edit a text element – whether while initially typing it or after double-clicking it to enter *Text edit* mode – a toolbar appears at the bottom of the MuseScore that provides control over the formatting on a per-character basis.

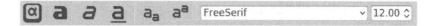

The controls on this toolbar allow you to change the formatting of selected characters within the text.

- ⟨α⟩ – display *Insert Special Characters* dialog
- **a** – toggle bold for selected characters
- *a* – toggle italics for selected characters
- <u>a</u> – toggle underlining for selected characters
- a_a – toggle subscript for selected characters
- aª – toggle superscript for selected characters
- font family
- font size

Chapter 14

Lyrics

Lyrics are form of text, but MuseScore provides special commands for entering them to make it easier to attach words note by note as well as to handle the hyphens, extenders, and other symbols and conventions used in lyrics.

Entering Lyrics

To enter lyrics into your score, click the first note you wish to add a lyric to, then press `Ctrl`+`L` (Mac: `Cmd`+`L`) or use `Add` ⟩ `Text` ⟩ `Lyrics`. This places you into *Lyrics edit* mode, which is similar to *Text edit* mode but with special handling for lyrics.

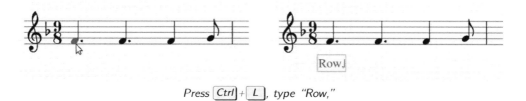

Press `Ctrl`+`L`, type "Row,"

One of the special feature of *Lyrics edit* mode is that pressing `Space` advances the cursor to the next note, allowing you to type the next syllable.

Press `Space`, type "row,"

Pressing `Esc` ends lyrics edit mode, as does clicking somewhere else on the score.

177

Hyphenation

To enter a hyphenated word, simply press the ⊟ (hyphen) key instead of ⎀Space⎀ to move to the next syllable. You can then type the next syllable normally.

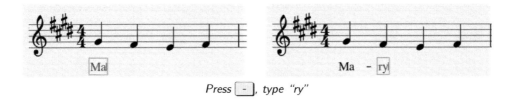

Press ⊟, *type "ry"*

If the hyphenated word is a *melisma* – a syllable that is held out over more than note – then keep entering hyphens to move note by note until you reach the note for the next syllable.

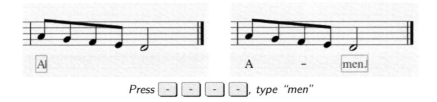

Press ⊟ ⊟ ⊟ ⊟, *type "men"*

If the syllables are close enough together, MuseScore inserts just a single hyphen; if the syllables are far apart, MuseScore automatically inserts a series of evenly-spaced hyphens.

If you should need to enter a hyphen into a single lyric syllable rather than as a separator, you can enter it as ⎀Ctrl⎀+⊟ (Mac: ⎀Cmd⎀+⊟).

Extenders

When a melisma occurs at the end of a word, an extender line is used to show the duration of the melisma. These are entered using the ⊟ (underscore) key. As with hyphens, press ⊟ as many times as you need to reach the next word.

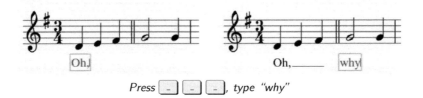

Press ⊟ ⊟ ⊟, *type "why"*

If you should need to enter an underscore into a single lyric syllable rather than as an extender, you can enter it as Ctrl + _ (Mac: Cmd + _).

Verses

To enter multiple verses or otherwise create multiple lines of lyrics, press Enter while in *Lyrics edit* mode to move down to the next line. You can then start entering lyrics for the next verse.

Press Enter, *type "How"*

A new line of lyrics is also created if you press Ctrl + L (or use Add ⟩ Text ⟩ Lyrics) to enter *Lyrics edit* mode while on a note that already has a lyric.

Once multiple lines of lyrics have been entered, you can use the ↑ and ↓ cursor keys to navigate between them.

If you wish to number your verses, simply type the number (and optionally a period or other punctuation) as part of the syllable. If you wish to enter a space between the number and the syllable, use Ctrl + Space .

Type "1.", press Ctrl + Space , *type "She"*

Copy and paste

Sometimes it can be simpler to enter lyrics into a separate text editor and then add them to your score using copy and paste. When pasting text in *Lyrics edit* mode, MuseScore pastes one syllable at a time and automatically moves on to the next syllable. To take advantage of this useful facility, type your lyrics with spaces and hyphens in any text editor, then copy them to your clipboard.

In the example below, I started by typing and then selecting the following text into a text editor:

Just say the word,_ _ soft-ly

As I press Ctrl + V in *Lyrics edit* mode, the lyrics are pasted one syllable at a time.

Press Ctrl + V repeatedly

If you copy and paste a range that includes lyrics, the lyrics are copied as part of the range unless you exclude them using the *Selection Filter*. You can also copy a group of lyrics to another set of notes. For more information, see *Copy, Cut, and Paste* in the chapter on *Editing*.

Editing Lyrics

Just as with other text elements, double-clicking an existing lyric syllable puts you back into *Lyrics edit* mode, thus allowing you to make changes.

While editing lyrics in *Lyrics edit* mode, ← and → move the cursor within the current syllable, or to the previous or next note once you reach the end of the current syllable. Ctrl + ← and Ctrl + ← move a note at a time. ↑ and ↓ move up and down through verses.

You can also move through lyrics using Space, - , and _ . Pressing Space on a syllable that previously had a hyphen or extender will delete it.

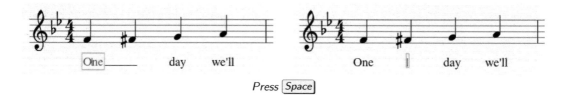

Press Space

Changing Appearance and Behavior

Lyrics are a form of text, and therefore, the standard text formatting facility applies. See the chapter *Text* for more information. Lyrics formatting uses two different text styles: *Lyrics Odd Lines* and *Lyrics Even Lines*. This allows you to have the font alternate between regular and italics, for example.

The standard MuseScore controls can be used to adjust the position of lyrics: you can drag them, click them and move them with the arrow keys, use the Inspector, etc. But due to the special nature of lyrics, there are also some controls and techniques specific to lyrics that you should know.

Global lyrics settings

Aside from the text styles, other relevant settings for lyrics are found in [Style]⟩[General]⟩[Page].

Lyrics top margin – additional margin to add to default vertical position of lyrics as set in text style

Lyrics bottom margin – minimum distance between lyrics and top of staff below (extra space is added to enforce this)

Lyrics line height – distance between lyric lines (as a percentage of default line spacing)

Alignment

While lyrics honor most of the standard text style settings, including alignment, there is some special handling to allow lyrics to obey traditional music engraving practices without your needing to set the alignment for syllables manually. For instance, any syllable that represents a melisma – whether hyphenated or not – is automatically left-aligned. Leading and trailing punctuation characters are ignored when centering or left-aligning syllables. Lyrics that begin with a number are assumed to represent the beginnings of verses, so the numbers are aligned.

Vertical alignment is also treated specially by MuseScore in order to work as expected in the presence of multiple verses, the line height style setting, odd and even text styles, hyphens, and extenders.

Common Tasks

To move lyrics to avoid notes below the staff

The default vertical position for lyrics as controlled by the text style and the *Lyrics upper margin* in [Style]⟩[General]⟩[Page] is sufficient to ensure that lyrics can clear notes one ledger line below the staff. However, if your music goes lower than that, lyrics may collide with notes. Traditional music engraving practice is to move the entire line of lyrics down.

Changing the text style or margin setting would affect all lyrics on the score, which might be good if you have these collisions throughout the score. However, it may happen that there is only system that needs adjustment, and you may wonder how to accomplish this most easily. Dragging syllables individually is possible, but time-consuming, and it would be hard to ensure they all line up properly. Instead, it usually makes sense to select them all and move them together. You can try to select the syllables as a group using Shift+drag, but this will probably be difficult due to the fact that they are overlapping the notes. You can also Ctrl+click (Mac: Cmd+click) them one by one, but this too could be time-consuming.

A reliable way to select and move all syllables on a given system is the following:

1. Right-click a single syllable
2. Select ≫ More
3. Check the *Same system* option
4. Press OK
5. Use the *Inspector* to change the *Vertical offset* of the selected syllables

No matter how you select the syllables, the real key to making the adjustment is to use the *Insepctor* to move them all together.

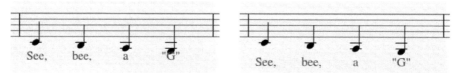

Increase Vertical offset using the Inspector

To create lyrics above the staff

In choral writing, it is common to have multiple parts – for example, soprano and alto – in different voices on the same staff. If the rhythms and lyrics are similar, then they can share the same lyrics. However, if the rhythms or lyrics differ, then lyrics for the top part would normally be written above the staff. While MuseScore provides no direct automatic way of doing this, it does provides controls that make the job straightforward.

1. Enter the lyrics for the top voice
2. Select the range over which you wish to move the lyrics (optional)
3. Right-click one syllable
4. Select ≫ More
5. Check the *Same voice* option
6. If you selected a range first, check the *In selection* option
7. Press OK
8. Use the *Inspector* to change the *Vertical offset* of the selected syllables
9. Enter the lyrics for the bottom voice normally

You can of course select the syllables using any other method you like if that happens to be easier. For instance, if you are careful to enter all voice 1 lyrics first and can move them all at once before entering any voice 2 notes, you can omit step 2 and replace steps 4-7 with Select ⟩

All similar elements . But the steps above should always work well, even if you prefer to work a few measures at a time and/or to alternate between voices.

In any case, once the lyrics are selected, the *Inspector* is always an easy way to move them all up together.

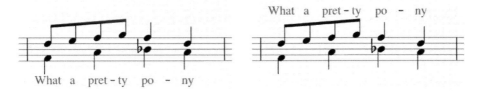

Decrease Vertical offset using the Inspector

Chapter 15

Chord Symbols

MuseScore allows you to enter symbols representing chords into your score with a great deal of flexibility, understanding virtually all common variations on syntax, offering a choice of different fonts (including a "handwritten" style), and providing an optional jazz style that does automatic superscripting and other formatting.

Standard versus Jazz chord symbol styles

See *Changing Appearance and Behavior* for more information on the different formatting options available.

Entering Chord Symbols

To enter chord symbols, click the note or rest above which you wish the chord symbol to appear, then press Ctrl + K (Mac: Cmd + K) or use Add ⟩ Text ⟩ Chord Symbol . This will place you in *Chord symbol edit* mode, displaying a text cursor above the staff. You can then type a chord symbol as text.

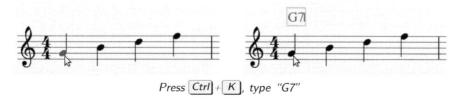

Press Ctrl + K , type "G7"

When you have completed entry of a chord symbol, you can press any of the following keys:

- Space – move cursor to next note, rest, or beat
- Shift+Space – move cursor to previous note, rest, or beat
- ; – move cursor to next beat
- : – move cursor to previous beat
- Tab – move cursor to next measure
- Shift+Tab – move cursor to previous measure
- Ctrl plus number (1 - 9) – move cursor by duration corresponding to number (e.g., half note for 6)
- Esc – exit *Chord symbol edit* mode

These shortcuts allow you to enter chord symbols much as you do lyrics – moving on to the next chord symbol without ever leaving *Chord symbol edit* mode.

Press Tab, *type "A7"*

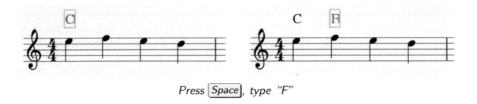

Press Space, *type "F"*

Note that Space, Shift+Space, ;, :, and the Ctrl plus number (1 - 9) shortcuts all allow you to enter chords on beats where there are no notes. This allows you to have multiple chords per measure even in measures containing only a whole note or measure rest.

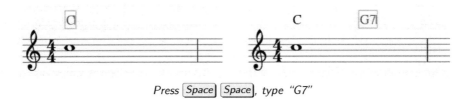

Press Space Space, *type "G7"*

The [;], [:], and [Ctrl] plus number ([1] - [9]) shortcuts are especially useful in that they allow you to quickly enter chords at regular intervals regardless of how many notes might be present.

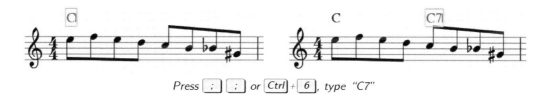

Press [;] [;] or [Ctrl]+[6], type "C7"

Chord Symbol Syntax

In order for a chord symbol to correctly display, transpose, and export to other formats like MusicXML, MuseScore needs to be able to understand what you have typed. MuseScore supports a wide variety of different chord symbol syntaxes, so for the most part, you can type chords as you expect and they will be understood correctly. There is ordinarily no need to adhere any particular set of rules for chord symbol syntax. However, you will probably want to know how to create some of the special symbols used in chord symbols, and to be familiar with the basic rules of chord symbol construction.

Flats and sharps

When typing, use the letter "b" to indicate a flat sign and it will automatically be rendered as such when you finish entering the chord symbol. Similarly, use the "#" character to indicate a sharp sign.

Press [Esc]

Double flats and double sharps and can be entered as "bb" and either "x" or "##".

Chord quality

MuseScore understands the commonly used abbreviations for the basic chord qualities of major, minor, augmented, diminished, and half-diminished. Most of these abbreviations can be typed directly. A few special symbols can be created using easy-to-remember shortcuts: "o" for the diminished symbol, "0" for the half-diminished symbol, "ˆ" or "t" for the triangle that is sometimes used to indicate a major chord. Here is the full list of accepted abbreviations for the standard chord qualities:

major – M, Ma, Maj, ma, maj, Δ (type: "ˆ" or "t")
minor – m, mi, min, -
augmented – aug, +
diminished – dim, o (type: letter "o")
half-diminished – m7b5, mi7b5, min7b5, -7b5, ø (type: number "0")

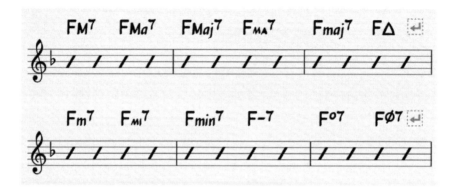

Special keywords

In addition to the standard abbreviations for major, minor, augmented, diminished, and half-diminished, MuseScore also understands most of the special keywords commonly used in chord symbols, plus a few that are not particularly common but are found in some other programs and/or are supported by MusicXML:

sus – suspended (replace third)
alt – altered (include only altered fifths and ninths)
add – add the specified degree
no – omit the specified degree
omit – omit the specified degree
lyd – major seventh chord with ♯11
phryg – minor seventh chord with ♭9
blues – dominant seventh chord with ♯9
Tristan – chord of the form 1 ♯4 ♯6 ♯9

Of these, "add," "no," and "omit" must be followed by a number specifying a chord tone to add or leave out. "sus" may be followed by a number specifying a chord tone to replace the third, but if there is no number immediately after the "sus," 4 is assumed.

MuseScore does not limit you to just these keywords. As long as it can read the initial characters as a root name, it will render the rest as well as it can, and the chord will still transpose normally. However, only chords that are understandable can be exported reasonably to MusicXML.

Extensions and alterations

MuseScore understands the common extensions and alterations (e.g., 13, ♭9, ♯11) to chord symbols. Parentheses and commas may be used freely but are optional.

Alternate bass notes

A chord may be specified with a note other than the root in the bass by following the name of the chord with a slash and the name of the bass note.

Note names

By default, the chord symbol facility in MuseScore uses the note naming convention used in most English-speaking countries as well as much of the rest of the world: *A, B, C, D, E, F,* and *G*, always spelled using capital letters, and flat and sharp denoted with ♭ and ♯. However, MuseScore also supports alternate note spelling options such as those used in many French-speaking, Spanish-speaking, and other countries (*Do, Re* or *Ré, Mi, ...*) as well as Germany (*H; es* and *is*). MuseScore also supports the convention, used by some musicians, in which lower case letters are used for minor and diminished chords and/or alternate bass notes, and it also supports all caps spelling.

If you wish to use any of these note naming conventions in your chord symbols, go to [Style] [General] [Chord Symbols, Fretboard Diagrams] and select the appropriate option, which are described below under *Changing Appearance and Behavior*.

Parenthesized chords

You can indicate optional chords by enclosing them in parentheses. Simply type the parentheses when entering the chord symbol. Additional space is automatically added when you complete entry. If several optional chords occur in a row, you can enclose the whole sequence in parentheses.

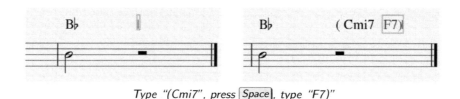

Type "(Cmi7", press Space, type "F7)"

Capo chords

For guitar music in which you wish to provide a capo version of your chords, MuseScore can automatically generate these and display them in parentheses after the main chords. To enable this feature, go to Style ⟩ General ⟩ Chord Symbols, Fretboard Diagrams and enter a value for *Capo fret position*. You can then type the chords as you intend them to sound, and MuseScore will automatically calculate the appropriate chord to play in order to get that sound. It will also add the capo version to any chord symbols you have already entered.

For example, with *Capo fret position* set to "1", MuseScore calculates that you need to play an *A* chord in order for a *B♭* chord to result, and the *A* chord will automatically be displayed in parentheses next to the *B♭* chord.

Enter "1" for Capo fret position

Changing Appearance and Behavior

Chord symbols are a special form of text, and therefore most of the ordinary text formatting options are available. The relevant text style is *Chord Symbol*. See the chapter *Text* for more information.

There are also a number of additional options unique to the special handling of chord symbols.

Global chord symbol settings

Aside from the text style, other relevant settings for chord symbols can be found in [Style⟩ ⟩General⟩⟩ Chord Symbols, Fretboard Diagrams].

Appearance

Standard – chord symbols are displayed normally according the text style

Jazz – chord symbols are displayed with special formatting (see below)

Custom – chord symbols are displayed with custom formatting

Chord symbols style file – XML file with definitions for custom formatting

Load chords.xml – specify whether chords.xml needs to be loaded (for compatibility with custom chord symbol files created for earlier versions of MuseScore)

Note Spelling

Standard – A, B♭, B, C, C♯

German – A, B♭, H, C, C♯

Full German – A, B, H, C, Cis

Solfeggio – Do, Re, Mi

French – Do, Ré, Mi

Automatic Capitalization – automatically capitalize chords according to the options set below

Lower case minor chord – use lower case for minor and diminished chords

Lower case bass notes – use lower case for alternate bass notes

All caps note names – use all caps for note names

Position

Default vertical position – baseline for chord symbols (text style vertical offset is relative to this)

Distance to fretboard diagram – distance of chord symbols above fretboard diagrams if present

Minimum chord spacing – minimum space between chord symbols (notes are automatically spaced to enforce this)

Maximum barline distance – maximum distance from chord symbol to barline (barline is automatically spaced to enforce this)

Capo

Capo fret position – automatically calculate capo chords from this fret position

A few of these options bear further explanation.

Capitalization

When the *Automatic Capitalization* option is on (as it is by default), MuseScore will capitalize root and alternate bass note names in chord symbols according to the other options in that group. This means that even if you type chords all lower case, MuseScore will automatically capitalize note names by default unless you use one of the options to force lower case or all caps. However, if you turn the *Automatic Capitalization* option off, MuseScore will preserve the capitalization of chords as you type them, thus allowing for mixed capitalization within the same score. This can be useful, for example, in accordion music.

Spacing

By default, MuseScore will automatically space your music to avoid collision between chord symbols. The *Minimum chord spacing* setting controls how much space MuseScore will preserve around chord symbols. Negative numbers here will cause MuseScore to allow chord symbols to overlap by the specified amount. You may wish to do this if you want your music spaced as tightly as possible and plan to position chords manually to avoid collisions.

Also, by default, MuseScore will allow chord symbols to overlap the barline, which may cause the last chord of one measure to collide with the first of another measure. The *Maximum barline distance* setting controls how much space MuseScore will use after a chord symbol before drawing the barline. The default value here is on the low side, which is what allows chord symbols to overlap the barline. By increasing this setting, you can force MuseScore to add more space before the barline where chord symbols are present, thus preventing chord symbols from overlapping. Depending on the nature of your music, you might consider that a simple solution, or you might find it simpler to adjust the position of individual chord symbols manually.

Common Tasks

To use jazz chord symbol formatting

MuseScore includes a font called *MuseJazz* that can provide a handwritten appearance to your score. This font can be used for any type of text in your score by selecting it normally under Style ⟩ Text , and this works for chord symbols just as it does for other types of text.

Change both Lyrics Odd Lines and Chord Symbol text styles to MuseJazz

However, in order to take full advantage of this font, set the *Jazz* option under *Appearance* in Style ⟩ General ⟩ Chord Symbols, Fretboard Diagrams . Setting this option not only changes the font used in rendering chord symbols to *MuseJazz*; it also enables a number of special formatting techniques such as superscripting of alterations.

Set Jazz option under Appearance

This is all set up for you when using any of the jazz templates when first creating your score. In addition, the font size for chord symbols is raised to 15 point.

To enter substitute chord symbols

By entering multiple chord symbols on the same beat, and setting different text style or properties for them, you can create substitute chord symbols. You can do this for individual chord symbols by moving chord symbols as you go, but there are shortcuts that can simplify the task of entering a complete set of substitute chord symbols.

While there are different ways of going about this, here is one method that should work well:

1. Enter the original chords
2. Select them all (e.g., Select ⟩ All Similar Elements in Same Staff)
3. Cut (optionally paste them elsewhere for safety)
4. Enter substitute chords
5. Select them all
6. Use the *Inspector* to change the vertical position and/or text style
7. Select first note
8. Paste

In the example below, I used this technique with a custom text style I created called "Alternate Chord Symbol" – based on the regular *Chord Symbol* text style but with a font size of 12 point and a vertical offset of -3.50*sp*.

Chapter 16

Lines

A number of musical symbols are essentially just lines drawn in the score with various embellishments. Some also contain text, some have hooks, some are angled, some are curved, etc. Some of the specific types of lines will be discussed in later chapters, but there are a few general types of lines – as well as some concepts and techniques common to all lines in MuseScore – that we will look at here first.

Placing Lines

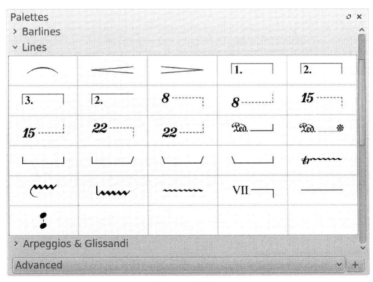

Lines palette

Most lines can be placed by selecting a range in your score then double-clicking the icon for the line in the palette. The line will be applied to the entire range.

You can also apply them by dragging and dropping them from the *Lines* palette to the specific note on which you wish the line to begin.

When using drag and drop, MuseScore tries to pick a sensible default initial length for the line, but you are usually better off selecting the range first then double-clicking the icon.

A few lines, such as slurs and hairpins, can also be added via [Add ⟩ Lines] or have keyboard shortcuts that allow them to be placed more easily. Line types that support these entry method will be discussed as we encounter them.

Editing Lines

In most cases, the only alteration you will need to make to a line is to change the end anchor point. Some lines are attached to measures, others to notes, but in either case, the end anchor point is changed in the same way: double-click the line to enter *Edit* mode, then press [Shift] + [→] or [Shift] + [←] to change end anchor point. Lines attached to measures (like voltas) are extended a measure at a time; lines attached to notes (like slurs) are extended a note at a time.

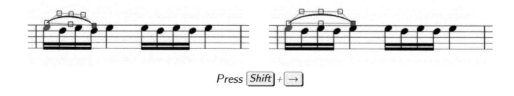

Press [Shift] + [→]

Lines can be extended across multiple systems, or even multiple pages. Just keep extending the line with Shift + → and MuseScore will automatically continue it as necessary.

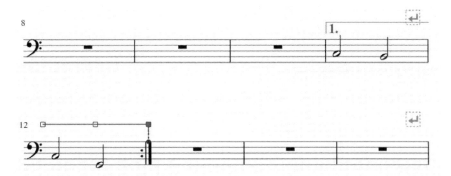

If you change your mind about where you want the line to start, you can move the left handle in the same way.

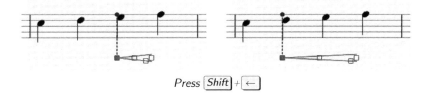

Press Shift + ←

Once you have set the start and end anchor points for a line, you can also fine-tune the length of the line by using the arrow keys without Shift, or by dragging the handles.

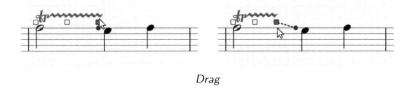

Drag

Dragging is for fine-tuning the length of the line only; it does not change the actual anchor points. Do not use dragging as a substitute for changing the anchor points. If you do, playback will not be correct, multimeasure rests may not be handled correctly, and layout may not be correct if a measure subsequently moves to a different system. You must use Shift + → and Shift + ← to change the anchor points.

The center handle provides a convenient way to adjust the position of a line using the arrow keys. Position can also be adjusted by dragging or by using the *Inspector*.

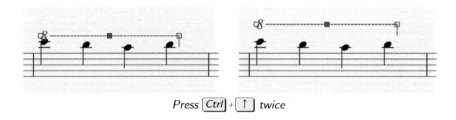

Press `Ctrl` + `↑` *twice*

Line Types

As mentioned above, a few of the line types will be covered in more detail in later chapters where they are more relevant. For example, voltas are discussed in *Repeats*, hairpins in *Dynamics*, and slurs, pedals, and trills in *Articulations and Other Symbols*. But a few more general lines types are discussed here.

Text lines

A number of line types provided by MuseScore allow text to be incorporated with the line. This includes voltas, ottavas, and pedal lines, each of which is discussed in a subsequent chapter. However, MuseScore also provides a generic text line that will be discussed here. The facilities for manipulating the text in all of these line types is similar. So the discussion here will be referenced in the chapters covering those other line types as well.

Text lines are created like other line types – select a range and double-click the line icon, or drag the line icon from the palette to your score. There are actually two versions on the palette: one with sample text ("VII") already provided, and one with no text. Either version is attached to a specific note, so when using drag and drop, be sure to release when the desired note highlights.

To edit the text attached to the line, right-click the line and choose `Line Properties` from the resulting context menu to display the *Line Properties* dialog.

The *Begin* and *End* sections of this dialog allow you to specify text to be used at the beginning and ending of the line. The *Continue* section allows you to be specify text to be used at the beginning of each system for lines that are continued over more than one system.

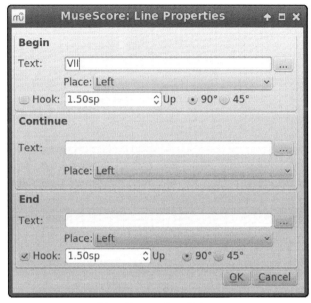

Line Properties dialog

For each section, you can type the desired text into space provided. The ⌐⌐⌐ button displays the standard *Text Properties* dialog, allowing you to customize the font and alignment of the text as described in the chapter on *Text*. In addition, there is a drop-down menu to select whether the text is displayed to the left of the line or above/below the line.

Note that in order for the text to actually be displayed above or below the line, you need to set appropriate vertical alignment in the text properties as well. What the drop-down actually controls is whether the line starts immediately or not until after the text. With *Left*, the line starts after the text; otherwise it starts immediately. Whether the text actually displays above or below the line depends on the vertical alignment in the text properties.

In addition to the text itself, text lines support optional hooks on either end of the line to clarify the exact extent of the line. The *Line Properties* dialog also contains options, shown above, to control the presence, length, and angle for hooks at the beginning and end of lines.

The follow example shows the result of setting the *Begin* text to "Optional", with *Placement* set to *Below*, *Text Properties* set to align the top of text, and the *End* hook set to a length of 3*sp*.

Ottava

An ottava line is a special type of text line that is used to indicate that a passage is to be played one or more octaves higher or lower than written. The lines *8va*, *15ma*, and *22ma* tell the performer to play one, two, or three octaves higher than written; *8vb*, *15mb*, and *22mb* tell the performer to play lower.

MuseScore automatically places ottava lines above the staff for lines that indicate notes should be played higher than written, or below the staff for lines that indicate notes should be played lower than written. You can override this – and also change the basic type of marking between *8va*, *8vb*, *15ma*, etc. – using the controls in the *Inspector*, as discussed below.

In addition to the standard methods of applying ottava lines (double-click, drag and drop), you can also place some ottava lines via [Add⟩Lines] or the keyboard shortcuts listed in that menu.

Changing Appearance and Behavior

Global line settings

There are no global settings common to all line types. Certain line types such as voltas and hairpins do support some global settings. Of the line types discussed in this chapter, here are the settings available:

- [Style⟩General⟩Hairpins, Volta, Ottava]

  Ottava
  Default vertical position – default height above the staff
  Hook height – default length of hook
  Line thickness – default line thickness

Line style – default line style (*Continuous, Dashed, Dotted, Dash-Dotted, Dash-Dot-Dotted*)

Individual line properties

The following properties, found in the *Inspector*, are common to all lines types:

Line

Line visible – control whether the line itself is visible, or just the text
Allow diagonal – allow line to be drawn diagonally (by moving the end handles)
Line color – color of line
Line thickness – thickness of line
Line style – style of line (*Continuous, Dashed, Dotted, Dash-Dotted, Dash-Dot-Dotted*)

In addition, for ottava lines, the following properties are available:

Ottava

Type – *8va, 8vb, 15ma, 15mb, 22ma, 22mb*
Placement – placement relative to staff (*Above, Below*)
Numbers only – specify whether the "va", "vb", "ma", or "mb" text is displayed by default

Shortcuts

There are a few predefined keyboard shortcuts that can used to enter lines directly, both in *Note input* and *Normal* modes. These are two-character sequences, entered by pressing the keys in succession.

- `Ctrl`+`Y` `Ctrl`+`O` `Ctrl`+`A` – ottava 8va
- `Ctrl`+`Y` `Ctrl`+`O` `Ctrl`+`B` – ottava 8vb

Chapter 17

Repeats

MuseScore supports the standard symbols used to indicate repeated passages, and most of these symbols work for playback as well. The symbols used share attributes with other types of markings: repeat barlines are just a special type of barline, "D.C. al fine" is just a special type of text, voltas (endings) are just a special type of line, etc.

Repeat Barlines

The most common way to indicate a repeated section is with repeat barlines. These are located within the *Barlines* palette and are added like other barlines; see *Barlines* in the chapter on *Measure Operations* for more information.

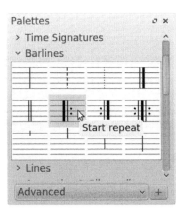

Start repeats are added by applying the barline to the first measure of the repeated section. You can do this either by dragging the palette icon to the measure or by selecting the existing left barline and double-clicking the palette icon.

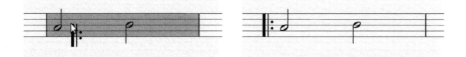

The corresponding end repeat barline should be added to the last measure of the repeated section; it will appear at the right of the measure.

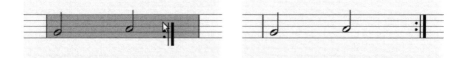

When one repeated passage is followed immediately by another, add the two-sided *End-start repeat* symbol to the end of the first section.

Playback

By default, each repeated section will be played twice. To specify a different number of repeats, right-click the measure with the closing repeat and choose $\boxed{\textsf{Measure Properties}}$. The *Repeat count* setting controls the total number of times the section ending at that repeat sign is played.

Mid-Measure Repeats

If a piece starts with a pickup measure, it may be necessary for a closing repeat to appear mid-measure. Mid-measure repeats are created like other types of mid-measure barlines. Either click the note or rest before which you wish the repeat to appear and then double-click the repeat sign in the palette, or drag the icon to the note or rest.

Mid-measure repeats created in this manner do not play back. If you would like to hear the playback, then use the Edit ≫ Measure ≫ Split Measure command (discussed in the chapter *Measure Operations*) to split the measure into two parts. Then you can add the repeat barline to the first part normally, and playback will work.

Voltas (Endings)

If a passage is to be repeated with a different ending each time, use a volta symbol to indicate this. The volta symbols are located within the *Lines* palette.

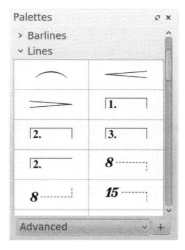

For more information on how lines work in MuseScore, see the chapter on *Lines*.

Voltas are normally attached only to the top staff of a score, and they are automatically copied and linked to all parts (see the chapter on *Parts*). But in particularly large scores – such as for a full orchestra – you may wish to place additional voltas at the top of each section. MuseScore allows you to do this. Only voltas attached to the top staff will be copied to parts.

Placing a volta

To place a volta, select the range of measures and double-click the palette icon, or drag the icon from the palette to the measure that you wish to begin the volta.

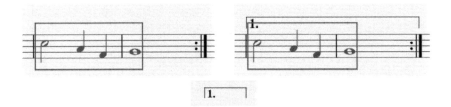

Extending a volta

If you wish to extend a volta to cover more measures than you originally attached it to, double-click the symbol after placing it. This places the volta in *Edit* mode. You can then press Shift+→ to move the endpoint of the volta one measure at a time to the right.

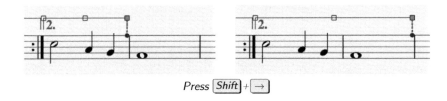

Press Shift + →

Changing the ending number

The palette provides symbols for first, second, and third endings. If you need other endings, such as a fourth ending, or an ending to be used for the first through third repetitions, place the volta using one of the existing symbols, then right-click the symbol and select Volta Properties. This will bring up a dialog that allows you to enter the text that will appear as well as select the exact repetitions for which this ending should be used.

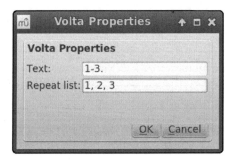

D.C., D.S., Segno, Coda, Fine

To place a D.C., D.S., segno, coda, or similar marking, use the *Repeats & Jumps* palette.

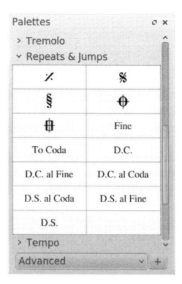

Drag a marking from this palette to the desired measure of your score, releasing when the measure highlights. The marking will automatically be placed above the measure, aligned either to the left or to the right as appropriate for the marking.

Note that while some editors use the coda sign alone to indicate where a performer should jump forward, MuseScore requires you to use the *To Coda* marking in order for playback to work correctly. However, if you prefer to use the coda sign instead of (or in addition to) text, go ahead and add the *To Coda* marking, then double-click it to edit the text. To insert the coda sign, press F2 to bring up the *Special Characters* palette, then double-click the coda sign.

MuseScore normally interprets these symbols automatically when it comes it playback, but if you have an especially complicated road map with multiple segnos and/or codas, you may need to use the *Inspector* to tell MuseScore which D.S. goes with which segno, etc. Each segno and coda marking has a label you can set, and each D.S. and D.C. lets you specify the labels they jump to.

Measure Repeat

The measure repeat symbol can used when you wish to repeat a single measure. It is located on the *Repeats & Jumps* palette, and you can add one to your score by dragging it to the desired measure or by selecting the measure and double-clicking the symbol in the palette. The latter approach also allows you to insert several measure repeat symbols at once, by selecting a range of measures before double-clicking the palette icon.

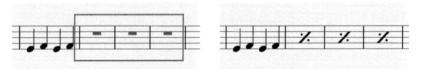

Double click measure repeat icon in palette

MuseScore does not contain native support for two-bar or four-bar repeats. However, the symbols themselves are present in the *Bravura* font and can be added to your score using the *Symbols* palette. To add one of these symbols, press ⟨ Z ⟩ to display the palette. The symbols in question are found toward the very end, so scroll down until you find them.

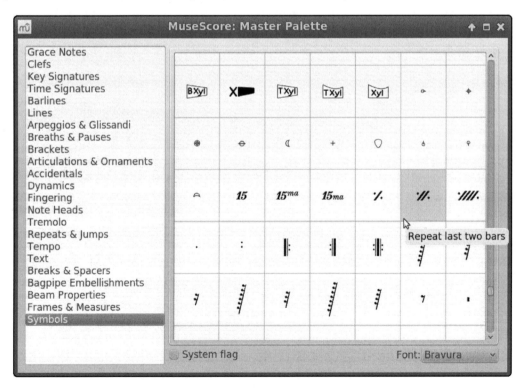

This symbol is usually centered directly on the barline between two measures, indicating that those two measures are to be replaced with the contents of the previous two. You can attach the symbol to a barline in your score by dragging it and releasing when the dotted line is drawn to the correct barline.

If you use this symbol a lot, you may wish to add it to your *Repeats* palette as described in the chapter on *Customization*.

Although MuseScore does not position this symbol automatically, you can do so manually in a reliable way without too much trouble, as follows:

1. Click the symbol to select it
2. Press Ctrl + R to reset the position to the default (to top right of barline)
3. Double-click symbol to enter *Edit* mode
4. Press Ctrl + ↓ twice to move the symbol to the middle line
5. Press Ctrl + ← followed by ← five times to center it on the barline

You can accomplish the same results with the *Inspector*, entering offsets of -1.50*sp* horizontal and 2.00*sp* vertical.

Once you have positioned the symbol appropriately in your score, you can mark the rests invisible and then copy and paste those two measures or use the R command to repeat the passage as often as desired.

In no time at all, you can fill entire pages with these.

Although these symbols do not playback, you can use separate invisible staves to contain the playback for these and other symbols for which playback is not defined. See the chapter *Staves and Instruments* for more information.

Changing Appearance and Behavior

The appearance of repeats can be customized in the same basic ways as for other element types, but there are some special properties for repeats, to support playback for instance.

Global repeat settings

The text-based repeating markings such as D.C., Fine, and the segno and coda signs themselves use the *Repeat Text Left* and *Repeat Text Right* text styles, depending on whether they are normally aligned to the left or the right of the measure. Global settings for repeat barlines are discussed in the chapter *Measure Operations*. Addition global settings for repeats are as follows:

- Style ⟫ General ⟫ Hairpins, Volta, Ottava

  Volta
  Default vertical position – default height above the staff
  Hook height – default length of hook
  Line thickness – default line thickness
  Line style – default line style (*Continuous, Dashed, Dotted, Dash-Dotted, Dash-Dot-Dotted*)

Individual repeat properties

Barline settings have already been discussed in the chapter on *Measure Operations*, text settings in *Text*, and line settings in *Lines*, but there are a few additional properties for repeats that you can set in the *Inspector*.

- **Volta**

  Volta
  Type – *Open, Closed*

- **D.C., D.S.**

  Jump
  Jump to – label of marker to jump to
  Play until – label of marker to play until after jump to above marker
  Continue at – label of marker to continue at after playing until above marker

- **Segno, Coda, To Coda, Fine**

  Marker
  Marker type – type of this marker (controls label and default text)
  Label – label of this marker (for use by jump elements such as *D.C.* and *D.S.*)

Chapter 18

Dynamics

Dynamics indicate the relative volume of a passage – how soft or loud it should be played. Dynamic indications fall into two categories: text markings like *mf* that most often indicate the overall volume of a passage, and lines called *hairpins* used to indicate a gradual change in volume. The former are found in the *Dynamics* palette; the latter in the *Lines* palette. All of these symbols are understood and applied to playback, with certain limitations in the case of hairpins.

Dynamics Text Markings

The standard dynamics text markings (e.g., *mp*, *ff*) are found in the Dynamics palette.

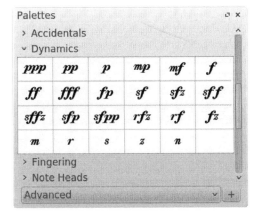

These markings can be added to your score in the same way as most palette items: either drag and drop one to a specific note, or else click one or more notes then double-click the icon.

Double-click sfz in palette

You may also wish to add text markings like "cresc." or "crescendo" rather than using a hairpin symbol. You can do this by adding an ordinary dynamics text marking like f and then double-clicking it to edit the text.

As mentioned in the chapter on *Text*, the special versions of the letters $\boldsymbol{f}$, $\boldsymbol{m}$, $\boldsymbol{n}$, $\boldsymbol{p}$, $\boldsymbol{r}$, $\boldsymbol{s}$, and $\boldsymbol{z}$ can be entered while editing text by pressing Ctrl + Shift while typing the letter.

Hairpins (Crescendo and Diminuendo)

A gradual change in dynamics – crescendo or diminuendo (decrescendo) – can be indicated with a hairpin symbol. These are found on the *Lines* palette and generally work as described in the chapter on *Lines*.

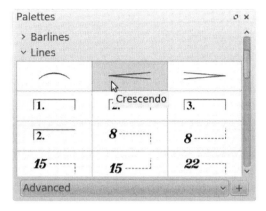

Hairpins can be added to a score like other lines: either select a range then double-click the icon, or drag the icon to a specific note in your score. In the latter case, you will need to adjust the end anchor manually (double-click and use [Shift]+[←] and [Shift]+[→]).

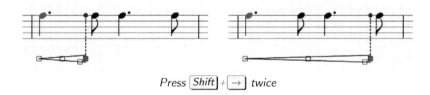

Press [Shift]+[→] *twice*

However, you can also add hairpins via [Add][Lines], or using keyboard shortcuts. The latter method is especially convenient First select the range, then press [<] for crescendo or [>] for diminuendo.

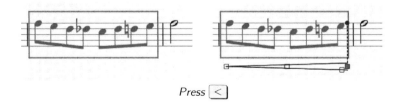

Press [<]

When a hairpin is in *Edit* mode, there is a special handle that appears at the open end to control the height of the hairpin.

Drag

Changing Appearance and Behavior

The standard text markings are a form of text and hence can be customized similarly to other text markings. Hairpins are a form of line and hence can be customized similarly to other lines. But there are also some specific settings unique to dynamics.

Global dynamics settings

The standard text markings use the text style *Dynamics* to control position and font.
Settings for hairpins are as follows:

- Style ⟩⟩ General ⟩⟩ Hairpins, Volta, Ottava

    Hairpins
    Default vertical position – position relative to top of staff
    Line thickness – thickness of line
    Height – height of hairpin at wide end
    Continue height – height of hairpin at narrow end when continued across systems

Individual dynamics properties

A variety of properties relating specifically to dynamics can be set in the *Inspector*. Note that the more general properties of dynamics as text or lines are available as well. These are documents in the chapters on *Text* and *Lines* respectively.

- **Standard text markings**

    Dynamic
    Dynamic range – scope of playback effect (*Staff*, *Part*, *System*)
    Velocity – MIDI velocity (volume on scale of 1-127)

- **Hairpins**

    Hairpin
    Circled tip – display small circle on closed end (indicating silence)
    Dynamic range – scope of playback effect (*Staff*, *Part*, *System*)
    Velocity change – change in velocity from start to end; 0 indicates automatic determination
       from surrounding dynamics

Height – height of hairpin at wide end
Continue height – height of hairpin at narrow end when continued across systems

Chapter 19

Fretboard Diagrams

Music for guitar and similar instruments often includes diagrams showing how to finger the chords on the fretboard. MuseScore allows you to create these fretboard diagrams with a straightforward fretboard diagram editor.

Creating a Fretboard Diagram

Fretboard diagrams are added to your score using the *Fretboard Diagrams* palette.

Initially, this palette contains only a single fretboard diagram, but after adding one to your score, you can modify it as we will see below. As you build a collection of chords, you can add them to your palette as described in *Palettes* in the chapter on *Customization* to make it easy to reuse these fretboard diagrams.

To add a fretboard diagram to your score, drag it from the palette to a note or rest, or click the note or rest then double-click the palette icon.

The chord already provided on the palette is a *C* chord, but of course, you will be wanting other chords too. To edit a fretboard diagram, right-click it and choose Fretboard Diagram Properties. This displays an editor that allows you to create your own chords easily.

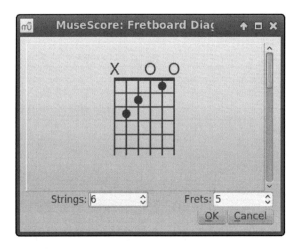

By default, this editor displays six strings and five frets, but you can customize this using the controls at the bottom of the dialog. You can also use the scroll bar to set the topmost fret.

Fret marks

To add a fret mark to a string, simply click where you want the mark to appear.

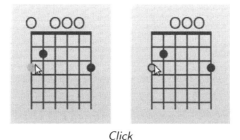

Click

   If there is already an existing mark on another fret for that string, the existing one is deleted automatically.

Open and unused string indicators

If you wish to remove a fret mark and leave the string open, either click on the mark you wish to delete or click above the string where you would like the open string indicator (the letter "O") to appear.

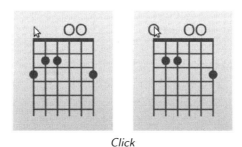

Click

To mark an open string as unused, click the "O" and it will turn into an "X".

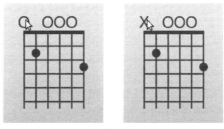

Click

If you click the "X", it will be deleted, leaving you with an unmarked string.

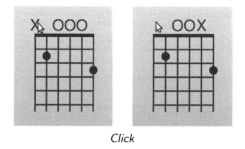

Click

Barré chords

To create the symbol for a barré, Shift+click the string/fret where you would like the barré to end.

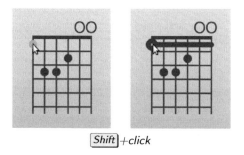

Shift+click

Chord symbols

Chord symbols and fret diagrams can be used together and entered in either order. Chord symbols will automatically display above a fret diagram if present.

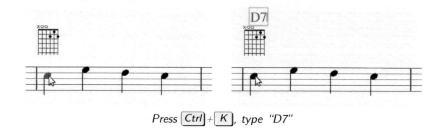

Press Ctrl+K, type "D7"

When using chord symbols in conjunction with fretboard diagrams, you will probably want to set the *Chord Symbol* text style to centered rather than left-aligned. See *Text style* in the chapter on *Text* for more information.

Changing Appearance and Behavior

The options that control the appearance of fretboard diagrams are found in $\boxed{\text{Style}}\rangle\boxed{\text{General}}\rangle$ $\boxed{\text{Chord Symbols, Fretboard Diagrams}}$.

Default vertical position – position above staff
Scale – relative size of fretboard diagram (1.0 = standard)
Fret offset number font size – size of fret offset number relative to size used for "X" and "O"
Position – display fret offset number to *Left* or *Right* of diagram
Barré line thickness – relative thickness of barré line (1.0 = standard)

Chapter 20

Figured Bass

Figured bass is a style of notation, commonly used in Baroque music, in which notes are written for a bass instrument and symbols are placed below the staff to indicate a harmony that is to be supplied by a keyboard player or other musician. MuseScore supports the most common types of figured bass notation.

Entering Figured Bass

Figured bass notation can be created in MuseScore in a similar manner as for chord symbols. To begin figured bass entry, click a note then press Ctrl + G (Mac: Cmd + G) or use the menu item Add 》 Text 》 Figured Bass . This places a text cursor under the staff, allowing you to type a figured bass symbol.

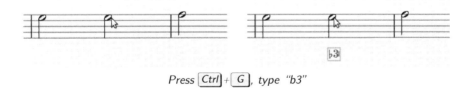

Press Ctrl + G , *type "b3"*

As with chord symbol entry, a similar set of shortcuts exist to move the cursor when entering figured bass.

- Space – move cursor to next note, rest, or beat
- Shift + Space – move cursor to previous note, rest, or beat
- Tab – move cursor to next measure
- Shift + Tab – move cursor to previous measure
- Ctrl plus number (1 - 9) – extend duration corresponding to number (e.g., half note for 6)

- Esc – exit *Figured bass edit* mode

Note that as you enter figures, a gray horizontal bar appears on screen above each figure to show its duration. These bars do not print but are there to help you visualize how your figures relate to the bass notes above. See *Duration* below for more information.

To edit a figured bass element that has already been entered, you can either navigate back to it while still in *Figured bass edit* mode, or you can double-click it if you have already exited to *Normal* mode.

Figured Bass Syntax

Figured bass symbols include digits, accidentals, and a variety of other special symbols.

Digits

Digits are entered normally. Stacked digits are entered by pressing Enter after each line.

Type "6", press Enter*, type "4"*

When you complete entry of the figure, it will be reformatted automatically.

Accidentals

Accidentals are entered using ordinary characters that will be automatically converted to the proper symbols when you complete entry of the figure. Use "b" for flat, "#" for sharp, "h" for natural, "bb" for double flat, and "##" for double sharp. Accidentals can be placed before or after a digit, or used in place of a digit (which by convention implies a 3). Parentheses – both round and square – can be used freely around accidentals.

Combined shapes

Digits can be combined with a slash or cross by typing "/", "\", or "+" as appropriate, either before or after the digit. For example, to produce a 6 with a slash through it, type "6\", and it will be converted when you complete entry of the figure.

Duration

Figured bass elements have a specific duration, shown on screen by the gray horizontal line above each figure. Although MuseScore does not currently use this value for anything, the duration can be used by plugins and is also exported to MusicXML, so one should take care to set these correctly. By default, each figure lasts the duration of the note to which it is attached, and this is set when you use Space or Tab to move to the next note or measure or Esc to exit *Figured bass edit* mode.

You can explicitly enter a longer or shorter duration while entering a figure by pressing Ctrl (Mac: Cmd) in conjunction with the number key corresponding to the duration you wish to set. Using one of these shortcuts upon entering a figure will both set the duration as specified and move the cursor forward by that same amount. This allows you to enter multiple figures under a single note, or to enter a single figure that extends for multiple notes.

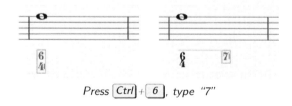

Press Ctrl + 6 , type "7"

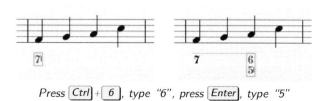

Press Ctrl + 6 , type "6", press Enter , type "5"

In order to make the duration visually explicit in the final score (not just the gray line on screen), you can enter a continuation line by typing an underscore after the figure, and then using Ctrl and a number as usual to specify the duration.

Type "_", press Ctrl + 6 *, type "6", press* Enter *, type "5"*

Changing Appearance and Behavior

Although figured bass elements are a form of text, rendering requirements are special enough that the usual text style mechanism does not apply. Instead, all relevant settings are part of the general style.

Global figured bass settings

Most of the options for controlling the appearance of figured bass are found in Style ⟩ General ⟩ Figured Bass , which is described in detail below. Although figured bass is a form of text, there is no corresponding *Figured Bass* text style. The relevant controls are all found in the general style options.

- Style ⟩ General ⟩ Figured Bass

  Figured Bass
  Font – currently the only option is *MuseScore Figured Bass*
  Size – size of font
  Vertical position – default position of figures relative to top of staff
  Line height – spacing between lines for multi-line figures, expressed as a percentage of font size
  Alignment – specify whether *Top* or *Bottom* of figure is aligned to reference point
  Style – specify *Modern* or *Historic* rendering styles for combined shapes

Chapter 21

Articulations and Other Symbols

MuseScore supports a very large number of markings, including articulations such as staccato dots or tenuto lines, ornaments such as mordents and trills, and other symbols such as arpeggios, tremolo, and even a set of bagpipe embellishments.

Rather than overwhelm you with a single palette containing hundreds of symbols, MuseScore divides them up into a number of separate palettes. The way MuseScore divides the markings up has as much to do with how they are created in the program as with what they actually mean, which can sometimes make things hard to find at first. This book presents a compromise between these two different ways of categorizing markings.

Most of the markings discussed in this chapter support the standard adjustments to position that can be made using the keyboard, mouse, or the *Inspector*, as described in *Manual Adjustments* in the chapter on *Editing*. Most require a double-click to be placed into *Edit* mode before nudging with the keyboard becomes possible; exceptions include markings that are actually based on text (eg, fingerings).

The examples below often make use of the *Advanced* workspace, which contains the fullest set of markings. If your palettes contain fewer symbols than shown here and you need to use one of the missing ones, be sure to select the *Advanced* workspace using the control at the bottom of the palette window.

Articulations

The term *articulation* refers to the manner in which individual notes are played. Articulation symbols in MuseScore are found in the *Articulations & Ornaments* palette.

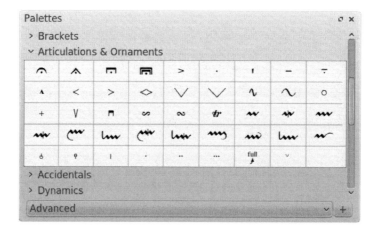

Placing articulations

Markings on the *Articulations & Ornaments* palette can be added to your score in the usual ways: by dragging and dropping a palette element onto a single note or rest, or by selecting one or more notes or rests and then double-clicking the palette icon.

Certain articulations can also be entered via keyboard shortcuts, both in *Note input* and in *Normal* modes.

- Shift + S – staccato
- Ctrl + Alt + N – tenuto
- Ctrl + Alt + O – marcato

Editing articulations

In addition to the standard adjustments, most articulations can be flipped upside down and/or to the opposite side of the note (stem side versus note head side) using the keyboard command X .

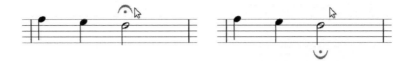

Playback

Certain articulations – such as staccato – will play back automatically. Play back for other articulations may be simulated by using the *Inspector* to set appropriate properties (e.g., to increase the velocity for notes under a down bow marking).

The fermata is special in that it has built-in playback support that is not enabled by default. To make a fermata play back, increase its *Time stretch* property in the *Inspector*. A value of 2.00, for instance, will cause the note under the fermata to be held twice as long as usual.

Slurs

Slurs (not to be confused with ties, which look similar but are entirely different – see *Ties* in the chapter on *Entering Notes and Rests*) can be considered a form of articulation, but they are special in that they are not applied to individual notes but instead to groups of consecutive notes. They are found on the *Lines* palette.

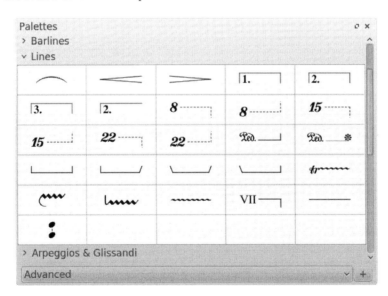

Placing slurs

The easiest way to apply a slur to a group of consecutive notes is to first select them and then press the keyboard command $\boxed{\text{S}}$.

Press [S]

Slurs can also be entered directly during note entry. Press [S] after entering a note and a slur will be started. The slur continues as you enter more notes, until you press [S] again to terminate it.

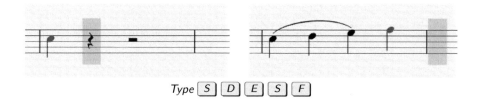

Type [S] [D] [E] [S] [F]

You can also enter a slur from the *Lines* palette as described in the chapter on *Lines*, or via [Add] ⟩ [Lines] ⟩ [Slur].

Editing slurs

Slurs can be edited as described in *Lines*. Although I recommend that you use [Shift]+[←] and [Shift]+[→] when adjusting the endpoints of any lines, slurs are unlike other line types in that you can also drag an endpoint with the mouse to a different note, and the slur will automatically adjust. Just be sure to release when the anchor point (as shown by the dotted line) changes to the desired note.

Drag right

Fine tuning can be done by adjusting the handles without holding [Shift]. Slurs are different from other lines in that they are curved and thus contain additional handles that can be used to customize the shape of the slur.

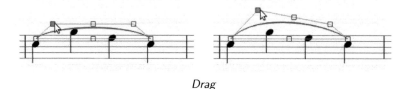

Drag

Slurs can also be flipped above or below the notes to which they apply using the keyboard command ⌐X⌐.

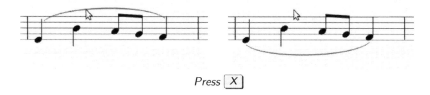

Press ⌐X⌐

Cross staff slurs

For instruments like piano that use multiple staves, slurs can cross from one staff to the other. To create a cross staff slur, place the slur normally, and then while in *Edit* mode, use ⌐Shift⌐+ ⌐↑⌐ and ⌐Shift⌐+⌐↓⌐ to move the anchor point to a note or rest on the staff above or below.

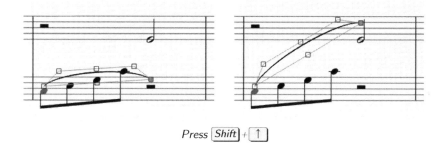

Press ⌐Shift⌐ + ⌐↑⌐

Ornaments

Ornaments that have a fixed shape and size are found on the *Articulations & Ornaments* palette. Ornaments like trills that can be extended in length are found on the *Lines* palette.

Placing ornaments

The ornaments on the *Articulations & Ornaments* palette are attached to individual notes in your score and are placed just like articulations and most other palette elements: drag and drop from the palette to a note or rest, or select a note or rest then double-click the palette icon.

The ornaments on the *Lines* palette – various forms of trills – are placed by selecting a range and then double-clicking the icon or by using drag and drop, as discussed in the chapter on *Lines*.

Editing ornaments

Ornaments placed from the *Lines* palette can be extended as described in the chapter on *Lines*: double-click to enter *Edit* mode, then use Shift + ← and Shift + → to change the anchor points.

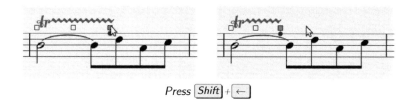

Press Shift + ←

Fine tuning can be done by adjusting the handles without holding Shift.

Playback

Certain ornaments, such as mordents and turns, will play back automatically. However, interpretation of ornaments is highly subjective, and the automatic playback is unlikely to be satisfactory to everyone in all cases. The *Ornament Style* control in the *Inspector* enables you to customize the playback of ornaments. You can also disable playback of an ornament completely using the *Play* control, and you can optionally provide your own interpretation of the ornament by adding invisible notes in another voice or on another staff.

Pedal Markings

MuseScore supports the standard pedal markings used for piano. These markings are found on the *Lines* palette.

Placing pedal markings

Pedal marking are placed like other lines, as described in the chapter on *Lines*: select a region then double-click the palette icon, or drag from the palette to the desired start note.

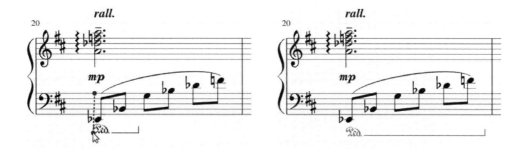

Editing pedal markings

By default, a pedal marking extends to the end of the measure, but the anchor point can be edited as for other lines: double-click then use Shift + ← or Shift + → .

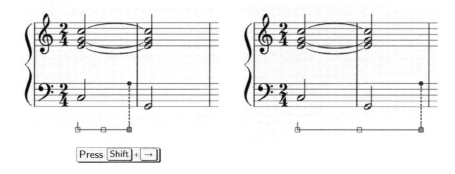

Press Shift + →

Pedal change markings

The angle bracket used to indicate a pedal change can be created in MuseScore by combining two pedal lines: one ending with an angle hook where you want the change to occur, and another starting with an angle hook at that same location.

Pedal release markings

Some editors prefer to use the symbol "*" to indicate where the pedal is released, instead of using a line with a hook at the end. This symbol can be added from the *Lines* palette even though no actual line will appear in your score. The line is marked invisible and will appear grayed-out on screen.

Other pedal types

MuseScore includes built-in support (including palette icons and playback) for the standard damper pedal only, but you can add generic text lines for other types of pedal marking such as sostenuto pedal, using Line Properties to set the text and other attributes however you like.

Fingering

Fingering markings are found on the *Fingering* palette.

Although all the markings on this palette are placed and edited the same way, there are actually four different types of fingering markings with different handling in terms of the automatic positioning that is applied. The first set of numbers (0-5) is intended for piano. The next set of letters (p, i, m, a, c) are for guitar right hand, the next set of numbers (0-5) are for guitar left hand, and the set of numbers in circles (0-6) are for guitar string numbers. The tooltip that appears when you hover over one of these markings is intended to help you tell which fingering is intended for which purpose. In truth, it does not actually matter if you use the "wrong" fingering style, but the automatic placement of the markings is optimized to work best when used as intended.

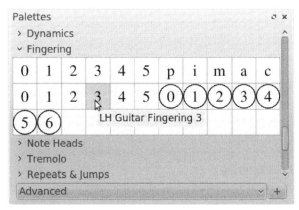

Fingering palette

Placing a fingering

Fingerings are placed like most palette elements: either drag a symbol to the desired note, or select one or more notes then double-click the appropriate fingering.

2

Editing a fingering

Fingerings are ordinary text and can be edited using the standard text tools. See the chapter on *Text* for more information. The text styles used by the different fingering types are *Fingering*, *RH Guitar Fingering*, *LH Guitar Fingering*, and *String Number*.

Breaths and Pauses

Markings to indicate breaths and pauses are found on the *Breaths & Pauses* palette.

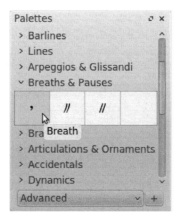

If you are looking for the fermata marking – which could be considered a type of pause as well – see the section on *Articulations* above. If you are looking for the rest symbols – which are sometimes called pauses – see the section *Entering Rests* in the chapter on *Entering Notes and Rests*.

Placing a breath or pause

Breaths and pauses are placed just as for most other markings – drag and drop or double-click. Just be sure to attach the marking to the note or rest *before* where you want the marking to appear.

Tremolo and Rolls

Tremolo markings consist of a series of diagonal slashes. A tremolo marking can be placed through the stem or above or below a single note to indicate rapid repetition of that note (in which case, it is the same as a roll for percussion), or it can be placed between two notes to indicate rapid alternation between them. These markings are found on the *Tremolo* palette.

The markings that show the stem are the type that can be applied to individual notes; the ones without the stem are the type that are applied between two notes.

Placing a tremolo or roll on individual notes

Tremolo markings can be placed on individual notes in the usual way: by dragging a marking from the palette to a note, or by selecting one or more notes then double-clicking a palette icon.

Placing a tremolo between two notes

Tremolo markings that occur between two notes – indicating rapid succession between them – work a bit differently. By convention, the notes being alternated are notated with both notes shown at the full rhythmic value. Thus it may look like there are too many beats in the measure. For example, the notation for a whole note tremolo in 4/4 time shows both notes as whole notes, making it appear there are eight beats in the measure. MuseScore uses a special method to enter this notation:

1. Enter the notes as if each were to take half the total length of the tremolo
2. Apply the tremolo to the first note of the pair (drag and drop or select and double-click)

When you apply the tremolo, MuseScore will automatically convert the notes to the correct notation.

Arpeggios

Arpeggio markings are found on the *Arpeggios & Glissandi* palette.

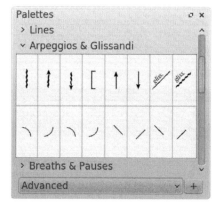

The first few symbols on this palette are for arpeggions; the remainder are discussed later in the sections on *Glissandi* and *Falls, Doits, Scoops, Plops, and Slides*.

Placing an arpeggio

These markings are placed in the usual way: either drag the icon to a chord, or select one or more chords then double-click the palette icon.

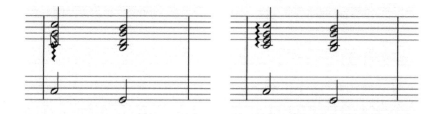

Editing an arpeggio

Arpeggios can be edited for length and position much like other lines: double-click and drag the handles.

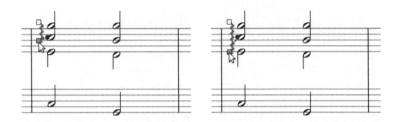

They can also be extended across staves of a single instrument such as piano using [Shift]+ [↑] and [Shift]+[↓].

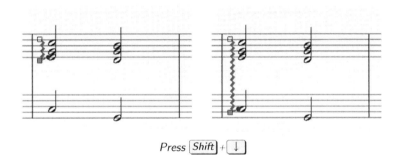

Press [Shift]+[↓]

Playback

Arpeggios will playback by default, but this can be disabled via the *Play* property in the *Inspector*.

Glissandi

Glissandi – lines connecting two chords to indicate a sliding in pitch between them – are found on the *Arpeggios & Glissandi* palette, shown above in the section on *Arpeggios*. They are placed by attaching them to the first note of the pair in the usual way: select and double-click or drag and drop.

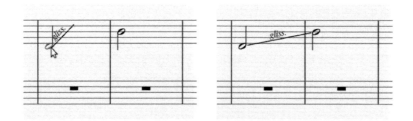

Although glissandi appear to be a form of line, they are not editable via *Edit* mode.

Playback

Glissandi will playback by default, but this can be disabled via the *Play* property in the *Inspector*.

Falls, Doits, Scoops, Plops, and Slides

These symbols are attached to individual notes to indicate a bend in pitch preceding or following the note. They are found on the *Arpeggios & Glissandi* palette, shown above in the section on *Arpeggios*.

These symbols are added in the usual way: drag and drop to a note, or select one or more notes then double-click. Because they attach to a single note, there is no need for Shift + ← and Shift + → to move the anchor points, but the shape of the symbols can be edited by double-clicking and then dragging the handles.

Drag

Guitar Bends

Guitar notation – and tablature in particular (see *Tablature*) – uses a few special notations to indicate different types of bends. MuseScore provides support for two different types of customizable bend markings.

Bends

The most common type of bend notation used in guitar music consists of one or more arrows indicating the direction of the bend and text indicating the magnitude. MuseScore provides one default bend marking but allows you to customize it. To do this, first add the default version to your score from the *Articulations & Ornaments* palette.

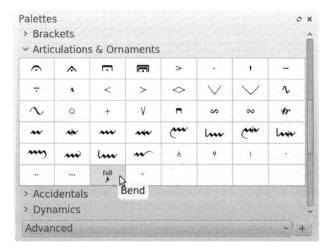

This marking is placed like other articulations: drag the icon to a note, or click the note then double-click the icon.

The default bend marking shows an upward bend of a full fret. Once you have placed a bend marking, you can customize it to show a bend of a half fret or some other magnitude, a bend up and back down, a bend up to the note, or other types of bend. To do this, right-click the bend marking and select Bend Properties, which displays the *Bend Properties* dialog.

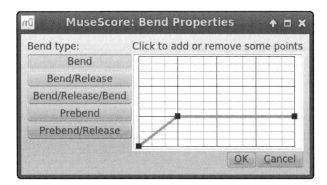

The thick gray line with the blue control points depicts the overall shape of the bend, plotted on a grid. The darker horizontal lines on the grid indicate frets; the lighter ones indicate intermediate points between frets. So the example above – the default bend marking – shows a bend of one full fret. To change this to a half fret bend, simply click to move the control points down to the horizontal line half way between the current line and the bottom.

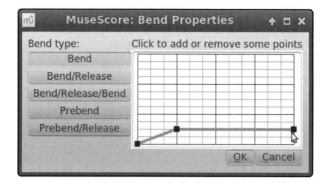

When you press OK, the marking in the score automatically updates to show "1/2" instead of "full":

More complex bends are possible by adding more control points. The buttons to the left of the dialog provide presets for a number of common bend types. For instance, the Bend/Release button generates the following graph:

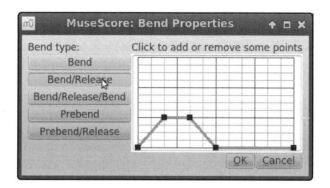

This creates the following marking:

Tremolo bar markings

Tremolo bar markings are similar to bends in how they are applied and customized, but the specific controls differ. Tremolo bar markings are also added to your score from the *Articulations & Ornaments* palette.

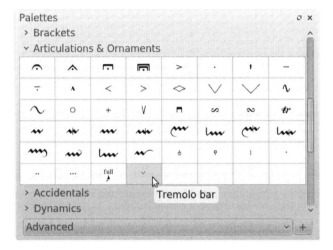

This marking can be placed via drag and drop or by double-clicking.

You can then customize them by right-clicking and selecting *Tremolo Bar Properties*. This brings up a dialog that looks and works much the same as for bends.

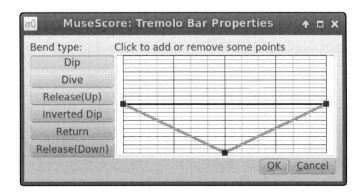

Playback

Bends will playback by default, but this can be disabled via the *Play* property in the *Inspector*.

Ambitus

MuseScore supports the symbol used in some early music editions to indicate the ambitus or range of a part. This symbol is found in the *Lines* palette.

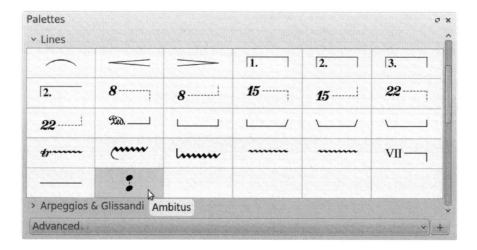

MuseScore can indicate this automatically at the beginning of the part. To do this, either click the clef at the beginning of the system and then double-click the icon, or drag the icon to the clef:

MuseScore creates this symbol based on the highest and lowest note found on the staff. You can then change this using the *Inspector* if necessary.

Bagpipe Embellishments

Bagpipe music uses a series of embellishments that are similar to grace notes but that occur is very specific combinations. MuseScore provides a whole palette of these.

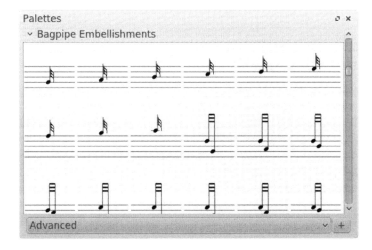

These can be added to your score in the usual ways: either drag and drop to a specific note, or select one or more notes then double-click the icon.

Once added to your score, these are ordinary grace notes and can be edited as such.

Miscellaneous Symbols

MuseScore provides a number of other symbols that can be used for various purposes.

Other symbols

There are a large number of other symbols that can be found by going to View ⟩ Master Palette ⟩ Symbols or pressing the keyboard shortcut Z .

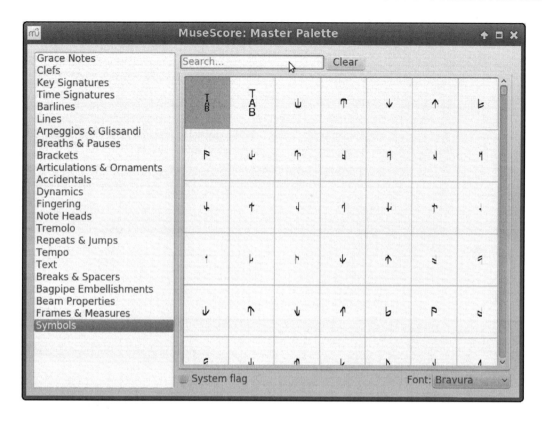

These can be placed in your score as usual: by drag and drop to an element in your score, or by selecting one or more notes then double-clicking the symbol in the palette.

You can then move the symbol into the desired position.

By default, MuseScore will show you symbols from the *Bravura* font, which contains such a large number of symbols that it can be overwhelming. To help you find what you are looking for, there is a search box at the top of the dialog that you can use to filter the list if you can guess at part of the name of the symbol. For example, typing "pedal" into the search box will display only the symbols with that term in the name.

If the symbol you are adding is a common one that is supported more directly by MuseScore in another context – for instance, if you are trying to add a clef somewhere a clef would not normally appear – then you may also find it easier to find the symbol in the *Emmentaler* font, which is the default used in MuseScore for most symbols in their usual context. To select from the *Emmentaler* font, select it in the drop-down menu at the bottom right of this dialog.

> Do not confuse this palette with the *Special Characters* palette described in the chapter on *Text*. That palette is specifically for including a symbol within text; the *Symbols* palette discussed here is for attaching symbols directly to notes, rests, or other elements.

You can also add any of these symbols to a custom palette to make them easier to find later, as described in *Palettes* in the chapter on *Customization*.

Graphics

When all else fails, MuseScore allows you to insert graphics from image files into your score. This allows you to create whatever notation you like in a graphics editor and then add it into your score. For best results, use transparent PNG or SVG formats. Graphics can be added to frames as described in the chapter on *Page Layout*, but they can also be added to any note or rest in your score via drag and drop or copy and paste from another program.

In the following example, I first created a drawing using *Inkscape*, a free and open source vector graphics editor, and copied it to my clipboard. I can then paste it into my score.

Press Ctrl + V

As with symbols, you can then move the graphic into the desired position.

Changing Appearance and Behavior

The different types of markings discussed in this chapter all have different settings, properties, and methods of customization. The most important adjustments for each type of marking have already been covered in the corresponding sections above.

Global settings

The default settings for the markings covered in this chapter are found in different pages of the Style ⟩ General dialog.

- Style ⟩ General ⟩ Articulations, Ornaments

    Note head distance – distance from note head for multiple articulations placed relative to chord
    Staff distance – distance from staff for multiple articulations placed relative to staff

Articulation distance – distance from articulation to chord, staff, or other articulation
Articulation size – relative size of articulations
Anchor – reference point for articulation placement (*Above Staff, Below Staff, Chord Automatic, Above Chord, Below Chord*)

- Style ⟩ General ⟩ Slurs/Ties

Line thickness at end – thickness of end of tie or slur
Line thickness middle – thickness at middle of tie or slur
Dotted line thickness – thickness of dotted line for ties or slurs

- Style ⟩ General ⟩ Arpeggios

Distance to note – distance from arpeggio to chord
Line thickness – thickness of line
Hook length – length of hook for bracket form of arpeggio

- Style ⟩ General ⟩ Pedal, Trill

Pedal
Default vertical position – position relative to staff
Line thickness – thickness of line
Line style – *Continuous, Dashed, Dotted, Dash-dotted, Dash-dot-dotted*
Trill
Default vertical position – position relative to staff

Individual properties

The various types of markings support different property settings in the *Inspector*. The settings are arranged by group. For line markings, see the chapter on *Lines* for more information on their available properties.

Articulation
Direction – *Auto, Up, Down*
Anchor – reference point for articulation placement (*Above Staff, Below Staff, Chord Automatic, Above Chord, Below Chord*)
Time stretch – relative amount to extend duration of notes (for fermatas)
Ornament style – select from different playback interpretations where supported
Play – controls whether ornament affects playback

Slur/Tie
Line type – *Continuous, Dotted, Dashed*

Trill
Type – *Trill Line, Up Prall, Down Prall, Prall Prall*
Ornament style – select from different playback interpretations
Play – controls whether trill affects playback

Arpeggio

Play – controls whether arpeggio affects playback

Glissando
Type – *Straight* or *Wavy*
Text – text to display with line (if room)
Show text – controls whether text is displayed with line (if room)
Play – controls whether glissando affects playback

Ambitus
Head group – same as for notes; see *Changing Appearance and Behavior* in the chapter on Editing
Head type – same as for notes
Direction – *Upright, Leaning Left, Leaning Right*
Has line – controls whether a line is drawn between top and bottom note
Line thickness – thickness of line
Top note / Oct – pitch and octave of top note
Bottom note / Oct – pitch and octave of bottom note
Update range – recalculate top and bottom notes automatically

Part IV

Staves and Layout

Chapter 22

Staves and Instruments

MuseScore allows you to write music for a single instrument or for as many instruments as you like. Most instruments will use only a single staff, but some – like piano, or guitar if you opt for linked standard notation and tablature staves – use multiple staves. The set of staves for all instruments in a score is referred to as a *system*.

Each staff in your score is associated with an *instrument* (which might actually be a voice, or some sort of sound effect). The instrument associated with a staff determines the name displayed on the staff, the sound used for playback, the transposition used when toggling *Concert Pitch* (see the chapter on *Transposition*), the usable pitch range (so MuseScore can flag notes that are too high or too low for the instrument), and other staff properties.

MuseScore also uses the term *part* in some places in the interface. For now, we will assume a part and an instrument are essentially the same thing. In the chapter on *Parts*, we will see that is possible to define a part containing multiple instruments, and that an instrument can belong to more than one part.

The staves for the instruments in your score can be grouped together using brackets or barlines that extend through them, and MuseScore can automatically hide empty staves to save space. Each staff can be sized and spaced independently, and staves can have any number of lines. Staves can be defined to use standard notation, percussion notation (see the chapter on *Percussion*), or any of a variety of types of tablature (see the chapter on *Tablature*). MuseScore can also link staves together for simultaneous display of standard notation and tablature (see *Adding, Removing, and Reordering Instruments and Staves* below).

The example below contains five instruments: two violins, one viola, one cello, and one piano. The first four instruments contain one staff each, but the piano instrument contains two staves (connected with a curly brace), making a system of six staves in all.

Depending the size of your page and the number, size, and spacing of your staves, there might be only one system per page, or there might be many. For more information, see the chapter on *Page Layout*.

In most cases, the *Create New Score* wizard already sets up everything you need for the staves in your score. See the chapter on *Creating a New Score* for more information. But if you need to make changes after your score has already been set up – such as adding more staves, changing the instrument assigned to a staff, adding brackets between staves, or hiding empty staves – then this chapter and the ones that follow cover everything else you will need.

Adding, Removing, and Reordering Instruments and Staves

When creating a new score from scratch, you would normally have selected the instruments you want in the *Create New Score* wizard. If you change your mind later, or if you created your score from a template and need to customize the instrument and staff selection, go to [Edit⟩ ⟩Instruments] or press the keyboard shortcut [I].

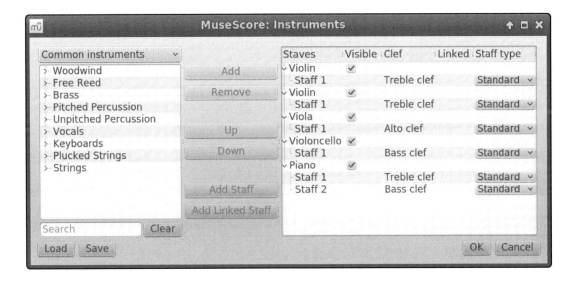

This dialog is virtually identical to the one that appears in the *Create New Score* wizard when creating a score from scratch. You can add and remove instruments from your score with the Add and Remove buttons; add staves to instruments with the Add Staff button, add linked staves with the Add Linked Staff button; and reorder instruments and staves with the Up and Down buttons.

For more information on how the various controls in this dialog work, please see the chapter on *Creating a New Score*.

MuseScore has a long list of instruments it knows about, although only the most commonly used instruments are displayed in this dialog by default. To see the full list, select *All instruments* from the drop-down menu at the top of the *Instruments* dialog. You can also customize the instrument list to add your favorites if they are missing. See *Score* in the chapter on *Customization* for more information. But you can also simply choose a similar instrument and use *Staff Properties* to change the name.

Splitting a Single Staff into a Grand Staff

Sometimes it happens that you have music written on a single staff that you decide you would rather have split into two staves. This can happen for imported MIDI files that are not automatically recognized as being for piano, for instance. MuseScore provides a facility to automatically create a second staff within the same instrument and move all notes to it that are below a certain split point.

To do this, simply right-click the staff you wish to split and select Split Staff from the context menu. A dialog appears that allows you to select the point at which the staff will be split.

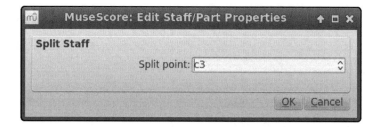

When you press OK, a new staff with bass clef will be created below the current staff. Notes lower than the split point will be moved to the new staff.

Split staff at c3

Grouping Staves

In a score for multiple instruments, it is common to group related staves together, either with brackets at the start of each system or by extending barlines through the staves or by some combination of the methods. MuseScore supports all of these options.

Brackets

You can add a bracket in front of a group of staves using the *Brackets* palette.

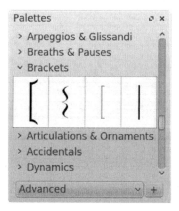

To add one of these brackets to your score, add the icon from the palette to the topmost staff you want included.

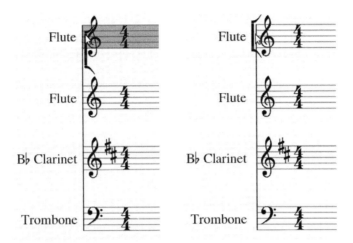

The bracket can then be extended to include additional staves by double-clicking it and dragging the handle downward. The bottom of the bracket will automatically snap into place at an appropriate position.

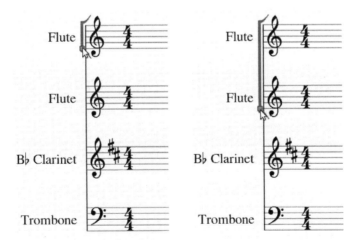

Brackets can be nested, allowing a bracket group to include other bracketed sub-groups. To create nested brackets, work from the inside out. First add the inner brackets, then add the outer.

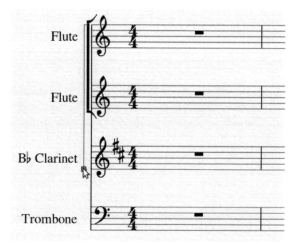

Extending barlines

Barlines are typically extended through the staves of bracketed groups, except for vocal staves where the barlines would interfere with lyrics. To extend barlines through staves, double-click any barline on the topmost staff you want included in the group, then drag downward.

For more information, see *Barlines* in the chapter on *Measure Operations*.

Hiding Staves

By default, all staves of instruments added to a score will display on screen and print. However, there are situations where you might wish to hide certain staves, or only show certain staves. One such case is in a score for multiple instruments where you wish to print and hand out individual parts. MuseScore provides special facilities for this purpose; see the chapter *Parts* for more information.

In this chapter, I will focus on two different situations where you might want to hide staves. One is creating a condensed score by automatically hiding empty staves in each system, and the other is creating staves to be used for playback purposes only.

Creating a condensed score

A full score shows all staves for all instruments in each system, even if some of the instruments are not actually playing during that passage. A condensed score, on the other hand, omits the staves for instruments that are not playing at any given point. This can save space, allowing you to fit more systems per page and thus require fewer pages.

Condensed score

MuseScore can turn your score into a condensed score (aka short score) automatically. To do this, go to Style ⟩ General ⟩ Score and enable the *Hide empty staves* option. You will note there is an additional *Don't hide empty staves in first system* option underneath that allows you to control whether empty staves are hidden in the first system. The default – and the norm in published condensed scores – is to always shows all staves in the first system.

There are also options to control the behavior of individual staves with respect to the *Hide empty staves* option. For more information on these options, see *Changing Appearance and Behavior* below.

Creating a staff for playback only

Sometimes you may wish to create a staff that will be used for playback purposes but not otherwise be displayed or printed. For example, in a jazz arrangement, you might want to have the notated parts for rhythm section instruments just show chords symbols and slashes (see *Slash Notation* in the chapter on *Alternative Notation*) but also create separate parts with actual notes for playback. MuseScore allows you to make these playback staves completely invisible. To do this, go to Edit ⟩ Instruments (keyboard shortcut I) and uncheck the *Visible* option for the staff or staves you wish to hide. The staff will not be displayed or printed, but will still be heard on playback.

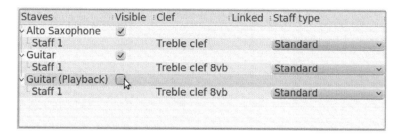

Changing the Instrument and Sound for a Staff

As discussed above, each staff in MuseScore belongs to a particular instrument. Usually there is one staff per instrument, but some instruments may contain multiple staves. The instrument is what controls the sound used for playback as well as other attributes such as transposition and usable range. The instrument is also what shows up in the *Mixer* (see below); an instrument may have three staves but still have only one entry in the *Mixer*.

There are several ways of changing the sound used for playback of a staff, depending on whether you are also interested in changing the transposition and other attributes as well, and whether you want the change to affect all the music on the staff throughout the score or whether you want the sound to change mid-score.

Note that with all of these methods, if the instrument to which a staff was originally assigned had more than one staff, changing the instrument assigned to one staff will affect all staves assigned to that instrument. So for example, if you have a piano part with two staves and you changing the instrument assigned to top staff to an electric piano, this will affect the bottom staff as well. If you wish to have different sounds for different staves, they should be added as separate instruments.

Changing instrument for an entire staff

You can change the instrument assigned to a staff by right-clicking the staff and selecting Staff Properties. The *Edit Staff/Part Properties* dialog box appears, and the Change Instrument button in this dialog allows you to change the instrument assigned to this staff. It displays an instrument dialog similar to the one you use when selecting instruments for your score.

Selecting an instrument in this dialog changes the listing in the *Mixer* (see below) for the instrument to which this staff belongs. It also changes other instrument-related properties including playback sound and transposition. The change affects the entire staff from the beginning to the end of your score.

Changing playback sounds only for an entire staff

If you wish to change the playback sound for a staff but leave the transposition and other settings alone, and you wish this to affect the entire score from beginning to end, the place to do this is the *Mixer*. Go to View ≫ Mixer or press the keyboard shortcut F10.

Most instruments will have only a single entry in the *Mixer*, regardless of how many staves they have. For example, there is only one entry for the piano shown above even though that instrument has two staves.

To change the sound used for a given instrument, simply select a different sound from the drop-down menu.

The list of available sounds is controlled by the soundfont(s) you have loaded into the *Synthesizer* window. The *Mixer* window contains a number of other controls that should be familiar to anyone who has used a real mixer. See the chapter *Playback and Audio Output* for more information on the *Synthesizer* and *Mixer* windows.

Changing instrument for a staff mid-score

There are two main ways to change the sound of a staff mid-score. The first way literally changes the instrument and works for all instruments, while the second keeps the same instrument but just changes between different sound variants that are predefined for that particular instrument in MuseScore (e.g., regular and muted trumpet).

In order to change the sound for an instrument mid-score, you first need to place a special instrument text in your score from the *Text* palette. The idea is that you would need this text to tell a human performer to change instruments, so MuseScore uses this same text to control its own playback as well.

This element can be added to your score like most other palette items: either click a note then double-click the palette item, or drag the palette item directly to the note. The text will initially read simply "Instrument", but you can then double-click it to edit it as for any text. See the chapter on *Text* for more on text editing and formatting.

Adding an instrument text to your score automatically creates a new *Mixer* entry for the staff to which you have attached the text. It is basically like another instrument that is defined to start at the point where you added the text, replacing the instrument that was originally defined for the staff in *Staff Properties*. However, this new instrument affects playback only. You cannot define different transposition or other characteristics currently.

To change the playback associated with this new instrument, you can right-click the text and select Change Instrument from the context menu. This will display the same instrument selection dialog as shown above. You can also simply change the playback sound in the *Mixer*.

Changing between sound variants for a single instrument

Certain instruments can make different sounds depending on how they are played. For example, a trumpet sounds very different depending on whether it is played with a mute or not, and a violin sounds very different depending on whether it is bowed (arco) or plucked (pizzicato). MuseScore knows about these and other similar variants. If you view the *Mixer* entry for one of these instruments, you will see there are actually multiple entries – one for each variant. For example, trumpets will show both a normal and muted entry.

MuseScore allows you to change between these different sounds for the same instrument using staff text. To accomplish this, first place a staff text element normally – e.g., select a note and press [Ctrl]+[T] (Mac: [Cmd]+[T]). Then right-click it and choose [Staff Text Properties] from the context menu. This brings up a dialog that allows you to choose between the different sound variants (MuseScore calls them *channels*) that are predefined for the instrument.

You can then select from the other channels on a per-voice basis. **Important**: note that you must select a voice for each channel change; simply selecting a different sound without telling MuseScore which voice or voices you wish it to apply to will have no effect.

Changing Appearance and Behavior

Global staff settings

In addition to options like *Hide empty staves* discussed above, there are a number of settings that affect the actual appearance of staves – distance between lines, thickness of lines, etc.

- [Layout]⟩[Page Settings]

    Staff space – distance between staff lines; used as a unit of measurement throughout MuseScore

- Style 》 General 》 Score

Hide empty staves – hide staves containing no notes for a given system
Don't hide empty staves in first system – keep all staves on first system
Hide instrument name if there is only 1 instrument – control whether instrument names
    are displayed for scores with only one instrument

- Style 》 General 》 System

System bracket thickness – thickness of square brackets
System bracket distance – space to right of square brackets
Brace thickness – thickness of curly braces
Brace distance – space to right of curly braces

- Style 》 General 》 Measure

Staff line thickness – thickness of staff lines

- Style 》 General 》 Sizes

Small staff size – relative size for staves marked Small (see below)

In addition to the settings described here, see the chapter on *Page Layout* for more information on controlling different aspects of staves.

Individual staff and instrument properties

There are a number of properties that control various aspects of how staves and instruments are handled. To access these properties, right-click an instrument name or empty place in a staff and select Staff Properties from the context menu. The *Edit Staff/Part Properties* dialog is then displayed.

The settings in this dialog are divided into two groups. The settings in the first group – labeled *Staff Properties* – affect the current staff only. The settings in the second group – labeled *Part Properties* – are actually instrument properties, and they affect all staves assigned to the same instrument as the current staff.

Staff properties

Lines – number of staff lines

Line distance – space between staff lines (relative to score default given by *Staff space*)

Extra distance above staff – extra space above this staff throughout all systems

Scale – size of staff and contents (relative to score default given by *Staff space*)

Never hide – do not hide with *Hide empty staves* option even if empty

Show clef – show clefs

Show time signature – show time signatures

Show barlines – show barlines

Hide system barline – do not draw system barline through this staff (if at top of system)

Do not hide if system is empty – keep this staff if entire system is empty

Small staff – display the staff and its contents at small size (see Syle ⟩ General ⟩ Sizes)

Invisible staff lines – hide the staff lines

Staff line color – color of staff lines

Advanced style properties

In addition to the settings available directly within the *Staff Properties* dialog, there is an Advanced Style Properties button that displays a dialog with further settings that are dependent on the staff type – standard, percussion (see the chapter on *Percussion*), or tablature (see the chapter on *Tablature*). Options specific to percussion and tablature staff types will be discussed in the relevant chapters. This section covers the options for standard staves.

Lines – number of staff lines
Line distance – space between staff lines (relative to score default given by *Staff space*)
Show clef – show clefs on this staff
Show time signature – show time signatures
Show barlines – show barlines
Show key signature – show key signatures
Show ledger lines – show ledger lines
Stemless – do not show stems

Note that the first several options are duplicated from the ordinary *Staff Properties* dialog; changing the option in one place automatically updates the other.

Part properties

Changing the instrument via the Change Instrument button in this dialog sets most of these properties at once based on the default for that instrument in MuseScore. However, you can also override these settings manually.

Part name – name used for this instrument in the *Mixer* and as default name for the generated part (see chapter on *Parts*)
Long instrument name – name displayed to the left of this staff at the start on the first system
Short instrument name – name displayed to the left of this staff on subsequent systems
Amateur range – notes outside this range are colored dark yellow
Professional range – notes outside this range are colored red
Play transposition – interval to play back relative to written pitch (see chapter on *Transposition*)
Octave – octave to add to *Play transposition* interval
Up / Down – direction for *Play transposition*
Number of strings – number of strings (for stringed instruments with string data defined only; see *String data* in the chapter on *Tablature*)

Chapter 23

Transposition

MuseScore provides a number of different facilities for transposition. If you have written a piece in the key of E major and then decide you rather have it in $A\flat$, MuseScore can transpose your score or any selected range of it into any key or by any interval you specify. It can also automatically handle the transposition necessary when writing for transposing instruments – instruments that produce sounding pitches that are different from their written pitches.

Transposing a Selection

In the chapter on *Editing*, we have already seen a number of commands that MuseScore provides to transpose a selection by step or octave. The ↑ and ↓ keys – alone or in conjunction with Ctrl (Mac: Cmd) or Alt+Shift – will transpose the notes in the selection up or down a semitone, octave, or diatonic step. But these operations do not transpose the key signature or chord symbols – they affect the notes only. For a more complete transposition, we need the facility described in this section.

To transpose your score or a range of it, select a range you wish to transpose – or, if nothing is selected, the entire score will be transposed. Then go to Notes ⟩ Transpose, which will display the *Transpose* dialog.

This dialog contains a number of options to control the transposition to be performed.

Transpose Chromatically – keep the same relative intervals when transposing

> **By Key** – transpose into a specified key
> *Closest / Up / Down* – direction of transposition
> **By Interval** – transpose by a specified interval
> *Up / Down* – direction of transposition

Transpose key signatures – transpose any key signatures already present within the range (does not create a new key signature)

Transpose Diatonically – adjust intervals when transposing to keep the notes in the current key

> *Up / Down* – direction of transposition
> *Keep degree alterations* – do not convert notes with accidentals to diatonic pitches

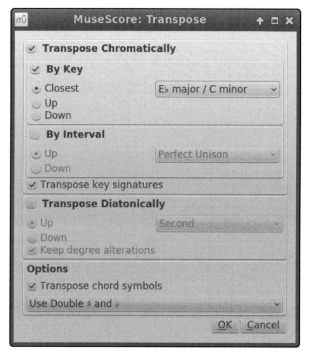

Transpose dialog

Options

Transpose chord symbols – transpose chord symbols as well as notes

Single ♯ and ♭ only / Use double ♯ and ♭ – allow double sharp and flat or respell

Transposing Instruments

Music for certain instruments – especially brass instruments like trumpets and horns, and woodwind instruments like clarinets and saxophones – is written at a different pitch than the instrument actually sounds. For example, alto saxophone sounds a major sixth lower than written, and French horn sounds a perfect fifth lower. This means that in order to produce the sound of a *G*, you would need to write an *E* for alto saxophone or a *D* for the French horn. So the following notes all produce the same sounding pitch:

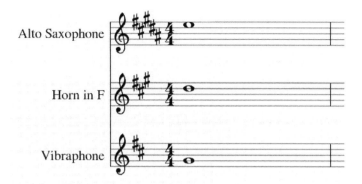

Switching between written and concert pitch

MuseScore allows you to easily switch the display of your score between written pitch and sounding pitch. The button that performs this function is labeled Concert Pitch, because that is the term used by players of these instruments to describe the sounding pitch. When the Concert Pitch button is off, your score displays using the written pitch, as shown above. But when you turn Concert Pitch on, your score displays using the sounding pitch.

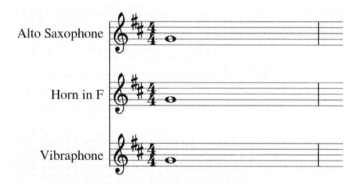

Notice that the key signature transposes as well. The actual sounding key of the piece is *D* major, and this is how it is displayed with Concert Pitch turned on. But this translates to *A* major for French horn and *B* major for alto saxophone, so that is how it was displayed with Concert Pitch turned off as in the previous example.

Whether Concert Pitch is turned off or on, your score will playback using the sounding pitch – the transposition affects the display only. So your score should always sound correct.

By default, when you create a new score, it will be displayed with Concert Pitch turned off. Unless you are more comfortable transposing for the various instruments yourself, you should immediately turn on Concert Pitch upon creating a new score that includes transposing instruments. Then you can enter notes at the desired sounding pitches. Leave it on until you are done entering the notes, then turn it off before doing any final formatting or before printing.

As discussed previously, MuseScore will highlight any pitches that are outside the playable ranges for their respective instruments. This check works correctly regardless of the state of the Concert Pitch button.

Changing the transposition for a staff

MuseScore knows the usual transposition for each instrument and its sets this up for you when you add a staff to your score. If you change the instrument assigned to the staff later as described below, MuseScore automatically updates the transposition information. So you should never normally need to alter the transposition settings yourself.

However, if for some reason a situation arises where you wish to override the default transposition for an instrument, the controls to do so can be found in the *Staff Properties* dialog, as described in *Changing Appearance and Behavior* in the chapter on *Staves and Instruments*.

Changing the enharmonic spelling of a note

There may be notes where you wish the transposed spelling to be "wrong" relative to the concert pitch spelling. For example, music for a $B\flat$ instrument normally is written a major second higher than it sounds. But if you have a score that includes an $A\sharp$ at concert pitch, you may wish to spell this as C rather than $B\sharp$ when transposed. MuseScore provides a special command to change the enharmonic spelling in the current mode only.

You may recall that the J command will change the enharmonic spelling of selected notes. This normally affects both the concert pitch and transposed spellings. So if you have Concert Pitch turned off, and you select a $B\sharp$ and press J, this will change the spelling to C, but the concert pitch spelling will also be changed, to $B\flat$.

If you wish to change the transposed spelling to C but leave the concert pitch spelling at $A\sharp$, use the Ctrl + J command instead of J.

Press Ctrl + J

You will then find if you enable concert pitch, the original spelling is retained.

Enable Concert Pitch

Chapter 24

Percussion

Unpitched percussion instruments – and drumsets in particular – use a somewhat different style of notation than most other instruments. MuseScore supports this type of notation, and provides a special *Drum input* mode to facilitate entering it. It also allows you to customize the particulars of how different instruments are notated.

Drum Notation

Before explaining how to create percussion notation, it helps to have a clear understanding of the concepts.

Individual unpitched percussion instruments are normally notated on a one-line staff. Many of these instruments use standard note heads, but a few use different note heads to indicate different playing techniques. Some use notes above and below the line to indicate different pitches.

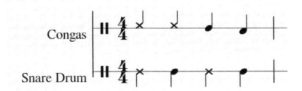

Drumsets are collections of multiple percussion instruments. Music for drumsets is normally notated on a five-line staff, with each staff line or space representing a different drum, and again, different note heads to indicate different playing techniques. It is also common to use multiple voices – voice 1 with stems up, voice 2 with stems down – to allow multiple rhythms to be notated clearly on the same staff.

In either case, the music is notated on a special percussion clef to make it clear the lines and spaces do not represent pitches in the usual sense. Unfortunately, there are no universal standards for which lines correspond to which drums, which note heads correspond to which playing techniques, or which notes to put in which voice.

By default, MuseScore employs a convention that is common in the US and some other countries. In this convention, notes near the bottom of the staff are for instruments played with the feet and are placed in voice 2 with stems down; the rest of the notes are for instruments played with the hands and are placed in voice 1 with stems up. Drums are notated with normal note heads, and cymbals are notated with "x" note heads. Other heads are used to indicate alternate playing techniques.

Within this basic set of guidelines, however, it seems everyone has different ideas on which drums or cymbals should be notated on which lines. And some people prefer an entirely different convention, such as one in which everything is notated in voice 1 with stems up. Luckily, MuseScore provides customization options that allow you to specify how you like your drum notation to work. See the section on *Changing Appearance and Behavior* below for more information.

> Music for drums in a jazz or pop/rock context often makes uses of slash notation, and MuseScore includes native support for this as well. See *Slash Notation* in the chapter on *Alternative Notation* for more information.

Percussion Staves

In order to enter percussion notation on a staff, it has to be designated as a percussion staff. You can add a percussion staff to your score when creating a new score, or at any time thereafter using [Edit ⟩ Instruments]. Any staff you add to your score from the *Unpitched Percussion* section of the instrument list will be added as a percussion staff.

The *Drumset* instrument defaults to a five-line staff; the other percussion instruments default to a one-line staff. You can override this by selecting a different staff type in that same dialog or by using *Staff Properties* dialog discussed in the chapter on *Staves and Instruments*.

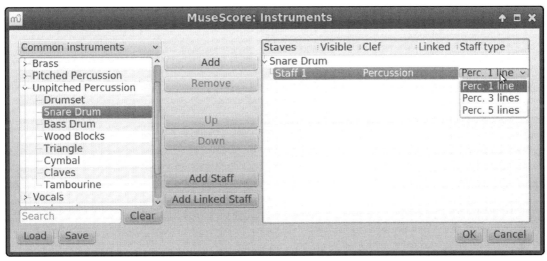

Unpitched percussion instruments

Drum Input Mode

Now that you have a percussion staff, you can enter percussion notation onto it. The process is somewhat different than for standard notation due to the unique nature of percussion notation, but still, you should begin by familiarizing yourself with the concepts presented in the chapter *Entering Notes and Rests*.

As with standard note entry, the first step in percussion note entry is to enter *Note input* mode by selecting a note or measure and then pressing N or clicking the N icon. When in *Note input* mode for a percussion staff, the drum palette should display at the bottom of the screen. This palette contains the notes defined for the instrument associated with that staff and lists the keyboard shortcuts where appropriate.

Drum palette

The basic steps after entering *Note input* mode are analogous to those for standard notation as well:

1. Select duration
2. Enter notes

Just as with standard notation, there are three ways of entering notes: with the mouse, with the computer keyboard, or via MIDI. But the specifics of how you enter the notes is different from standard notation no matter which entry method you select. Furthermore, the way MuseScore treats multiple voices is different for each of these note entry methods. The sections below will explain all of this.

Selecting duration

The process of selection duration is exactly the same as for standard notation, so I will refer you back to the corresponding section *Selecting Duration* in the chapter on *Entering Notes and Rests* for more information on this subject. But to summarize, you can click on the appropriate icon in the note input toolbar, or you can use the corresponding keyboard shortcuts (number keys 1 - 9).

Entering notes

Once you have selected the duration, you can enter the specific drum note you want. For each drum, MuseScore automatically selects the proper staff line and note head to use based on the drumset definition for the staff. As we will see below, multiple voices are handled differently accordingly to which note input method you choose.

Entering notes using the mouse

To enter a drum note using the mouse, select a palette icon and then click within the staff at the desired time position. It does not matter what staff line you click; the drum note you selected will be placed using the staff line and note head depicted in the icon. In the example below, the *Closed Hi-Hat* icon was selected first, as shown in the toolbar image above. This automatically selects the voice that is predefined for this drum in the drumset definition and sets the mouse cursor to an image of the predefined note head for this drum.

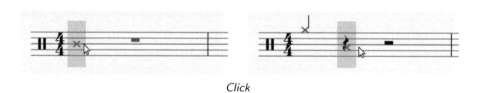

Click

Drum notes, like standard notes, are normally entered left to right for each voice, so you may need to enter leading rests before you can enter a note in the middle of a measure.

Click

If you wish to add a drum note in a voice other than the one predefined for that drum, simply change voices after clicking the palette icon but before entering the note into your score.

In the following example, I first selected the snare drum icon, then changed to voice 2 before entering the note.

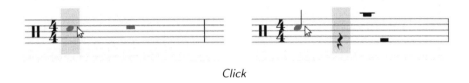

Click

Drum notes can be combined to form "chords" just as pitched notes can. To add a drum note to a chord, select the icon for the drum note you wish want to add, select the voice of the chord to which you are adding the note, then click the chord.

Click

You can also enter a drum note at the current cursor position by double-clicking the palette icon. However, this replaces any drum note already present at that position rather than adding to the chord.

Double-click Acoustic Snare icon

Drum entry on one-line and other staff types works the same way.

Entering notes using the computer keyboard

MuseScore allows you to use the keys [A]–[G] to enter drum notes. The drum palette shows the shortcuts that are defined by the current drumset. These shortcuts can be customized; see *Changing Appearance and Behavior* below. Pressing one of these shortcuts automatically selects that drum and enters the note into your score.

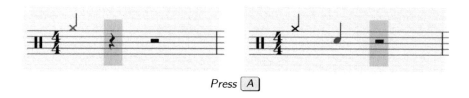

Press A

Drum note input using the keyboard always uses the voice predefined for that drum in the drumset definition for the staff. If it is not possible to enter a note in this voice at the current cursor position, the cursor will automatically back up to an appropriate position.

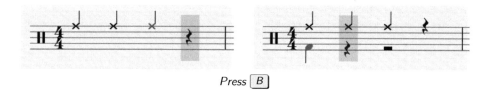

Press B

To add a note to a chord, move the selection cursor to that chord if necessary, and then press Shift while entering the note.

Press Shift + G

Even though only seven shortcuts can be defined, you can actually enter other drum notes by keyboard as well. Enter the closest note using its shortcut, then use the up and down arrow keys to cycle through the other notes in the order they are shown on the palette.

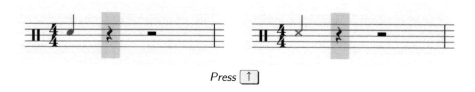

Press ↑

Entering notes using a MIDI device

If you have a MIDI input device such as a keyboard or drum pad, then you can use it to enter drum notes. Simply press the key, pad, or button corresponding to the drum you want, and the corresponding note will be placed in the score at the cursor position.

Play snare drum on MIDI device

When entering notes via MIDI, the line and note head are taken from the drumset definition, but the voice and stem direction are not. Instead, the currently selected voice is used, and stem direction is set automatically according to position on the staff – just as for standard notation.

Changing Appearance and Behavior

The customizations available for standard notation are available for drum notes and staves as well, so see the chapters *Entering Notes and Rests*, *Editing*, and *Staves and Instruments* for more information. But as discussed elsewhere in this chapter, many aspects of drum notation are customized in the drumset definition, and this is unique to percussion staves.

Editing a drumset definition

To edit the drumset definition for a staff, either right-click the staff and choose Edit Drumset, or click the Edit Drumset button within the drum palette while in *Note input* mode. The resulting *Edit Drumset* dialog allows you to define how each drum note is displayed and whether one of the available shortcuts can be used to enter it.

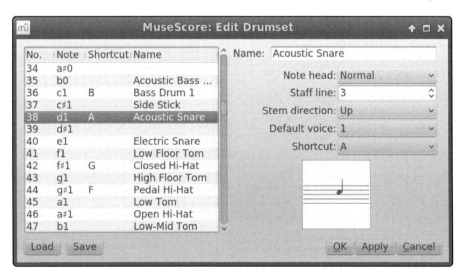

On the left is a list of the 128 possible MIDI pitch numbers. Each of these potentially corresponds to one drum sound, although many of them may not actually produce any sound in any given soundfont (see *Synthesizer* in *Playback and Audio Output*). On the right are the settings that define how the drum note corresponding to the selected MIDI pitch is displayed.

In the preceding image, we can see that MIDI pitch 38 is defined as *Acoustic snare drum* and will display with a normal note head on staff line 3 (second space from top – see below) with stem up, in voice 1 by default. The keyboard shortcut $\boxed{A}$ can be used to enter this note.

Most drumsets will not actually define drum notes for all 128 possible MIDI pitches. A drum note is defined only if its note head is set to something other than *invalid*. It normally makes sense to enter a name only for the drums that are actually defined by a drumset. This makes it easy to see which MIDI pitches in the list at left have defined drum notes.

To add a drum note to the drumset, or to modify the settings for an existing note in the drumset, select the MIDI pitch from the list at left and then define the various attributes on the right.

Name – name that appears in the drum palette tooltip and status bar
Note Head – note head group
Staff Line – staff line, where the lines and spaces are numbered consecutively (see below)
Stem Direction – *Auto, Up, Down*
Default Voice – voice to use when entering by mouse or keyboard
Shortcut – keyboard shortcut

A preview of the note as defined will display in the box below these settings.

The staff lines and spaces are numbered consecutively, and staff line 0 is always the top staff line. So in a five-line staff, the lines are numbered 0, 2, 4, 6, 8, and the spaces 1, 3, 5, 7. For a one-line staff, the line is 0. For a three-line staff, the lines are 0, 2, and 4. Spaces or ledger lines above or below the staff are numbered relative to this – one ledger line above any staff is -2, one ledger line below a three-line staff is 6, etc.

The mapping between MIDI pitch numbers and drum sounds depends on the specific soundfont you are using (see *Synthesizer* in *Playback and Audio Output*). However, most soundfonts you are likely to want to use – including the one provided with MuseScore – use a standard called General MIDI and have the same list of sounds at the same MIDI pitch numbers. See below for a list of drum sounds defined by General MIDI.

Saving and loading drumset definitions

The *Edit Drumset* dialog also contains $\boxed{\text{Load}}$ and $\boxed{\text{Save}}$ buttons. These enable you to save the current drumset definition to a file (with the extension *.drm*) or to load previously saved drumset files, thus allowing you to easily share drumset definitions between staves or scores.

MuseScore provides alternate drumset definitions for to handle a few specific needs. For example, the *drumset_fr.drm* file uses French names and conventions, whereas *orchestral.drm* works with the orchestral drumsets that you can select using the *Mixer*. You can find these drumsets by pressing the $\boxed{\text{Load}}$ button and navigating to the `templates` folder under your main installation folder.

General MIDI

The mapping between MIDI pitch numbers and drum sounds defined by General MIDI and used by MuseScore is as follows:

35   Bass Drum 2

36	Bass Drum 1
37	Side Stick/Rimshot
38	Snare Drum 1
39	Hand Clap
40	Snare Drum 2
41	Low Tom 2
42	Closed Hi-hat
43	Low Tom 1
44	Pedal Hi-hat
45	Mid Tom 2
46	Open Hi-hat
47	Mid Tom 1
48	High Tom 2
49	Crash Cymbal 1
50	High Tom 1
51	Ride Cymbal 1
52	Chinese Cymbal
53	Ride Bell
54	Tambourine
55	Splash Cymbal
56	Cowbell
57	Crash Cymbal 2
58	Vibra Slap
59	Ride Cymbal 2
60	High Bongo
61	Low Bongo
62	Mute High Conga
63	Open High Conga
64	Low Conga
65	High Timbale
66	Low Timbale
67	High Agogô
68	Low Agogô
69	Cabasa
70	Maracas
71	Short Whistle
72	Long Whistle
73	Short Güiro
74	Long Güiro
75	Claves
76	High Wood Block
77	Low Wood Block
78	Mute Cuíca
79	Open Cuíca
80	Mute Triangle
81	Open Triangle

Chapter 25

Tablature

Tablature (a.k.a. "tab") is a form of notation sometimes used for stringed instruments in which the lines represent strings and the symbols placed on those lines indicate frets. MuseScore allows you to create tablature staves and to enter notes onto them directly. It also supports linked staves (see the chapter on *Staves and Instruments*) so you can have your music displayed on a tablature staff as well as a standard staff and only have to enter it once. With linked staves, any notes entered onto one staff automatically appear on the other, so you can enter notes in standard notation and have them displayed in tablature notation or vice versa. Changes made on one staff are automatically reflected on the other as well.

Tablature notation

There are many different varieties of tablature, and MuseScore supports all the common ones – including three different forms of tablature for guitar and bass, tablatures for ukulele and for balalaika, and two different styles of Renaissance lute tablature. See *Tablature staff types* below for more information.

Tablature notation

Before explaining how to create tablature notation, it helps to have a clear understanding of the concepts.

String and fret

Tablature notation, like standard notation, is read from left to right, but the lines of the staff represent strings on the instrument rather than pitches. The top-most line generally indicates the highest string, although some people like to reverse that. A number placed on a line indicates you are to play that string at that fret, with "0" indicating the string is to be played open.

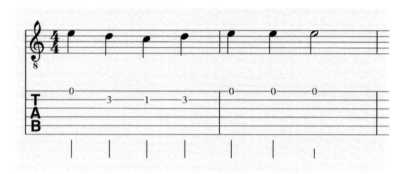

Many variations on this idea are possible. For example, in some styles of lute tablature, script letters are used instead of numbers to indicate frets, the fret marks are placed above the corresponding lines rather than directly on them.

MuseScore supports both of these styles and more; see *Tablature staff types*.

Rhythm

From the examples above, we can see that rhythm is indicated in different ways in different styles of tablature. Tablature for rock guitar often contains no indication of rhythm at all; a player is expected to have heard the piece and learn the rhythm by ear. However, it is also possible to indicate rhythms using stems that resemble standard notation.

Again, MuseScore supports a variety of different ways of indicating rhythm, as we will see in *Tablature staff types*.

Tablature Staves

In order to enter tablature notation on a staff, it has to be designated as a tablature staff. You can add a new tablature staff to a score, add a tablature staff that is linked to a standard staff, or convert an existing standard staff to tablature.

Adding a tablature staff

You can add a tablature staff to your score when creating a new score from scratch, or at any time thereafter using [Edit] ⟩ [Instruments]. For most instruments that use tablature notation, you will see both a standard and a tablature version in the instrument list. Simply select the tablature version.

You can also add a tablature staff to an existing instrument by selecting the existing staff in this same dialog, clicking the [Add Staff] button, then selecting one of the tablature types from the *Staff type* drop-down menu.

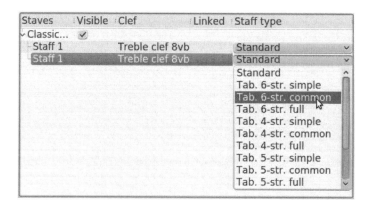

See the chapter on *Staves and Instruments* for more information on adding staves.

Adding a linked tablature staff

If you wish to have your music displayed both in tablature and in standard notation, the process is similar.

1. Go to [Edit ⟩ Instruments]
2. Add the standard instrument if you have not done so already
3. Select the standard staff
4. Click [Add Linked Staff] button
5. Select the new linked staff
6. Change staff type to one of the tablature types using the drop-down menu

If you prefer, you can enter the staves in the opposite order – first the tablature staff, then a linked standard staff. You can also rearrange the staves after adding them. See the chapter on *Staves and Instruments* for more information.

Once you have created linked standard and tablature staves, any notes added to one automatically appear on the other. If you are more comfortable with tablature than standard notation, you can enter notes onto the tablature staff and they will automatically appear in standard notation on the other. Conversely, if you are more comfortable with standard notation, you can enter notes that way and they will automatically appear in tablature as well. MuseScore will automatically attempt to figure out appropriate string and fret combinations for the notes in your standard staff. There is no guarantee the automatic choices are optimal, or even playable, however!

Converting an existing staff into a tablature staff

You can convert an existing standard staff into a tablature staff. The easiest way to do to do that is using [Edit ⟩ Instruments] again. Simply select the staff then change the staff type using the drop-down menu as shown previously.

The staff has to be for an instrument that is defined to allow tablature, since it has to have string data defined in order for many of the tablature commands to work. See *String data* below for more information. However, if the current instrument does not have string data, you can first change to an instrument that does. Right-click the staff and choose Staff Properties, then click the Change Instrument button. Even if you choose one of the tablature versions of an instrument, this will not immediately change the staff type, but now that the instrument has appropriate string data, you can go to Edit ⟩ Instruments and change the staff type there.

Tablature input mode

Once you have a tablature staff, you can enter tablature notation onto it. While this is done via similar basic steps as standard notation, the details are different. Even the duration and navigation shortcuts work differently in *TAB input* mode than in standard *Note input* or *Drum input* modes. However, even though there are differences, there are many more similarities, so you should start by familiarizing yourself with the concepts presented in the chapter *Entering Notes and Rests*. Most features – like tuplets, for example – work exactly the same way as for standard notation and hence are not discussed further here. Instead, we will focus on the differences.

Just as you do for standard or percussion notation, you begin note entry by clicking in a tablature staff and pressing N or the corresponding toolbar icon N to enter *TAB input* mode. After that, the steps for tablature note entry are:

1. Select duration
2. Select string
3. Enter fret
4. Repeat steps 2-3 as necessary to add more notes to chord
5. Move cursor to next input location

Selecting duration

The process of selecting duration is similar to that used for standard notation. However, because the number keys by themselves are used to enter frets when in *TAB input* mode, these shortcuts are not available for selecting duration. Instead, if you wish to use keyboard shortcuts for duration, you need to press Shift while pressing the desired number key, or use the keys on the numeric keypad if your computer has one.

So for example, to select a duration of a quarter note (crotchet), you would press Shift + 5 . The toolbar works in the usual way, as do dots, ties, and tuplets. See *Entering Notes and Rests* for more information.

String

When you are in tablature entry mode, the cursor indicates not just the time position but also the specific string on which a note can be entered. To select a different string, use the ↑ and ↓ cursor keys.

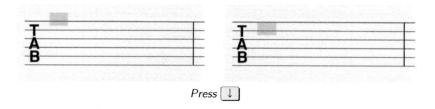

Press ↓

Fret

Once you have selected the duration and string, you may enter the specific fret you want. The most direct way to do this is to simply type the number.

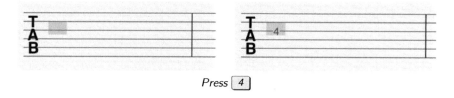

Press 4

You can enter two digit numbers by simply typing the two digits normally. MuseScore will not allow you to enter a number larger than the number of frets defined for the instrument (see *String data* below).

Instead of typing a fret number, you can also simply click the line itself to enter a "0" at the cursor position.

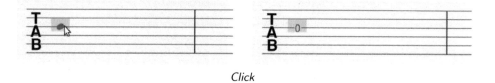

Click

You can then change the fret number by pressing [Alt]+[Shift]+[↑] and [Alt]+[Shift]+[↓], as discussed below.

For lute tablature, you can type fret letters instead of numbers, and if you have selected the French lute staff type, it will be rendered using an appropriate font.

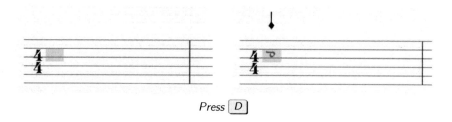

Press D

Lute tablature traditionally does not use the letter "j", but since the shortcut I is already used in MuseScore to access the *Instruments* dialog, you can use J to enter an "i".

Chords

You may have noticed that the cursor does not automatically advance after entry of a note in tablature as it does for standard notation. That is because in tablature, chords will be very common, and needing to back up the cursor and then change strings would make entry of chords a lot of work. So instead, you can enter a chord by simply changing strings after entering one note, then entering another note.

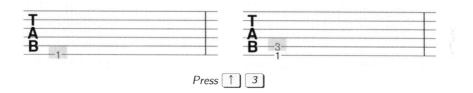

Press ↑   3

Repeat as desired to add more notes. Of course, you can only add one note per string. Attempting to enter another note on a string that is already used will simply replace the existing note.

Navigation

As mentioned above, the cursor does not automatically advance after adding a note in tablature entry mode. To advance the cursor, press the → cursor key.

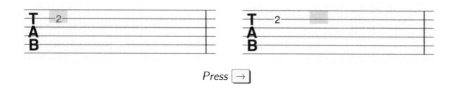

Press →

Should you need to back up, the ← cursor key accomplishes that. And just as with standard note entry, you can use Ctrl + → and Ctrl + ← (Mac: Cmd + → and Cmd + ←) to move the cursor a full measure at a time.

Ghost Notes

A note on a tablature staff can be converted into a ghost note by pressing the shortcut Shift + X .

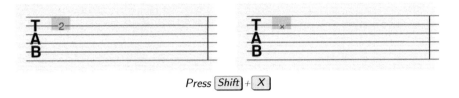

Press Shift + X

Rests

Rests are not displayed in some forms of tablature, although they are in the "Full" styles (see *Tablature staff types*, below). In any event, it may be necessary to enter a rest even though it is not displayed, such as to start a measure with a note somewhere other than the first beat. Since the keyboard shortcut 0 is already used to enter an open string, rests in tablature are instead entered using the keyboard shortcut ; (semicolon).

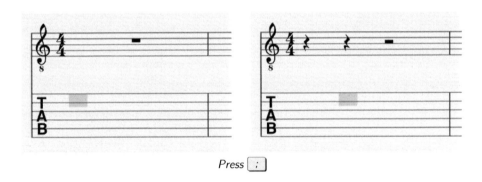

Press ;

Because it makes no sense to add more notes to the rest, the cursor does advance automatically after entering a rest.

Multiple voices

Tablature notation does not normally involve the use of multiple voices – complex polytonal music is usually better suited for standard notation. However, MuseScore does allow you to enter multiple voices onto a tablature staff, and music originally entered with multiple voices on a standard staff will be rendered as well as possible if converted or linked to a tablature staff.

When using one of the *Full* or *Common* tablature styles (see *Tablature staff types*, below), multiple voices will be indicated with stems up or above the staff for voice 1 and down or below for voice 2, similar to how music is notated on a standard staff.

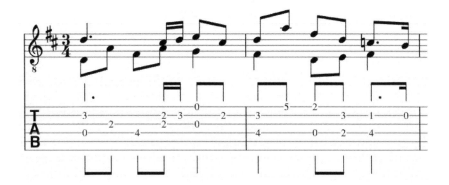

Any more voices than this, however, and it becomes more confusing.

The Simple style – which uses no stems at all – might be more suitable, even though it contains less information.

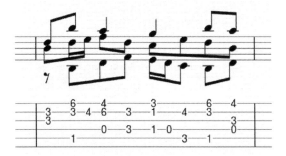

On the other hand, given that the notation of note lengths in guitar music tends to be less significant than in music for other instruments (most notes are assumed to ring until they decay naturally), this same passage could have been entered more simply and just as effectively with only two voices, by combining the notes of the top two voices into chords.

Regardless of which style you use or how you choose to assign notes to voices, actually entering notes in multiple voices on a tablature staff works just as it does for a standard staff. After entering tablature entry mode, press one of the voice icons on the note input toolbar or use one of the keyboard shortcuts [Ctrl]+[Alt]+[1] - [Ctrl]+[Alt]+[4] (Mac: [Cmd]+[Alt]+[1] - [Cmd]+[Alt]+[4]). Notes you enter will be entered in that voice until you change voices or leave *TAB input* mode.

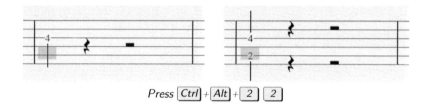

Press [Ctrl]+[Alt]+[2] [2]

Editing tablature

As with standard notation, there are some changes you can make while in *TAB input* mode and other changes that you can make while in *Normal* mode.

Making changes in TAB input mode

While you are in *TAB input* mode, you can move the cursor using the cursor keys as follows:

- [←] – move cursor to previous note or rest
- [→] – move cursor to next note or test
- [Ctrl]+[←] – move cursor to previous measure
- [Ctrl]+[→] – move cursor to next measure
- [↑] – move cursor to string above
- [↓] – move cursor to string below

With the cursor on a note, you can modify it using any of the following keys, several of which work the same as for standard notation:

- Delete – delete note
- Shift + ← – exchange with previous note or rest
- Shift + → – exchange with next note or rest
- Alt + Shift + ↑ – raise pitch (increase fret number or move note to next higher string)
- Alt + Shift + ↓ – lower pitch (decrease fret number or move note to next lower string)
- Ctrl + ↑ – move note to next higher string if possible
- Ctrl + ↓ – move note to next lower string if possible
- Shift + X – toggle ghost note

The behavior of Alt + Shift + ↑ and Alt + Shift + ↓ takes the tuning of the instrument into account (see *String data* below). For instance, on a guitar in standard tuning, playing the B string at fret 5 produces the same pitch as playing the high E string at fret 0. Using Alt + Shift + ↑ automatically takes this into account when it raises the pitch. It increases the fret number until you reach the pitch of the next string, and then it switches strings for you.

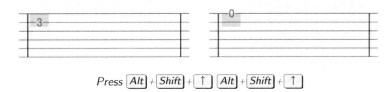

Press Alt + Shift + ↑   Alt + Shift + ↑

Similarly, lowering the pitch using Shift + ↓ decreases the fret number until you reach 0, and then it switches strings for you.

Ctrl + ↑ and Ctrl + ↓ (Mac: Cmd + ↑ and Cmd + ↓) also take the tuning into account when moving a note to a different string, so that the pitch remains the same.

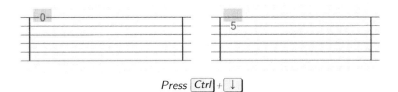

Press Ctrl + ↓

Making changes in Normal mode

Most other changes require you to leave *TAB input* mode, and this works just as it does for standard notation for the most part. For example, to change duration of a single selected note or chord, simply press the appropriate duration key or use the standard duration shortcut (without [Shift] – that is only needed while in *TAB input* mode). Working with selections – including copy and paste – also works just as it does for standard notation. So be sure to read the chapter *Editing* to learn the basic concepts.

There are a few special commands for tablature while in *Normal* mode:

- [↑] – raise pitch (increase fret number)

- [↓] – lower pitch (decrease fret number)

- [Alt]+[Shift]+[↑] – raise pitch (increase fret number or move note to next higher string)

- [Alt]+[Shift]+[↓] – lower pitch (decrease fret number or move note to next lower string)

- [Ctrl]+[↑] – move note to next higher string if possible

- [Ctrl]+[↓] – move note to next lower string if possible

- [Shift]+[X] – toggle ghost note

Changing Appearance and Behavior

The basic customizations available for other types of notes, such as position and visibility, are available for tablature notes as well, so see the chapter *Editing* for more information. Similarly, basic staff customizations (such as the long and short names and staff line color) are available for tablature staves just as for any others; see the chapter *Staves and Instruments* for more information. But there are a number of customizations unique to tablature. These are controlled by the staff type and the string data, which are described below.

Tablature staff types

MuseScore provides a number of predefined tablature staff types that control details like how rhythms are notated, whether frets are displayed as numbers or letters, the order of the strings, and more. We have already seen how you can change staff types by going to [Edit ⟩ Instruments] and using the *Staff type* drop-down menu.

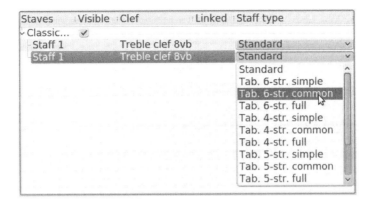

These predefined staff types should be sufficient for most purposes. However, MuseScore also allows you to customize the individual settings for each staff.

Predefined tablature staff types

MuseScore provides three predefined styles each for guitar, banjo, and bass tablature, two different predefined styles of lute tablature, and two more predefined styles for ukulele and balalaika that are based on the *Common* style for guitar and bass.

Simple (guitar, banjo, bass)   The *Simple* style includes numbers for the frets only, with no indication of rhythm.

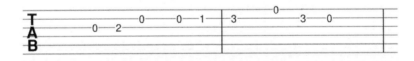

Common (guitar, banjo, bass, ukulele, balalaika)   The *Common* style adds stems below the staff to indicate rhythms. Eighth notes are indicated with flags or beams as appropriate; half notes with shorter stems. Rests are not indicated.

Full (guitar, banjo, bass) The *Full* style represents rhythm more completely, including time signatures and rests. Because rhythm is a more integral part of this style of tablature, the stems are connected to the frets rather than being written below the staff. Half notes are indicated with slashes through the stems.

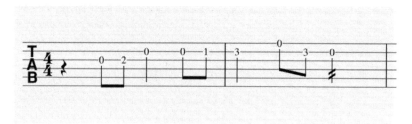

French (lute) In the *French* style, letters are used instead of numbers for the frets, with "a" indicating an open string, "b" indicating the first fret, "c" indicating the second fret, and so forth. The letter "j" is not used; the ninth fret is denoted by "k". The fret marks are placed in the spaces above the line for the corresponding string. Rhythms are indicated with symbols representing note values placed above the staff, but only where the duration changes. Rests are not indicated.

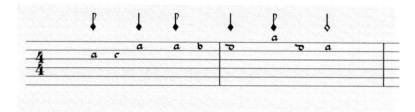

Italian (lute) In Italian lute tablature, frets are indicated with numbers on the lines as in modern guitar tablature, but the lines are reversed (highest string is the lowest line). Rhythms are indicated using symbols representing note values placed above the staff where the duration changes. Rests are indicated using symbols placed directly on the staff rather than above it.

Custom types

If one of the predefined tablature staff types does not suit your requirements, you can customize the settings for any particular staff by right-clicking the staff, choosing Staff Properties , and then clicking the Advanced Style Properties button. This brings up the *Edit Staff Properties* dialog.

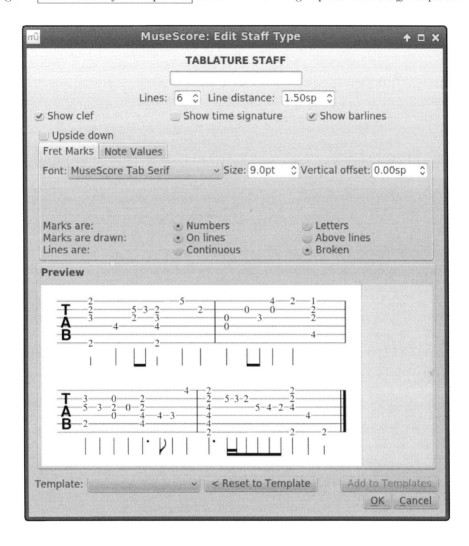

This dialog contains a number of different options, most of which are grouped into tabs for *Fret Marks* and *Note Values*.

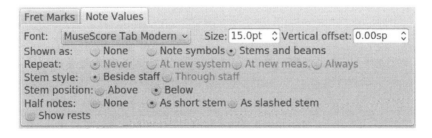

- *Upside down* – display highest string on bottom instead of on top

- **Fret Marks**

  Font – font for fret marks

  Size – size for fret marks

  Vertical offset – vertical offset for fret marks

  Marks are – *Numbers* or *Letters*

  Marks are drawn – *On lines* or *Above lines*

  Line are – *Continuous* (staff lines drawn through fret marks) or *Broken* (staff lines are broken for fret marks)

- **Note Values**

  Font – font for *Note symbols*

  Size – size for *Note symbols*

  Vertical offset – vertical offset for *Note symbols*

  Shown as – *None*, *Note symbols*, or *Stems and beams*

  Repeat – controls whether note symbols for repeated values are shown *Never*, *At new system*, *At new measure*, or *Always*

  Stem style – *Beside staff* or *Through staff* (for *Stems and beams*)

  Stem position – *Above* or *Below* staff (for *Stems and beams* with *Beside staff*)

  Half notes – *None*, *As short stem*, or *As slashed stem* (for *Stems and beams*)

  Show rests – controls whether or not rests are displayed

This dialog shows a preview of the results produced by the current settings, which can help in understanding how these settings will work together.

Underneath these options is the *Template* drop-down menu, which allows you to quickly change all settings in the dialog to those from a different staff type. Select the desired template and press the $\boxed{\text{Reset to Template}}$ button. This has the same effect as changing staff type in the *Instruments* dialog.

Note there is also an $\boxed{\text{Add to Templates}}$ button, but it is grayed out. Future versions of MuseScore may allow you define and re-use custom staff types.

String data

While it may not be common to need to customize the actual staff types, you will need to customize string data any time you wish to write tablature for an instrument using non-standard tuning (a.k.a. "scordatura"). The default tuning for each instrument is defined in *instruments.xml*, which can be customized as described in *Score* in the chapter on *Customization*. However, unless you know you will *always* want to use a particular non-standard tuning, it is better to leave the defaults in *instruments.xml* alone but instead override them for a particular staff. This is done by right-clicking the staff, choosing $\boxed{\text{Staff Properties}}$, and then clicking the $\boxed{\text{String Data}}$ button to display the *String Data* dialog.

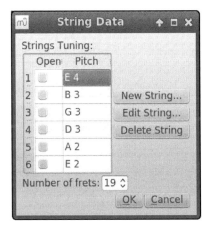

This dialog allows you to set the number of strings and the tuning for each, so MuseScore knows how to associate string and fret information with actual pitches. It also allows you to set the *Number of frets*, which MuseScore uses to prevent you from entering too high a fret number when creating tablature notation.

To change the tuning for an existing string, select the string and press the Edit String button. The *Note Selection* dialog will appear, allowing you to select the tuning for that string.

	C	C#	D	E♭	E	F	F#	G	A♭	A	B♭	B	»C
Octave 8	C 8	C# 8	D 8	E♭ 8	E 8	F 8	F# 8	G 8	A♭ 8	A 8	B♭ 8	B 8	
Octave 7	C 7	C# 7	D 7	E♭ 7	E 7	F 7	F# 7	G 7	A♭ 7	A 7	B♭ 7	B 7	C 8
Octave 6	C 6	C# 6	D 6	E♭ 6	E 6	F 6	F# 6	G 6	A♭ 6	A 6	B♭ 6	B 6	C 7
Octave 5	C 5	C# 5	D 5	E♭ 5	E 5	F 5	F# 5	G 5	A♭ 5	A 5	B♭ 5	B 5	C 6
Octave 4	C 4	C# 4	D 4	E♭ 4	E 4	F 4	F# 4	G 4	A♭ 4	A 4	B♭ 4	B 4	C 5
Octave 3	C 3	C# 3	D 3	E♭ 3	E 3	F 3	F# 3	G 3	A♭ 3	A 3	B♭ 3	B 3	C 4
Octave 2	C 2	C# 2	D 2	E♭ 2	E 2	F 2	F# 2	G 2	A♭ 2	A 2	B♭ 2	B 2	C 3
Octave 1	C 1	C# 1	D 1	E♭ 1	E 1	F 1	F# 1	G 1	A♭ 1	A 1	B♭ 1	B 1	C 2
Octave 0	C 0	C# 0	D 0	E♭ 0	E 0	F 0	F# 0	G 0	A♭ 0	A 0	B♭ 0	B 0	C 1
Octave -1	C -1	C# -1	D -1	E♭ -1	E -1	F -1	F# -1	G -1	A♭ -1	A -1	B♭ -1	B -1	C 0

For reference, a standard guitar is tuned from low *E* in octave 2 to high *E* in octave 4.

Enabling the *Open* option for a string tells MuseScore that the string cannot normally be fretted, so the algorithms that try to determine appropriate string and fret combinations for notes will not try to fret that string.

The *String Data* dialog also allows you to add and remove strings. To add a string below the selected string, press the New String button. This will display the same *Note Selection* dialog to allow you to select the tuning for the new string. To remove a string, press the $\boxed{\text{Delete String}}$ button.

Because new strings are always added below the selected string, adding a new high string requires you to edit the existing top string to set it to the new desired highest pitch, then add a new string below it to replace the old high string.

Chapter 26

Alternative Notation

In addition to *Percussion* and *Tablature*, MuseScore provides some support for a few other specific styles of notation. These are described in this chapter.

Slash Notation

There are two basic styles of slash notation supported by MuseScore. In one style, measures are filled with slashes, one per beat, to indicate that a musician is supposed to improvise his part (whether solo or accompaniment) as he or she sees fit. This style is created with the Edit ⟩ Tools ⟩ Fill With Slashes command in MuseScore. In the other style, specific rhythms are indicated. This second style can appear on its own within the staff or it can appear outside the staff combined with standard notation. The former variety is sometimes referred to as *rhythmic notation*; the latter as *accent notation*. Both of these varieties can be created with the Edit ⟩ Tools ⟩ Toggle Rhythmic Slash Notation command in MuseScore.

When using these commands to create slash notation, MuseScore will not normally transpose the slashes (see *Transposition*), nor will it play them back.

Fill With Slashes

To fill a measure or range with slashes, select the range and go to Edit ⟩ Tools ⟩ Fill With Slashes. Partial measure selections are allowed.

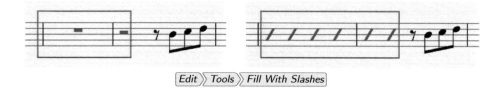

Edit ⟩ Tools ⟩ Fill With Slashes

The slashes are normally placed in voice 1, but if there are already notes present in the measure, they are preserved, and the slashes are placed in the next available voice.

Edit ⟩ Tools ⟩ Fill With Slashes

In compound meters, dotted quarter notes are used for the beat.

Rhythmic Slash Notation

To create rhythmic slash notation – where the slashes indicate the desired rhythm rather than beats in general – first enter notes for the rhythm, then select the range and go to Edit ⟩ Tools ⟩ Toggle Rhythmic Slash Notation.

Edit ⟩ Tools ⟩ Toggle Rhythmic Slash Notation

The original pitches are actually preserved, so if you run this command again, it will restore them.

MuseScore places the notes vertically according to a simple rule: notes in voices 1 and 2 are turned into full sized slashes within the staff; notes in voices 3 or 4 are turned into small slashes above or below the staff. So to create accent notation, enter the notes you wish to preserve into voices 1 or 2, the notes for the accents into voice 3, and use the *Selection Filter* (see the chapter on *Making Selections*) to exclude voices 1 and/or 2 before running Edit ⟩ Tools ⟩ Toggle Rhythmic Slash Notation.

As mentioned in the chapter on *Percussion*, music for drums often uses a combination of slash fill and accent notation. This is very easy to create in MuseScore as follows:

1. Enter notes for accents in voice 1 (e.g., using snare drum)
2. Select range
3. Edit ⟩ Voices ⟩ Exchange Voice 1-3
4. Edit ⟩ Tools ⟩ Toggle Rhythmic Slash Notation
5. Edit ⟩ Tools ⟩ Fill With Slashes

This places the accents above the staff and the beat slashes within the staff. In accordance with common conventions, the accents on percussion staves use regular note heads rather than slashes, and they are placed directly above the staff rather than floating slightly above as they are on standard staves.

Changing Appearance and Behavior

The slashes created in both styles of slash notation are actually just normal notes whose note heads have been set to *Slash* (except for drum accents, which are left *Normal*, as shown above). The heads can be overridden using the *Head group* setting in the *Inspector*. The *Fix to line* setting is what prevents the slash notation from transposing. The specific line used can be set using the *Line* setting.

> Remember, after selecting a range of music, you can restrict the selection to just the notes by clicking the Notes button in the *Inspector*. See the chapter on *Editing* for more information.

Shape Note Music

Shape note music notation is a system that associates each scale degree with a specific note head. MuseScore supports several different shape note systems through the use of a plugin. See *Plugins* in the chapter on *Customization* for more information on plugins. Once the *Shape notes* plugin has been downloaded and installed into MuseScore, converting standard notation into shape note notation is as simple as running the plugin. A dialog appears that allows you to choose between several different systems. The following examples shows the results of the *7 shape notes* option.

Plugins ⟩⟩ Notes ⟩⟩ Shape Notes , *7 shape notes*

Early Music

While MuseScore does not contain a full set of tools for notating Gregorian chant or other Renaissance and earlier forms of notation in anything like their original forms, it does provide a few features that can help in producing modern transcriptions of this type of music.

Mensuration

The term *mensuration* (also *menusural notation*) refers to the systems of indicating rhythms that were in use during the Renaissance. It is beyond the scope of this book to try to explain the different systems that existed, and as mentioned, MuseScore does not truly support these notations in their original formats. However, there are some features that you might find useful if you already have some idea of what you would like to do and are wondering how to accomplish or simulate it in MuseScore.

Time signatures

MuseScore uses the modern concept of a time signature as defining the length of a measure, not the older concept of tempus and prolatio as defining the lengths of the breve and minim. However, you can force a standard time signature to display using one of the older mensural symbols by right-clicking the time signature, choosing Time Signature Properties , and selecting the appropriate symbol under *Appearance*.

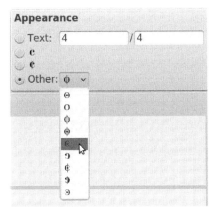

While nothing will change in the behavior or interpretation of the music, the time signature will be displayed using the selected symbol.

Meterless music

Much music of the era was notated with no time signature in the modern sense, and no barlines. In MuseScore, you can create this effect by notating your music in 4/4 but using the commands Edit ⟩ Measure ⟩ Join Measures and Edit ⟩ Measure ⟩ Split Measure to create one long measure for each system.

Edit ⟩ Measure ⟩ Join Measures

For more information on these commands, see *Splitting and Joining Measures* in the chapter on *Measure Operations*.

The time signature itself can be suppressed by right-clicking a staff, choosing Staff Properties, and turning off the *Show time signature* option.

You can also hide barlines individually (press $\boxed{V}$ or use the *Inspector, Visible*) or for an entire staff (*Staff Properties, Show barlines*).

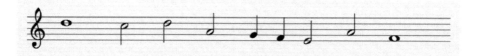

Mensurstrich

Mensurstrich is a form of notation that uses barlines between staves rather than within staves as a compromise between early and modern styles of notation. To create mensurstrich in MuseScore:

1. Style ⟩ General ⟩ Display note values across measure bar
2. Double-click a barline
3. Shift +drag handles to place barline between staves

The *Display note values across measure bar* option is experimental and may not always work, but it is intended to allow long notes that would be tied across the barline to be shown with their full value.

Note heads

While MuseScore does not contain a full set of early music note heads, it does support the square brevis that was commonly used instead of the more modern breve. To enable this, select a breve and use the *Inspector* to change the *Head group* to *Alt. Brevis*.

Set Head group to Alt. Brevis

Ambitus

MuseScore supports the ambitus symbol used to indicate the range of each staff. See *Ambitus* in the chapter on *Articulations and Other Symbols* for information on how to use this symbol.

Figured Bass

MuseScore provides a full-featured figured bass facility. See the chapter *Figured Bass* for more information.

Modified Stave Notation

The British organization Royal National Institute of Blind People (RNIB) has developed a set of guidelines for the production of large-print scores for the visually impaired. In Modified Stave Notation (MSN), the music is enlarged in general, but the proportions are altered to increase readability. For example, while notes are physically larger, the horizontal spacing is not increased as much as the vertical, and it is usually printed in landscape mode, in order to fit as many notes possible per system and thereby reduce the number of times your eyes have to track back to the beginning of the line. Smaller symbols are enlarged more proportionally than symbols that are already large. The guidelines also help minimize the size and number of pages required over what would result from a simple scaling, and symbols are placed in consistent positions where possible so the reader is less likely to miss them.

For example, here is an excerpt from a Mozart sonata that uses default settings in MuseScore:

Here is that same excerpt produced in MuseScore according to the MSN guidelines:

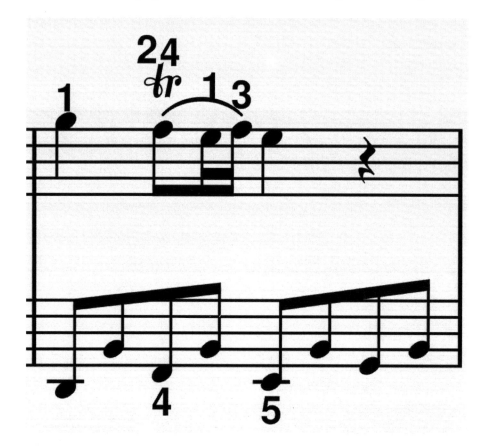

MuseScore has worked with RNIB to support as many of these guidelines as possible, so you can create scores in MSN by simply changing a few settings. The guidelines are subjective and finding the right settings for any given reader can be a matter of trial and error. But some of the settings you might wish to look at include:

- Layout ⟩ Page Settings

Page size
Landscape
Staff space

- `Style` ⟫ `General` ⟫ `Measure`

Spacing
Minimum note distance
Staff line thickness

- `Style` ⟫ `General` ⟫ `Barlines`

Barline thickness
End barline thickness
Double barline thickness

- `Style` ⟫ `General` ⟫ `Notes`

Dot size
Stem thickness
Ledger line thickness
Ledger line length

- `Style` ⟫ `General` ⟫ `Beams`

Beam thickness
Flatten all beams

- `Style` ⟫ `General` ⟫ `Slurs/Ties`

Line thickness at end
Line thickness middle
Minimum tie length

- `Style` ⟫ `General` ⟫ `Articulations, Ornaments`

Articulation size

In addition, the various text style settings under `Style` ⟫ `Text` can be worth looking at. MuseScore gives you control over many more settings that could be relevant as well, so check out the Changing Appearance and Behavior section of different chapters in this book to get an idea of what else is possible.

When you are done, you can save your modified settings via `Style` ⟫ `Save Style` and then load them into other scores via `Style` ⟫ `Load Style`, and you can specify this style to be used by default for all new scores in `Edit` ⟫ `Preferences` ⟫ `Score`. You can also save your score into your `Templates` folder and use it as a template for the creation of future scores.

Chapter 27

Other Editing Tools

There are a few editing commands provided by MuseScore that do not fit particularly well into any other chapter, so they will be covered here.

Explode

When writing for a group of related instruments, it is not uncommon to have passages where the parts have different pitches but the same rhythms. It can often be easiest to create the passages by first entering all parts onto one staff, then separating them out later. MuseScore provides a command to automate this process if you have written the parts as chords. If you have instead used multiple voices, there is no single command for this, but it can be done through creative use of other commands.

Exploding from chords

To explode a series of chords into individual notes on separate staves, first enter the chords on the topmost staff of the group. Then select the passage and go to Edit ⟩⟩ Tools ⟩⟩ Explode . The notes of the chords will be exploded onto the staves below.

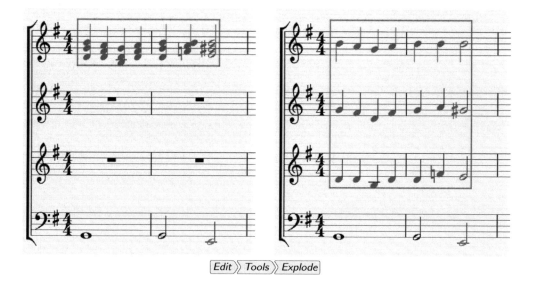

Exploding a staff in the this way will use as many staves as there are notes in the largest chord. If you would rather restrict the staves used, you can select just the staves you wish to use, and if there are extra notes, they will be ignored.

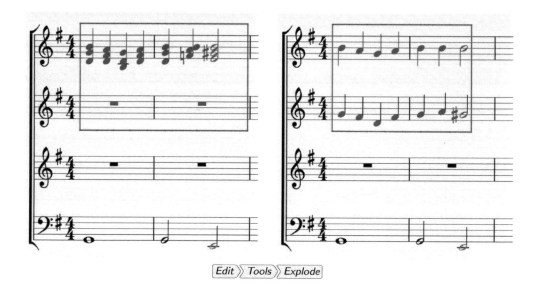

If on the other hand you select more staves than there are notes, the parts will be doubled as necessary.

Exploding from multiple voices

The *Explode* command does not work with multiple voices, but it is still possible to achieve the same effect if you have music on a single staff with multiple voices. Say you have a staff with two voices (voice 1 and voice 2) that you wish to separate into individual staves. You can do this via copy, paste, voice exchange, and the selection filter as follows:

1. Select passage to explode
2. Ctrl + C (Mac: Cmd + C) to copy
3. Click in destination staff
4. Ctrl + V (Mac: Cmd + V) to paste
5. Edit ≫ Voices ≫ Exchange Voice 1-2
6. Select the passage in both staves
7. Press F6 if necessary to display the *Selection Filter*
8. Exclude *Voice 1* in the *Selection Filter*
9. Press Delete to remove the contents of voice 2, keeping voice 1

The following images illustrate the process:

Copy to destination staff, exchange voices

Delete contents, keeping voice 1

The same technique can be extended to other voices as well.

When using the *Selection Filter* to exclude voice 1, it is important to remember to
enable it again when you are done, or else you will have trouble making selections!

Implode

Implode is the converse operation of explode – going from individual lines on separate staves or
in separate voices to a series of chords in one staff. MuseScore provides a command for this as
well.

Imploding from separate staves

To implode parts that were originally entered onto separate staves, enter the lines onto separate
staves, select the passage on all staves, and go to Edit ⟩ Tools ⟩ Implode . MuseScore will combine
the lines into chords on the top staff – the opposite of *Explode*.

Ideally, the parts should be identical in rhythm. If they are not, MuseScore will simply ignore notes that it cannot combine into chords on the top staff.

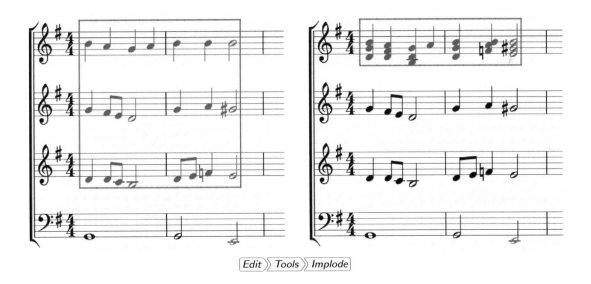

Imploding from multiple voices

You can also use Edit 〉 Tools 〉 Implode to combine multiple voices of one staff into chords on voice 1. As with imploding from separate staves, ideally the rhythms should be identical. But if a note from voice 2-4 cannot be added to a chord in voice 1, the note is left in its original voice, so the end result should still contain all the notes of the original.

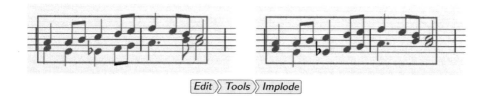

Chapter 28

Parts

A score may involve multiple instruments, and they are normally all displayed together one above the other, as we have seen in the chapter on *Staves and Instruments* (and indeed, in examples throughout this book). However, when it comes time for musicians to play your music, you will want to generate separate parts for each instrument in your score. MuseScore provides a powerful *linked parts* facility in which your parts can be displayed and printed individually, and changes to the score are automatically reflected in the parts (and vice versa).

In the following illustration, I have taken advantage of the View ⟩ Documents Side By Side option to show the score in one pane and one of the parts in the other:

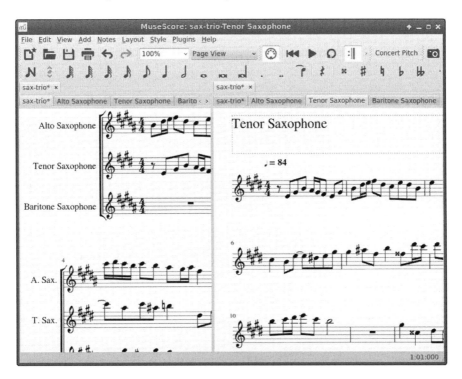

Creating Parts

In most cases, MuseScore can handle all details of part creation for you. Simply go to [File ≫ Parts] and press the [New All] button. MuseScore automatically defines one part for every instrument in your score, each named according to the *Part name* for that instrument (see the chapter on *Staves and Instruments*).

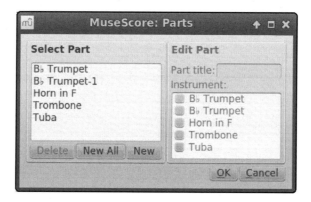

While this dialog box is still open, you can customize the part definitions as you see fit. You can delete parts you do not need using the [Delete] button, add new parts individually using the [New] button, rename a part using the *Part title* box, and change which instruments are assigned to which parts using the checkboxes in the list at right.

The instrument list allows you to produce a part containing the staves for multiple instruments. This might be useful, for instance, in a score for choir and instrumental ensemble, where you might want to generate a part containing all the vocal staves but none of the instrument staves.

You can also have the same instrument in multiple parts. For instance, you might want separate parts for all instruments in an orchestra, but also create an additional part for the winds as a section, another for brass, and another for strings. These parts might never be printed, but it might be convenient to be able to work with the parts in this way.

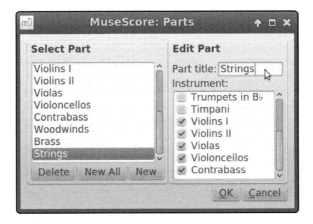

Again, though, in most cases, simply hitting the New All button is all you will need.

When you are done defining the parts, press OK to actually create them. You will now see separate tabs for each part.

The parts are automatically saved as part of your score, so there is no need to save them separately. Whether you are viewing the score or one of the parts, when you save, the score and all parts are saved together in the same file. However, the File ⟩ Save As and File ⟩ Export Parts commands both allow you to save a separate copy of one or more parts if you like. See the chapter on *File Operations* for more information.

Because your score and the parts are linked, it is not necessary to wait until you are done with your score before creating parts. You can create parts at any time, and as you continue to work on the score, the parts are automatically updated. However, especially for large scores, you might find it advantageous to wait until you are mostly done editing before creating parts, as performance can be a little sluggish on large scores with parts.

Once the parts have been created, you can still return to the *Parts* dialog to add or remove parts. But for parts that have already been created, you will no longer be able to edit the part titles or change which instruments are associated with which parts. This is another reason it usually makes sense to wait until you are mostly finished with your score before creating parts.

Working With Parts

Once parts are created, they are linked with the score so that most changes to one affect the other. You can freely move back and forth between working on the score and working on the parts, and MuseScore keeps things in sync for you. However, certain changes are deliberately not linked, to allow for formatting and other inherent differences between score and parts.

Changes that are linked

Any notes you add to any staff in the score will automatically show up in the corresponding part, and vice versa. Same for any text or other markings you add to those notes. Clef changes and other changes that affects the staff as a whole are also automatically linked.

If you make a change that affects the entire score rather than just a single staff, then this is reflected in the score as well as *all* parts. For example, time signature changes, adding or removing measures, repeat barlines, voltas on the top staff, and tempo markings – these affect the score as well as all parts, whether you make the change while viewing the score or while viewing any part. Note that, as discussed in the chapter on *Repeats*, voltas on staves other than the top are not copied or linked to parts.

Changes that are not linked

Certain types of changes are *not* linked, so that the formatting decisions made that are specific to the score do not affect the parts, and vice versa.

While manual adjustments to the position of score elements made *before* parts are created are copied to the parts, manual adjustments made *after* parts are created are not.

For example, it may make sense to move a dynamic in the score in order to avoid a collision with a note on a ledger line above the staff below.

However, this only makes sense in the score – in the part, the note that caused the conflict will not even be present, because it is in a different part.

Similarly, in the part, you might find a tempo marking conflicts with a multimeasure rest. But that multimeasure rest will not be present in the score, so again, that adjustment will not make sense to link.

In addition to manual adjustments to position, most other changes to individual element properties are not linked, either. This includes visibility, which allows you to add an element to the score that is invisible in the score or vice versa.

Changes to the *Concert Pitch* state of the score or parts are not automatically linked, thus allowing you to have a concert pitch score but transposed parts.

Line and page breaks not linked either, because they will not normally occur in the same places between the score and parts. The same is true for changes to other page layout settings, as well as for style settings. See below for more information.

Changing Appearance and Behavior

Global part settings

When a part is created, it inherits all style settings from the main score, so it will use the same fonts, position, etc. However, while the score might have been created with a custom page and staff size in order to fit all the staves for all of your instruments, the parts will use default page layout settings, because the page layout of the score is seldom appropriate for the parts.

As we will see in *Score* in the chapter on *Customization*, MuseScore allows you to specify a style file to control the default style and page layout for newly created scores. If you have done that, then this file will be used for newly created parts as well. You can also specify a different style file to be used for parts. These settings are located in Edit ⟩ Preferences ⟩ Score (*Style* and *Style for part*).

For more on the layout of both score and parts, see the chapter on *Page Layout*.

Individual part properties

As mentioned previously, if you change style settings after the parts are generated, these changes are not linked by default. This allows you to have differences in style settings between score and parts, which can be useful. However, chances are if you make a style change in one part, you will want that same change made in all parts. So MuseScore provides an Apply to all Parts button at the bottom of the *Edit Style* and *Edit Text Styles* dialogs.

 OK   Apply   Apply to all Parts   Cancel

The same is true for the *Page Settings* dialog.

The part name that that appears by default at the top left of each part is, of course, not linked between score and parts. This name is generated automatically when you create a part. But if you need to regenerate it later, you can do so via Add ⟩ Text ⟩ Part Name .

Chapter 29

Page Layout

Page layout is a complex topic, but MuseScore provides facilities to accomplish just about anything you might wish to do. You can control the overall page size and margins, with separate margins for odd and even page if you like. You can set the overall size of the music as well as the default horizontal spacing of notes, and you can increase or decrease the spacing where necessary. You can also control where line and page breaks occur. You can keep individual systems from extending all the way to the left or the right margin, and you can create gaps in the middle of systems. You can set the default distance between staves and between systems, and you can specify variable system spacing so that more space is added on pages that have room for it. You can also create additional space between certain staves or systems where necessary.

In this chapter, I will demonstrate how to accomplish each of these tasks and more. The following diagram may prove a helpful reference. It shows the MuseScore terms for some of the various concepts we will be discussing.

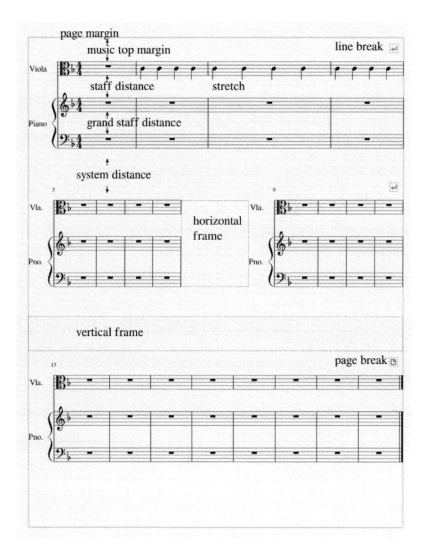

Page Size and Margins

If you create a score using a template, page size and margins for your score are determined by the template. Otherwise – when creating a score from scratch – MuseScore chooses a default page size and margins for you. Either way, you may wish to override these defaults for any given score. To do this, go to Layout ⟩ Page Settings to display the *Page Settings* dialog.

Most of the settings in this dialog should be familiar from word processors or other programs that deal with the printed page. The one that is unique to MuseScore is the *Staff space* setting under the *Scaling* heading. This literally controls the size of the spaces between staff lines, but more than that, this distance – also referred to as *spatium* and abbreviated *sp* – is used as a unit of measurement throughout MuseScore. See the section *Music Size* for more information.

Here is a full description of the settings in this dialog:

Page Settings dialog

MuseScore uses the default paper size for your default printer as the default page size when creating a new score from scratch. In addition, when creating a new score from a template that uses A4 or Letter page size, MuseScore will automatically substitute whichever is appropriate on your system.

Page Size – select from a variety of preset paper sizes using the drop-down menu
Width – manual paper width setting
Height – manual paper height setting
Landscape – select between portrait or landscape orientation
Two sided – enable separate margin settings for odd and even pages
Scaling
Staff space – set size of spaces between staff lines
First page number – set the page number to use for the first page of the score
mm / inch – select between millimeters and inches for display of units in this dialog
Odd Page Margins – margins for odd-numbered pages (all pages if *Two sided* is off)
Even Page Margins – margins for even-numbered pages

This dialog also includes thumbnail representations of the pages in your score so you can see the effect of changes to the various settings in real time.

MuseScore can optionally display the page margins on your score. Select [View] ⟩ [Show Margins], and the margins are shown with an outline, as in the example at the beginning of this chapter.

In addition to the *Page Settings* dialog, there are two settings in [Style] ⟩ [General] ⟩ [Page] that are relevant here.

Music top margin – additional space between top page margin and first system of page
Music bottom margin – additional space between bottom page margin and last system of page

Without this extra space, the top line of the staff would be placed right up against the top margin. Notes on ledger lines above the staff would extend into the margin, as would text and other markings normally placed above the staff. So these additional margins are intended to create room above and below the top and bottom staves of each page, to prevent the music and markings from extending into the margins.

> The *Music top margin* and *Music bottom margin* do not apply if there is a vertical frame at the top or bottom of the page. The distances above and below vertical frames are set independently. See *Vertical Frames* below for more information.

Music Size

As mentioned above, the *Staff space* setting in Layout ⟩ Page Settings controls the size of the spaces between staff lines, and this setting is used as a unit of measure throughout the score. This means that changing the *Staff space* setting actually scales just about everything in your score uniformly. The sizes of notes, rests, and most other elements, the vertical and horizontal positions of elements above or below the staff, the height of hairpins, the thickness of barlines – all these and more are specified in *sp* units and thus will scale with changes to the *Staff space* setting. In addition, most text styles use the *Size follows 'Staff space' setting* option, so even font sizes (which are specified in points) will scale with changes to the *Staff space* setting. The page size and margins, however, remain unchanged. As a result, changing the *Staff space* setting is often all you need to do in order to fit more or less music on a page than the default.

Change Staff space setting from 1.764mm to 1.364mm

Line, Page, and Section Breaks

MuseScore normally fits as many measures per system and as many systems per page as it can given its current spacing settings. If you wish to fit *more* music on a line or page, you will need to reduce the music size as described above, or reduce the music spacing as described in *Horizontal Spacing* and *Vertical Spacing* below. However, if you wish to fit *less* music on a system or page than MuseScore fits by default, you can place explicit line or page breaks using the *Breaks & Spacers* palette.

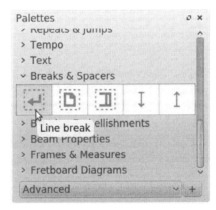

From left to right, the first three icons are for line break, page break, and section break. These are each described below. The last two icons are staff spacers, which will be discussed later under *Vertical Spacing*.

Line breaks

To add a line break to your score, you can drag the icon to the measure after which you want the break to occur, or select the measure then double-click the icon. You can also click the barline after you which you want the break to occur and then press Enter.

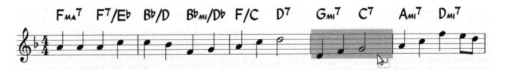

When you add a line break to a measure, MuseScore ends the system with the chosen measure, respaces the music on that system fill it out to the right margin, and reflows the music from that point onward. In addition, a line break icon will appear above the barline (on screen only) to show that an explicit break was placed there.

A line break can be removed by clicking it and pressing Delete.

MuseScore also provide a command to add or remove line breaks automatically throughout your score. Select a range of measures (if desired; otherwise the command works on the whole score) and go to Edit ⟫ Tools ⟫ Add/Remove Line Breaks.

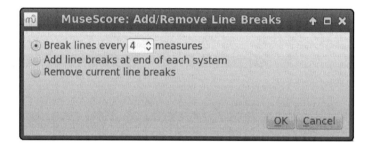

The dialog that is displayed contains three options:

Break lines every ... measures – insert line breaks at the specified interval within the selected range

Add line breaks at end of each system – locks in the current system layout by adding explicit line breaks within the selected range

Remove current line breaks – removes all line breaks from the selected measures

The first option allows you to create layouts with a consistent number of measures per system (although remember, if you want more measures on a system than MuseScore fits by default, you will need to change the music size or horizontal spacing). The second option can be useful when you have finished a score and wish to guarantee that the layout will not change in the future. The command adds line breaks at the end of each system, thus guaranteeing MuseScore will never try to fit more measures on any system. You can then reduce stretch as described in *Horizontal Spacing* to help ensure that MuseScore will not fit *fewer* measures on a system in the future.

Page breaks

Page breaks work in the same manner as line breaks. You can drag the page break icon to the measure after which you want the break to occur, or select the measure then double-click the icon. You can also click a barline and then press Ctrl+Enter (Mac: Cmd+Enter).

MuseScore ends the system with the chosen measure as with a line break, but it also ends the page with that system.

Depending on your settings MuseScore may also add space between systems to try to fill the page more and reduce or eliminate the empty space at the bottom of the page. See *Vertical Spacing* below for more information.

Section breaks

Line and page breaks should be familiar from word processors and other programs, but a section break is more specific to music notation. It is used to indicate an actual musical break, such as between movements of a sonata or between songs in a fakebook.

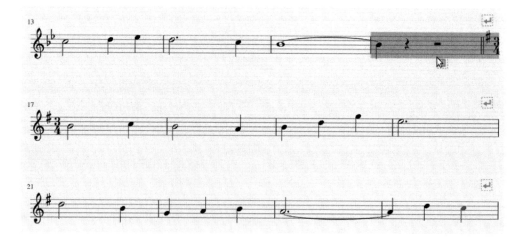

A section break in MuseScore acts like a line break – the next section will start on a new system – but it also causes MuseScore to treat the first section almost like a separate score. If the new section is in a different key or time signature, no courtesy signature will be displayed at the end of the previous section.

You can add a vertical frame with a new title before the first measure of the new section as well.

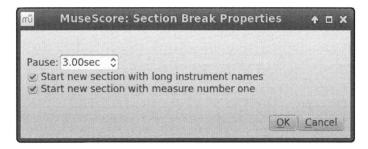

By default, a section break also adds a three-second pause between the sections during playback, and it resets the measure numbering so that the first measure of the new section is "1". In addition, long rather than short instrument names will be displayed before the first system of the new section if appropriate. You can customize these default behaviors of a section break by right-clicking the icon on your score and choosing [Section Break Properties] from the context menu.

Pause – set length of the pause between sections on playback

Start new section with long instrument names – select whether to use long instrument names for first system of new section

Start new section with measure number one – select whether to reset measure numbering for new section

Horizontal Spacing

MuseScore uses standard music engraving rules to determine how much space to place between notes, which in turn affects how many measures can fit on a system. MuseScore gives you a considerable degree of control over this process, both globally for the score and for locally specific systems and/or measures.

Changing the default horizontal spacing for the score

The settings MuseScore uses to control horizontal spacing are found in [Style]》[General]》[Measure]. Most of these settings have already been discussed in previous chapters. For example, the *Clef left margin* setting is documented in the chapter on *Clefs*. There are three specific settings worth discussing again here, however.

Minimum measure width – minimum width to render measures
Spacing – spacing factor; larger values result in more spacing between notes
Minimum note distance – minimum distance between notes

The *Spacing* setting provides a general control over how tightly notes are spaced. The smaller the value, the tighter the spacing, and the more measures you can fit on each system, while keeping the *size* of the music the same. The default *Spacing* of 1.200 should produce good results for most scores.

The minimum value is 1.000, and this produces very tight spacing with more measures per system that you would get by default.

A larger value like 1.600 (for example) produces much looser spacing with fewer measures per system.

In general, I find values between 1.100 and 1.400 usually work best. The default spacing of 1.200 works best for classical scores, while a value of 1.400 might be more appropriate for jazz lead sheets, for example. When in doubt, it is usually better to select a smaller value than you need, because you can always insert line breaks in your score and force looser spacing where you want it (see *Line, Page, and Section Breaks*).

In the above examples, even with a *Spacing* setting of 1.000 (which allows six measure on this system by default), if I add a line break after measure four, the result would be exactly the same as with a *Space* setting of 1.600 (which allows only four measure on this system by default). But the difference is that with a *Spacing* setting of 1.600, four measures are the maximum that can fit on that particular system, whereas with a *Spacing* setting of 1.000, you also have the choice of five or six.

However, instead of setting a low value for *Spacing* for the entire score, you may find it more useful to override the spacing for selected measures only as shown below.

Overriding the default horizontal spacing for selected measures

Often, the default spacing is fine for most of the score, but there may be individual measures or groups of measures where you may wish to alter it. This can be done by selecting the measure or measures you wish to adjust then pressing `{` (`Layout`〉`Decrease Stretch`) to tighten the spacing, or `}` (`Layout`〉`Increase Stretch`) to loosen it. You can also control stretch using the *Measure Properties* dialog (see the chapter on *Measure Operations*).

You can change the stretch settings anywhere you see fit, but there are some specific situations where this often comes in handy. Before discussing these, however, I should mention that after experimenting with stretch settings, you can reset the spacing in selected measures using `Layout`〉`Reset Stretch`.

Fitting more measures onto a system

As we have already seen, you can tell MuseScore to put fewer measures on a system than it otherwise would by adding explicit line breaks. However, there is no direct way to tell MuseScore to put more measures on a system than it would otherwise. Instead, the way to accomplish this is to select the measures you wish to appear on a single system and reduce stretch until the measures fit.

In the following example, I wish to fit the first measure of the second system onto the first system.

By pressing `{` as necessary, I can tighten up the spacing enough to convince MuseScore to combine them.

Creating uneven spacing within a system

Normally, MuseScore will space all measures within a system equally. Note that this is not to say all measures will be the same size (although see below if this is what you want). What I mean by equal spacing is, the amount of space allocated for any given note duration – say, eighth notes – will be consistent throughout any given system. This is standard practice in music engraving. But if you need to override this – to make a particular measure tighter or looser than the others on the same system – you can increase or decrease stretch for individual measures.

If I wish to make the selected measure narrower, I can simply press ⎡ { ⎤ as desired.

Although this is not standard engraving practice, some people like to force all measures on each system be the same width. You can accomplish this in MuseScore by individually increasing or decreasing stretch measure by measure as necessary.

Last system fill

MuseScore normally fills (right-justifies) all systems but the last. That is, MuseScore places as many measures on the line as it can given the spacing settings, and then it stretches the measures out to fill the width of the page. However, the last system might contain only a measure or two, and this would normally be left unfilled.

The last system in this example would look strange if it were stretched out to fill the width of the page.

On the other hand, if the last system is close to being full already, then it could be safely fill the width of the page like any other system. MuseScore provides a setting to control how close to full the last system needs to be before being automatically filled the rest of the way. To set this, go to Style 》 General 》 Page, and see *Last system fill threshold*. If the last system is more full than this, it will be filled the rest of the way; otherwise it will not.

Horizontal Frames

A system normally extends from the left margin of the page to the right margin. Horizontal frames can be used to create additional space to the left or right of a system or to create space between measures within a system. Frames can be added from the Add 》 Frames menu or from the *Frames & Measures* palette. When adding from the palette, the frame is inserted before the measure you are dragging to.

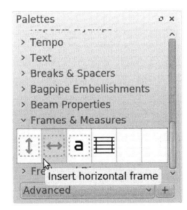

Adding space to the left of a system

When adding a frame to the beginning of a system, it is a good idea to first ensure there is a line break at the end of the previous system. Otherwise, when you add a frame to the beginning of the system, it might actually appear at the end of the previous system. Add the horizontal frame to the first measure of the system you want to indent (add from the palette or use Add 》 Frames 》 Insert Horizontal Frame).

Adding space between measures within a system

Add the horizontal frame to the measure you wish to appear after the gap.

This creates a gap:

By default, MuseScore repeats the staff names, brackets, clefs, and key signatures after the gap, but you can hide these elements if you wish by clicking them and pressing $\boxed{\text{V}}$ (or using the *Visible* property in the *Inspector*).

Adding space to the right of a system

Because horizontal frames are placed in front of the measure to which they are added, creating a horizontal frame at the end of a system is a little more tricky but can be done. First, follow the steps for adding a frame to the left of the *next* system. Delete the line break from the end of the system where you want the frame. At this point, there are three possibilities:

1. The frame may be exactly where you want it – at the end of the system
2. The frame might be on the system where you want it, but there might be other measures after it on that system as well
3. The frame might still be at the start of the next system (if there is not enough room at the end of the system where you want it)

In the third case, select the measures on the system where you want the frame.

Reduce stretch as necessary to create room for the frame. This may create *too* much space, and you may now be faced with the second case.

In this case – or if you see the second case from the beginning – simply drag a line break from the palette to the horizontal frame itself.

Changing Appearance and Behavior

A horizontal frame is invisible in itself, but it can be resized to create more or less space, and it can also contain text or graphics.

Resizing a horizontal frame

Once you have placed a horizontal frame, you can resize it by double-clicking it and dragging the handle.

Drag

You can also use the *Width* property in the *Inspector*.

Adding text or graphics to a horizontal frame

As mentioned in the chapter on *Text*, you can add text to a horizontal frame by right-clicking it and choosing Add ⟩ Text from the context menu. A cursor will appear and you can type your text.

You can also add graphics in a similar way, using Add ⟩ Picture. A standard file selection dialog will appear, allowing you to choose an image file.

Vertical Spacing

MuseScore provides independent control over the distance between staves within a system and the distance between systems on a page. You can set defaults but also override them for particular staves and/or systems.

Staff spacing

MuseScore provides control over the default distance between staves within a system as well as overrides that apply to a staff on a single system or across all systems.

Setting the default distance between staves

MuseScore normally spaces all staves within a system a fixed distance apart. This is controlled by settings in Style ⟩ General ⟩ Page. There are two relevant settings in this dialog – *Staff distance* and *Grand staff distance*. The former controls the distance between staves of different instruments. The latter controls the distance between staves of a single instrument, such as the treble and bass clef staves of a piano score. This allows you to have more or less space between the two piano staves in a score than between the other staves.

These parameters both affect all staves on all systems throughout the score. But MuseScore provides overrides to allow different spacing for a given staff within a given system, or for a given staff on all systems.

Changing distance between specific staves on a single system

If you need to increase the space between two specific staves in one system without affecting other staves or other systems – such as to make room for a special marking that appears only in that one place – the way to do this is with a staff spacer. These are found on the *Breaks & Spacers* palette.

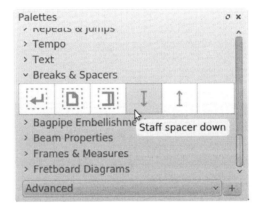

To use a staff spacer, add it from the palette to any measure on one of the staves you want to separate, then double-click it and drag the handle to control the amount of space added.

You can also use the *Height* property in the *Inspector* to set the spacer to a specific height.

The example above used a *Staff spacer down* attached to the upper staff and dragged downward. The exact same thing can be done in the other direction – attaching a *Staff spacer up* to the lower staff and dragging upward.

Changing distance between specific staves across all systems

A spacer is attached to a specific measure, and only the system containing that measure is affected by the spacer. If you wish to create additional space between two specific staves but

> It is not currently possible to *reduce* space between specific staves for a single system only. This is not a common thing to want to do, but if the need arises, you could decrease the distance between those staves across all systems (see below) and then add spacers to all other systems.

have this change affect *all* systems, you can simply drag the lower staff downward while holding Shift .

Adding vertical space by dragging a staff

The extra distance created in this manner is reflected in the *Extra distance above staff* setting in the *Staff Properties* for the staff you dragged. This can be used to accurately reset the spacing back to the default – just set *Extra distance above staff* to 0.00*sp*. This is more accurate than trying to do it by hand. Similarly, if you are working on a large score such as for an orchestra, you might wish to add a consistent amount of space between the different sections (i.e., between the woodwinds and brass, between the brass and percussion, and between the percussion and strings). This is also best done using *Staff Properties* rather than Shift +drag. See the chapter on *Staves and Instruments* for more on staff properties.

Note that whether dragging staves on the score or using *Staff Properties*, you can actually reduce the distance between staves as easily as you can increase it.

System spacing

System spacing is controlled in a similar manner as staff spacing: via defaults in $\boxed{\text{Style}}\rangle\boxed{\text{General}}$ $\rangle\boxed{\text{Page}}$ and the use of spacers for overrides.

Setting default distance between systems

MuseScore uses two settings to control the default distance between systems – the *Min. system distance* and *Max. system distance*, both found in $\boxed{\text{Style}}\rangle\boxed{\text{General}}\rangle\boxed{\text{Page}}$.

The reason there are two settings rather than just one is to allow for flexibility in system spacing from page to page. MuseScore will use the minimum system distance to compute the number of staves it can fit on a page. It will then add more space between systems (up to the specified maximum) in an effort to fill the page. MuseScore stops at the specified maximum system distance to avoid trying to fill the page if that would require excessive amounts of space.

For example (as shown above), if you have a score with a title frame on letter-sized paper, the default minimum system distance setting allows for up to nine single-staff systems on the first page, and these will be spaced to fill up the page. However, if you have only seven systems on the page, the default maximum system distance setting allows these to also be spaced to fill out the page.

On the other hand (as shown below), if you have only five systems, they are spaced only as far as allowed by the maximum system distance setting, creating a page that is not filled up completely but is still spaced more loosely than the page with nine systems.

A change to the minimum system distance thus affects how many systems MuseScore can fit on a page, whereas a change to the maximum system distance affects how hard MuseScore tries to fill the page with those systems.

For example, reducing the minimum system distance value to 8.0*sp* allows MuseScore to fit a tenth system on the page, whereas increasing the maximum system distance to 20.0*sp* allows MuseScore to fill the page with only six systems.

Taken together, the minimum and maximum system distance settings provide a powerful way of controlling system spacing. They allow one set of defaults to create pleasing layouts in a variety of different settings. Even if different pages within your score have different numbers of systems, or different sizes of systems, or if you use the same settings in different scores, most pages should all look good by default. Manual overrides to system distance should thus not be needed very often.

In most cases, the default settings will work well, but if you do need to change them, it may take a little while to get the hang of it, as these settings can admittedly be confusing at first. One potential cause for confusion is that changes to either of these settings might appear to have no effect at first. A change in minimum system distance, for instance, will have no visible effect unless you change it by enough to affect how many systems MuseScore can fit on the page. And on a page that is already being filled completely, a change in maximum system distance will have no effect unless you reduce it by enough to prevent the page from being completely filled. I encourage you to experiment with the settings to better understand how you can take advantage of the power and flexibility they provide.

Changing distance between specific systems

The same staff spacers that are used to add space between staves within a system can also be used to add space between systems. Add one from the palette to your score, double-click it, and drag in the direction of the arrow to increase the distance.

As when adding space between staves within a system, you can also use the *Inspector* to control the amount of space added.

Effect of lyrics on vertical spacing

If you add lyrics to your score, MuseScore automatically adds extra vertical space below the staff to accommodate them. This affects both staff spacing and system spacing. As discussed in the chapter *Lyrics*, you can control this via the *Lyrics top margin* and *Lyrics bottom margin* parameters in Style ⟩ General ⟩ Page .

Vertical Frames

Just as a horizontal frame creates space within a system, a vertical frame creates space between systems. If all you need is empty space, a staff spacer is a better choice, but a vertical frame can contain text or images. Vertical frames can be added from the Add ⟩ Frames menu or from the *Frames & Measures* palette.

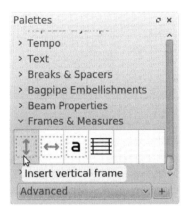

When adding from the palette, the frame will be inserted before the selected measure.

Insert vertical frame

Changing Appearance and Behavior

The options for changing the appearance of vertical frames are very much like those for horizontal frames. You can resize the frame by double-clicking and dragging the handle, you can add content by right-clicking and going to Add ⟩ Text or Add ⟩ Picture . But vertical frames provide additional options as well.

Global vertical frame settings

MuseScore provides global settings for the default space to leave above and below vertical frames. These are located in Style ⟩ General ⟩ Page .

Vertical frame top margin – space to leave above vertical frames
Vertical frame bottom margin – space to leave below vertical frames

Individual vertical frame properties

You can customize settings for individual vertical frames using the *Inspector*.

Top gap – additional space to leave above frame (negative values will decrease space)
Bottom gap – additional space to leave below frame (negative values will decrease space)
Height – height of frame
Left margin – space between left edge of frame and inserted elements
Right margin – space between right edge of frame and inserted elements
Top margin – space between top edge of frame and inserted elements
Bottom margin – space between bottom edge of frame and inserted elements

Adding text or graphics to a vertical frame

If you wish to add text to a vertical frame, right-click the frame and select Add from the menu
that appears. You will see that in addition to the plain Text option that is also available for
horizontal frames, there are also options for Title, Subtitle, Composer, Lyricist, and Part Name.
You can thus add these elements to frames other than the top frame for a score. This can be
useful when creating a score of multiple movements, or a collection of songs. See also *Creating
Albums* in the chapter on *File Operations* for another way to combine movements or songs into
a single score.

In addition to text, you can also add graphics to a vertical frame using Add ⟩ Picture.

Adding a horizontal frame to a vertical frame

In order to create more complex layouts, MuseScore allows you to insert a horizontal frame
within a vertical frames, via Add ⟩ Insert Horizontal Frame. One use for this is to create a table-like
layout with text that is right-aligned to some point within the vertical frame. Create a vertical
frame, add and resize a horizontal frame within it, add text to the horizontal frame, and use
Text Properties to right align the text.

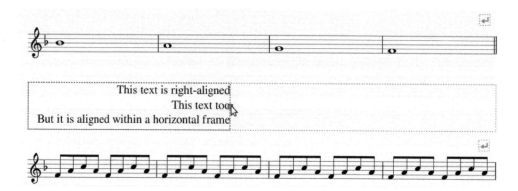

This is but one use for this facility. However, it should be emphasized that MuseScore is not
meant to replace a word processor or desktop publishing program. For more complex layouts
involving combinations of text and music, you may be better off creating a document another

program and inserting music from MuseScore using the facilities described in the chapter on *Printing and Graphic Output*.

Part V

Working with MuseScore

Chapter 30

Playback and Audio Output

While the primary purpose of MuseScore is to produce notation, MuseScore does include a built-in software synthesizer that aims to provide realistic playback using a high quality soundfont that is included. You can also find other soundfonts that may suit your needs better, and you can use these with the built-in synthesizer as well.

In addition to the built-in synthesizer, if you have your own MIDI-compatible synthesizer (whether hardware or software), you can configure MuseScore to use that instead. MuseScore can also be used as a playalong tool for practice, and it provides metronome and looping features for this purpose. It should be noted, however, that the mobile apps for Android and iOS are perhaps better suited for this purpose.

Playback Controls

The most commonly used playback controls offered by MuseScore are found on the *Transport Tools* toolbar. Other commands can also be found by going to `View`〉`Play Panel` (keyboard shortcut `F11`).

Play mode

To play your score, press `Space` or click the `▶` button on the *Transport Tools* toolbar or in the *Play Panel*. Playback commences from the beginning of the score by default. If you click a note first, playback will instead commence from that point.

Once started, the playback continues until the end of the score or until you hit `▶` or `Space` again to pause playback. If you then restart playback without first clicking another note, playback will continue from where it left off.

While your score is playing, MuseScore is in *Play* mode, and the following shortcuts can be used:

- `←` – seek to previous note
- `→` – seek to next note
- `Ctrl`+`←` – seek to previous measure

351

- Ctrl + → – seek to next measure

- Home – seek to start of score

In addition, a number of the buttons on the *Transport Tools* toolbar are relevant.

- ⏮ – rewind to beginning of score

- ↻ – toggle loop playback (see *Looping*)

- :∥ – toggle following repeats during playback

- ▶∥ – toggle automatic scrolling of score during playback

- *ℓ* – toggle metronome sound during playback

These controls can also be found in the *Play Panel*. This window contains a few other useful controls as well.

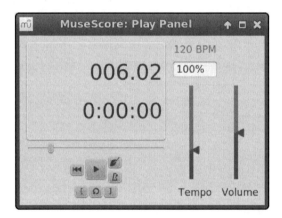

- [/] – set loop in/out points (see *Looping*)

- ⏼ – toggle count-in before playback

- *Tempo* – temporary scaling factor to apply to the actual tempo for the piece

- *Volume* – temporary override to the overall synthesizer volume

In addition, the horizontal slider in this window can be used to seek to a particular point in the score.

The *Play Panel* can be opened or closed at any time and is active during playback, allowing you to change any of these settings while listening to your score.

The basic tempo and dynamics for your piece should be set using tempo and dynamics markings placed directly on the score. Additional markings can be placed to change tempo and dynamics over the course of the piece. The tempo control in the *Play Panel* is intended to allow you to temporarily scale the tempos specified by the tempo markings in the piece by some fixed ratio. This can be useful for playalong purposes (see below). Do not use this as a substitute for placing tempo markings on your score. Similarly, the volume control in the *Play Panel* is for overriding the overall MuseScore playback volume (see *Synthesizer* below) for this particular score, and should not be used as a substitute for placing dynamics markings on your score.

Looping

As mentioned previously, your score normally plays until the end or until you pause playback by pressing [Space] or [▶]. However, MuseScore also provide a loop mode in which a specified passage is played over and over, thus allowing you to practice along with the playback. This loop mode can be enabled via the [Ω] button on the *Transport Tools* toolbar or in the *Play Panel*.

To set the range for the loop, you can select it before pressing the [Ω] button. You can also set the loop in and out points independently using the [[ ] and [ ]] buttons in the *Play Panel*. This will also automatically enable the loop mode.

When the loop mode is enabled, the in and out points are clearly marked in your score.

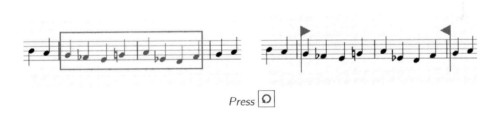

Press [Ω]

When the loop mode is enabled, playback will always start at the beginning of the loop and will continue until you stop it.

While the playback is looping you can adjust the tempo using the slider in the *Play Panel*, allowing you to start slowly and gradually increase the speed as you practice.

Although there are no default shortcuts defined for the loop controls, if you use this feature a lot, you can define shortcuts yourself as described in *Shortcuts* in the chapter on *Customization*.

Mixer

MuseScore includes a *Mixer* window that allows you to adjust a number of different playback parameters for the various instruments in your score, including the specific sounds used and relative volume levels of each instrument. To display this window, go to View ⟩ Mixer or press F10 .

Mixer window

The Mixer contains entries – called *channels* – for each instrument in your score. Instruments that define more than one variant will have separate channels for each. For example, in the above, we see separate channels for the normal and muted trumpet variants. These correspond to the same staff in your score, but the separate channels allow you to control the normal and muted sounds individually.

For each channel, the following parameters can be set:

Mute – when enabled, this channel will not playback
Solo – when enabled for any channel, only channels with this enabled will playback
Sound – select the sound to use for this channel
Volume – set the relative volume level for this channel
Pan – set the stereo panning for this channel (from left to right)
Reverb – set the amount of reverb to apply to this channel (external synthesizer only)
Chorus – set the amount of chorus to apply to this channel (external synthesizer only)

To set the parameters that use dials, click the dial and drag – up to turn to dial clockwise, down to turn the dial counterclockwise. You can also click the dial and use the up and down arrow keys. To reset any dial to its default value, just double-click it.

The *Sound* control displays a drop-down menu that lists all the sounds available.

The available sounds are determined by the soundfonts you have loaded. For more information, see the section *Synthesizer* below.

The *Mixer* window remains active during playback so you can adjust any of the parameters while your score is playing.

> Although you can change the sound used for a staff in the *Mixer*, in most cases this would only be done to change to related sounds, such as between the different types of guitar sounds. If you wish to actually change a staff from guitar to, say, accordion, you should normally do this via *Change Instrument* in *Staff Properties*. This will change the staff name, clef, transposition, and other important parameters that should be updated when making this type of change. For more information, see the chapter *Staves and Instruments*.

Synthesizer

The built-in synthesizer included with MuseScore allows you to use a variety of different *soundfonts* to define the sounds of the instruments used by MuseScore much in the way that a text font defines the appearance of characters used. The synthesizer in MuseScore also provides a customizable reverb effect and allows you to change the master tuning. To display the synthesizer controls, go to View ⟩ Synthesizer.

The two controls on the far right are for the volume of the playback as a whole and of the internal metronome. These controls affect the volume for all scores. The settings remain in effect for the duration of the current MuseScore session, but will reset to the defaults the next time you start MuseScore. If you wish to change the default volume for MuseScore, press the Save as Default button after setting the volume the way you like.

The other controls available within this dialog are explained below.

Soundfont

A soundfont is a file or set of files that define the sounds used in a synthesizer. MuseScore supports two types of soundfonts: the SF2 format (also known as *SoundFont*) and the SFZ format. These formats are used by the two different engines within the synthesizer. The SF2

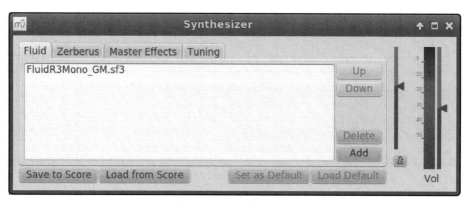

Synthesizer window

Although you might perceive the default volume to be on the low side, do keep in mind that MuseScore does not compress the dynamic range of its playback, so that music intended to be quiet really is quiet rather than being artificially amplified to bring it closer to the level of louder passages, as is common in much recorded music. Take care not to increase the default volume for MuseScore just to increase the volume for one particular piece that is marked *pp*, as this will likely result in pieces marked *ff* distorting badly.

engine is called *Fluid* and the SFZ engine is called *Zerberus*. The first two tabs in the *Synthesizer* window contain controls for loading different soundfonts into these two engines.

MuseScore allows you to load multiple soundfonts at once, and the sounds from all of the loaded soundfonts will be available in the *Mixer*. You can store soundfonts in the `Soundfonts` folder created for you by MuseScore, and these soundfonts will be available to load into the *Synthesizer*. See *Folders* in *File Operations*.

To load a soundfont, press the ⟨Add⟩ button and select the soundfont from the list that appears.

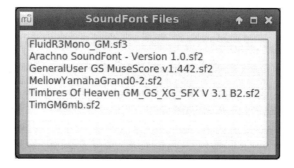

You can also load a soundfont directly from your operating system's file manager (e.g., Windows Explorer) by double-clicking it.

Once loaded into MuseScore, a soundfont is available to all scores for the duration of your current session – until you close MuseScore. The next time you start MuseScore, only the default soundfont will be loaded. If you wish your newly added soundfonts to be loaded each time you start MuseScore, click the [Save as Default] button after loading the soundfonts.

You can also save the current set of soundfonts directly into your score by pressing the [Save to Score] button. The soundfonts you save in this manner will not be loaded automatically next time you start MuseScore, nor even upon loading that score. But after loading a score to which you had previously saved soundfonts, you can return to [View] ⟩ [Synthesizer] and press [Load from Score] to restore the saved soundfonts. This can be useful if you have a large set of soundfonts that you do not want to load all the time for memory / performance reasons, but that you wish to be able to reload quickly for special occasions.

Fluid

By default, MuseScore uses the *Fluid* engine only, with a soundfont called *FluidR3*. This soundfont contains over 200 different instrument sounds, including the full set of 128 standard and 47 percussion sounds defined by the General MIDI standard. It should meet the needs of most users.

However, there are many SF2 soundfonts available that you may wish to investigate. Some simply provide different versions of the regular General MIDI sounds. Others provide sounds for just certain instruments, perhaps including instruments that are not part of the General MIDI standard.

You can load multiple soundfonts into *Fluid*. The one listed at the top will be used by default, and you can use the *Up* and *Down* buttons to arrange this list however you like. Regardless of the order of the soundfonts, all the sounds from all of the currently loaded soundfonts will be available in the *Mixer*.

> The *FluidR3* soundfont provided with MuseScore is actually in a special variation on the SF2 format in which the samples are compressed to save space. It is also customized a bit from the standard *FluidR3* soundfont that is available for download on other sites.

Zerberus

The *Zerberus* engine handles playback of SFZ soundfonts. However, MuseScore provides only partial support for this format currently. *Zerberus* is designed specifically to work with the free *Salamander* piano soundfont. Support for other soundfonts may be added in a future release. To load an SFZ file, simply switch to the *Zerberus* tab before pressing the [Add] button.

Effects

MuseScore includes a reverb effect called *Zita* that you can control by going to the *Master Effects* tab of the *Synthesizer* window.

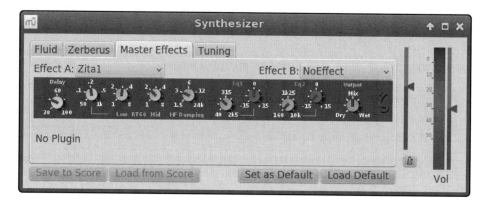

The various dials allow you to fine-tune the performance of the reverb.

Delay – time in milliseconds before the reverb is introduced for each note
Frequency / Time – set the length of the reverb effect for different frequency ranges
Eq1 / Eq2 – select specific frequency bands to boost or attenuate
Output – control the ratio of dry to wet signal

You can turn off the reverb completely by changing the *Effect A* to *No Effect*.

> If you are familiar with audio processing terminology, these controls should seem familiar. If not, you can try reading up on the subject or just experimenting. For most people, the defaults should be fine. If you have a general sense that you want "less" (or "more") reverb, the one setting you would want to play with is the *Output*. Turning the dial toward *Dry* will result in less reverb; turning it toward *Wet* will result in more.

Tuning

The *Tuning* tab of the *Synthesizer* window allows you to control the overall tuning of the synthesizer. The default is $A = 440Hz$. To change this, simply enter a different value into the *Master tuning* box and then press the Change Tuning button.

Exporting Audio

Once you have your score sounding the way you want it, you may want to export it to an audio format such as WAV or MP3 in order to share it with others. To do this, go to File ⟩ Export. This displays a standard file selection dialog that allows you to export your score to a variety of formats. Toward the bottom of the dialog is a drop-down menu that allows you to select the specific format.

The audio formats supported by MuseScore are:

Wave Audio – an uncompressed audio format; support by virtually all programs

FLAC Audio – an audio format that employs lossless compression that results in file sizes around 50% of WAV with no loss in audio quality; supported by many open source programs

Ogg Vorbis Audio – an audio format that employs lossy compression that results in files sizes only around 10% of WAV with only a modest loss in audio quality; supported by many open source programs

MP3 Audio – an audio format that employs lossy compression that results in files sizes only around 10% of WAV with only a modest loss in audio quality; supported by most programs

For formats that support the selection of a sample rate, you can set this in $\boxed{\text{Edit}}\rangle\boxed{\text{Preferences}}\rangle\boxed{\text{Export}}$. See *Export* in the chapter on *Customization*.

Exporting MIDI

In addition to the audio formats described above, MuseScore can also export to a standard MIDI file. It is important to understand that while MIDI can be used to produce sound, it does not contain actual audio information. Instead, it simply contains instructions as to what notes are to be played at what times and by what instruments. It is in that sense more similar to a score than it is to an audio file, except it contains none of the visual information (e.g., no information about whether a note is to be spelled *G♯* or *A♭*, no text, articulations, or other markings) that a score would normally contain. A score exported as a MIDI file and then loaded into another program will not sound the same as it does in MuseScore because the other program will be using a different synthesizer to create the various sounds. But if this is not important to you – or if you know the synthesizer used contains sounds you do want – then MIDI files can be convenient, because they are very small compared to even compressed audio files (often less than 1% of the size of an MP3 file).

To export a score to MIDI format, use the same $\boxed{\text{File}}\rangle\boxed{\text{Export}}$ dialog described above for audio, but specify *Standard MIDI File* as the file type.

MIDI Output

If you have your own MIDI synthesizer that provides sounds or other capabilities you wish to use, you may wish to have MuseScore play your score through your own synthesizer instead of the built-in one. MuseScore does not provide direct support for MIDI output, but you can do this via JACK, a free and open source program for Windows, Mac OS, and Linux. To configure MuseScore to use JACK, see the section on *I/O* in the chapter on *Customization*. A full discussion of how to use MuseScore with JACK is beyond the scope of this book, and the details may depend on what operating system you are using. For more information on using JACK with MuseScore, you may wish to try the support forums and other help resources on `musescore.org`.

Chapter 31

Printing and Graphic Output

Now that you have your score and parts looking and sounding great, you will probably want print everything out or convert to PDF and find musicians to play it for real! Or perhaps you are creating musical examples to include within web pages, exercise sheets, or other documents. MuseScore can print directly as well as export scores to PDF and a variety of image formats, and it provides an *Image capture* mode that allows you to define a region of a score and insert it as a graphic into other documents in other programs.

Printing

To print the current score or part, go to File ⟩ Print. A standard print dialog appears that allows you to select a printer and control basic parameters of how your score is printed.

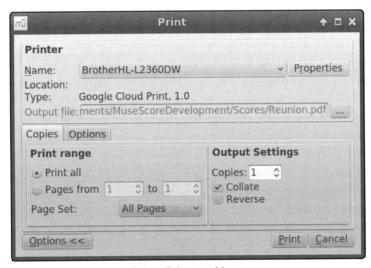

Print dialog on Linux

The specific controls provided will depend on your operating system and system configuration, but in general, you should expect to see options to select a printer, to set printer preferences, to limit the range of pages printed, to print multiple copies, etc.

Recall that the page size and margins within MuseScore are controlled by [Layout] ⟩ [Page Settings]. For more information, see the section on *Page Size and Margins* in the chapter on *Page Layout*. It is your responsibility to choose a page size that is compatible with your printer, or to choose appropriate printer options to resize the output, if your system supports this.

Exporting PDF or Graphics

To export the current score or part to PDF, go to [File] ⟩ [Export]. *PDF* is normally the default file type in the dialog that appears.

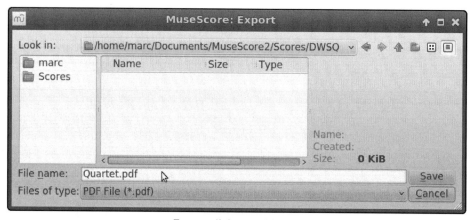

Export dialog on Linux

You can also export the score and all parts at once via [File] ⟩ [Export Parts]. This displays a similar dialog, but when you specify a file name for the export, one file for each part will be generated, with the name of the part appended. In addition, a copy of the score with all parts included will also be exported as a single file.

To export the current score or part to another graphic format such as PNG or SVG, use the same [File] ⟩ [Export] dialog as for PDF, but this time select PNG or SVG as the file type. To control the resolution and other details of how the score is exported, go to [Edit] ⟩ [Preferences] ⟩ [Export]. See the section on *Export* in the chapter on *Customization* for more information. Note that for PNG, a separate file for each page will be generated. For SVG, MuseScore will generate a single file that contains all pages.

Image Capture

To export a specific excerpt of your score as a graphic, MuseScore provides an *Image capture* mode. To enable this, press the 📷 button on the main toolbar. A cropping rectangle will appear that allows you to define the region to be captured.

You can resize this rectangle using the handles. For scores that consist of just the passage you wish to capture, you can right-click the rectangle and select Auto-resize to page to cause the rectangle to crop the region automatically.

There are also options to predefine up to four regions of the page, thus allowing you to capture the same region over and over as the content changes (see below).

Once you have defined the region you wish to capture, you can right-click the rectangle to display a menu of options that allow you to copy the region as an image to the clipboard or to save it to a file. The captured image can then be inserted into documents in other programs, such as the free and open source word processor LibreOffice Writer.

- Copy – copy the region as an image to the clipboard

- Resolution – set the resolution for the image capture

- Transparent background – render the paper as transparent pixels

- Auto-resize to page – crop the rectangle to the actual content of the page

- Resize to A/B/C/D – crop the rectangle to a preset region

- Set Standard Size – define the preset regions

- Save As (Print Mode) – save the region as a PNG, PDF, or SVG file as it would appear in print

- Save As (Screenshot Mode) – save the region as a PNG, PDF, or SVG file as it appears on screen (including icons for line breaks, grayed out invisible elements, etc.)

Unlike a traditional screen capture, the *Image capture* mode in MuseScore does not limit you to the resolution of your monitor. This facility allows you to create high resolution images suitable for inclusion in documents meant to be printed or displayed on high resolution devices, making it well-suited for creating music textbooks and similar documents.

However, if you are planning on producing a significant number of these types of document, or even a single such document with many musical examples, you may wish to check out the MuseScore Example Manager extension for LibreOffice and OpenOffice. This extension can help automate the process of inserting examples into text documents and keeping them linked with the original score files in MuseScore for easy updating later. You can install this extension via the extension managers built in to LibreOffice and OpenOffice.

Chapter 32

File Operations

In the chapter on *Creating a New Score*, we saw how you can create new scores in MuseScore. By now, you have probably figured out the basic file open and save dialogs as well. MuseScore provides a few additional facilities you may also find useful. These include the ability to save and share scores online, to define and use your own templates, and to create albums that join separate scores into one larger work (to produce a songbook, for example).

Folders

MuseScore creates a series of folders for you the first time it starts up. First, it creates a folder called MuseScore2 underneath your main documents folder. Within this folder, MuseScore creates the following folders, which are used as the default locations for the different types of files MuseScore uses:

- Scores – default location for opening and saving scores

- Styles – default location for loading and saving style and chord symbol style files (see *Style* in chapter on *Customization*)

- Templates – location searched for templates (see *Creating Templates* below)

- Plugins – location searched for plugins (see *Plugins* in chapter on *Customization*)

- SoundFonts – default location for soundfonts (see *Synthesizer* in chapter on *Playback and Audio Output*)

- Images – default location for saving image captures (see *Image Capture* in chapter on *Printing and Graphic Output*)

The location of these folders can be customized via [Edit ⟩ Preferences] as discussed in *Folders* in the chapter on *Customization*.

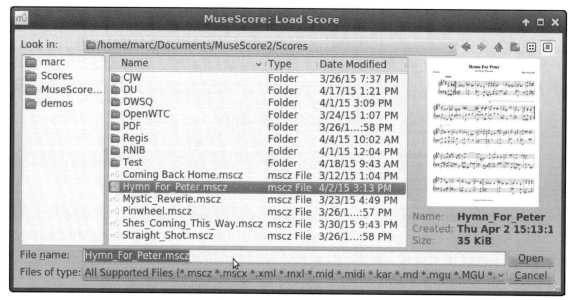

Open dialog on Linux

Opening Scores

The familiar [File] ⟩ [Open] command works as you would expect in MuseScore, displaying a standard file selection dialog box that allows you to choose a score. The standard shortcut [Ctrl] + [O] (Mac: [Cmd] + [O]) works as well.

There is also a list of recent scores you can access via [File] ⟩ [Open Recent]. You can clear the list of recent scores at any time via [File] ⟩ [Open Recent] ⟩ [Clear Recent Scores].

Another way to open a score from within MuseScore is to use the *Start Center*, which shows thumbnail images of all of your recent scores. To open the *Start Center*, go to [View] ⟩ [Start Center] or press the keyboard shortcut [F4]. You can then open any score shown by clicking its thumbnail. If the score you wish to open is not displayed, you can click the [Open a score] button to display the standard file selection dialog, just as if you had used [File] ⟩ [Open].

In addition, you can open scores directly from your operating system file by double-clicking the file name or icon.

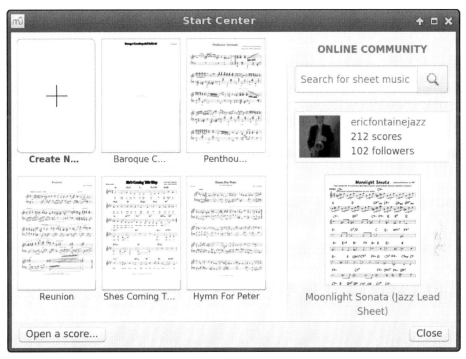

Start Center

Saving Scores

The standard File ⟩⟩ Save and File ⟩⟩ Save As commands work as you expect in MuseScore to save the current score, as do the keyboard shortcuts Ctrl + S and Ctrl + Shift + S (Mac: Cmd + S and Cmd + Shift + S). As discussed in the chapter on *Parts*, this automatically saves all parts as well if you have generated linked parts.

MuseScore also provides a few other options for saving scores:

- File ⟩⟩ Save a Copy – saves a copy of the current score under a different name, but leaves you editing the original score
- File ⟩⟩ Save Selection – creates and saves a new score consisting of the current selection only

Sharing Scores

An exciting feature of MuseScore is the ability to share scores online via the site musescore.com. Anyone can sign up for a free account, with more storage and features available with a Pro account as well. You can save your score to your account on musescore.com directly from within MuseScore. Once your score is saved online, it can be shared with others, accessed on mobile devices using a web browser or one of the dedicated MuseScore apps for Android or iOS, embedded within web sites, turned into a video score, and more. For more information on musescore.com, visit the site and browse around.

To save your score to `musescore.com` from within MuseScore, go to File ⟩ Save Online. If you have not already created an account or are not logged in, you will be prompted to do so. You will then be presented with a dialog that allows you to enter information about your score.

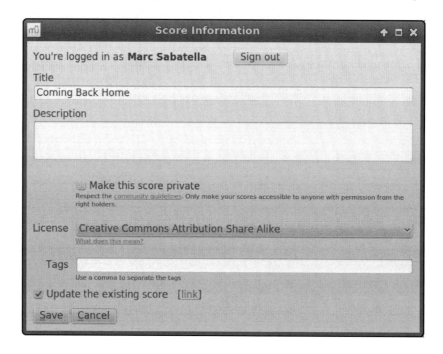

The information you enter in this dialog corresponds to the information you would enter when uploading a score via `musescore.com` itself.

Creating Templates

In the chapter *Creating a New Score*, we saw how you can use templates when starting a new score. Creating your own templates is very simple – just set up any score the way you like, go to File ⟩ Save As or File ⟩ Save a Copy, and save the score into your `Templates` folder. The new template will appear in the list when you create future scores – or at least, it will after you quit and restart MuseScore.

> When you create a score from a template, MuseScore will use the page layout and style settings, the list of instruments, and the properties of the title frame if present (size, margins, etc.) from the source score. No other information is used. So it is not necessary to delete measures, titles, or other content from an existing score before saving it as a template.

Creating Albums

The album feature allows you to join two or more scores into one longer score. This can be used to create a work of multiple movements, to create a collection, songbook or fakebook, or for any similar purpose.

An album in MuseScore consists of a list of scores that can be saved to a special *.album* file. This file is literally just a list of scores. MuseScore can print from this directly or use it as the basis for forming a new score composed of all the individual scores joined together.

Creating an album

To create an album, go to File ⟩ Album . The *Album Manager* dialog appears.

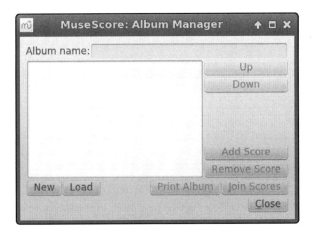

If you have previously created an album, you can load it now via the Load button. Otherwise, you will need to click the New button to create a new album. Once you have done that, you will be able to enter an *Album name*.

To add scores to the album, click the Add Score button. This will display a standard score selection dialog. You can select multiple scores in that dialog if you like, and you can repeat this process to add as many scores as you like.

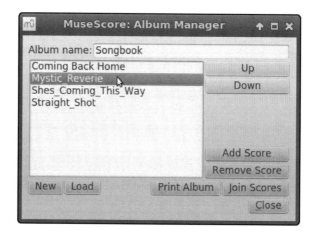

Newly added scores appear at the end of the list, but you can use the ⬚Up and ⬚Down buttons to arrange the scores into any desired order. You can also remove scores via the ⬚Remove Score button.

When you are satisfied with your album, you can either print or join the scores immediately (see below), or you can save the album for use later. To save the album, simply click the ⬚Close button and you will be prompted to save it to a *.album* file. As mentioned previously, this saves the list of scores only. If you make a change to one of the scores later, this change will be seen the next time you load the album.

Printing an album

You can print an album directly from the *Album Manager* by clicking the ⬚Print Album button. A standard print dialog will be displayed. Once you confirm the operation, the scores will be printed consecutively, with each score starting on a new page. The pages are numbered consecutively as well, so that if you have ten scores of one page each, the pages will be numbered 1, 2, 3, 4, 5, 6, 7, 8, 9, and 10.

Creating a joined score from an album

MuseScore also lets you join the scores of your album together to form a new score. To do this, click the ⬚Join Scores button. A standard file dialog will be displayed to allow you to save the joined score.

The joined score will have section breaks after each component score (see *Section breaks* in the chapter on *Page Layout*). Each score will begin on a new line, but not a new page.

Note that a joined album contains actual copies of the scores it comprises. Thus, changing any of the component scores later will not affect the joined score. But you can always load the album again and re-join the scores.

> In order for the album joining feature to work well, it is best if the scores in the album all have the same instrumentation. Whatever instrument is used for the top staff of the first score will be the instrument used for the top staff for all scores throughout the album, and the same for any subsequent staves.

Supported File Formats

MuseScore saves scores with a file name extension of *.mscz*. It can also optionally save to an uncompressed version of this format, by going to File ⟩ Save As and selecting the file type *.mscx*. The resulting file is plain text and can be examined in a text editor. This could be of value for those curious about the structure of a score in MuseScore, but note that the format is not documented and is subject to change from release to release. The *.mscz* format should be preferred in general.

In addition, MuseScore saves a backup copy of your score when it first saves your score during a session. This backup copy of the score has the same file name as the score itself except for a leading "." and trailing ",". This backup represents the state of your score when it was opened. MuseScore will not open this backup file directly, but if something happens to your score and you are unable to open it, you may be able to rename the backup file and open it to access an earlier version.

In addition to these native formats, MuseScore can also import from and export to certain other formats. Not all features can be supported when using a non-native format.

Importing from other file formats

MuseScore can import scores in a number of formats aside from its native *.mscz* and *.mscx*:

- MusicXML – *.xml, .mxl*
- MIDI – *.mid, .kar*
- MuseData – *.md*
- Capella – *.cap, .capx*
- Band-in-a-Box – *.mgu, .sgu*
- Overture / Score Writer – *.ove, .scw*
- Bagpipe Music Writer – *.bww*
- Guitar Pro / TuxGuitar – *.gtp, .gp3, .gp4, .gp5, .gpx*

To import a score in one of these formats, simply load it normally via File ⟩ Open.

Importing scores from other formats should not be expected to be perfect, as many of these formats are not documented. Plus, different programs have different feature sets and may have incompatible ways of representing scores. In addition, formats like MIDI simply cannot represent much of the information normally contained in a score. MuseScore does provide excellent support for MusicXML, which is the standard format for exchange between music notation programs. However, be forewarned that MusicXML files produced via optical music recognition (OMR) often contain many errors, as OMR technology is still in its infancy.

PDF

Although MuseScore cannot import PDF files directly, the score sharing site `musescore.com` provides an experimental service that can attempt to convert a PDF file to MusicXML via optical music recognition using the free and open source software Audiveris. To try this service, you can go to File ⟩ Import PDF within MuseScore and follow the prompts from there. If the conversion succeeds, you can download the converted MusicXML file to your computer and then open it normally.

MIDI

When importing a MIDI file, MuseScore employs a number of special techniques to try to produce readable notation. Because much of this basically involves guesswork, MuseScore provides a special set of controls to allow you to experiment with different conversions. Upon importing a MIDI file, a MIDI import panel is displayed, with a number of settings to guide the conversion of each track.

	Import	Channel	Sound	MuseScore instrument	Max. quantization	Max. voices	Tuplets	Is human performance	Split staff	Clef changes	Simplify durations	Show staccato	Dotted notes	Recognize pickup measure	Detect swing
All	☑				16th	4	3, 4, 5, 7, 9	☑		☑	☑	☑	☑	☑	None (1:1)
1	☑	1	Trumpet	Bb Cornet	16th	4	3, 4, 5, 7, 9			☑	☑	☑	☑		None (1:1)
2	☑	3	Alto Sax	Alto Saxophone	16th	4	3, 4, 5, 7, 9				☑	☑	☑		None (1:1)
3	☑	4	Tenor Sax	Tenor Saxophone	16th	4	3, 4, 5, 7, 9				☑	☑	☑		None (1:1)
4	☑	5	Trombone	Trombone	16th	4	3, 4, 5, 7, 9				☑	☑	☑		None (1:1)
5	☑	6	Clean Guitar	Electric Guitar	16th	4	3, 4, 5, 7, 9				☑	☑	☑		None (1:1)
6	☑	7	Grand Piano	Piano	16th	4	3, 4, 5, 7, 9				☑	☑	☑		None (1:1)
7	☑	7	Grand Piano	Piano	16th	4	3, 4, 5, 7, 9		☑		☑	☑	☑		None (1:1)
8	☑	8	Acoustic Bass	Contrabass	16th	4	3, 4, 5, 7, 9				☑	☑	☑		None (1:1)
9	☑	10	Percussion	Hi-hat	16th		3, 4, 5, 7, 9				☑	☑	☑		None (1:1)

The settings available for each track are:

MuseScore instrument – select the instrument to be used for this staff

Max. quantization – select the shortest note duration to use

Max. voices – limit the number of voices MuseScore will use if it detects overlapping notes

Tuplets – select what types of tuplets MuseScore will attempt to detect and create

Is human performance – attempt to ascertain the intended rhythms in a MIDI recording that was not recorded with a metronome

Split staff – split track into multiple staves

Clef changes – create clef changes if too many ledger lines would be needed

Simplify durations – round off note durations to minimize use of ties and/or rests

Show staccato – represent short notes using staccato

Dotted notes – recognize dotted rhythms

Recognize pickup measure – create pickup measure when appropriate

Detect swing – recognize and represent swung eighth notes as ordinary eighths rather than triplet or dotted rhythms

Exporting to other file formats

The native *.mscz* and *.mscx* formats are the only ones that are guaranteed to preserve all of the information present in a score. In order to facilitate interoperability with other programs, however, MuseScore allows you to export your score to a number of other formats. We have already discussed the audio (in the chapter on *Playback and Audio Output*) and graphic (in *Printing and Graphic Output*) formats supported by MuseScore. But aside from MIDI, none of these formats contain any of the type of information MuseScore or any other notation program would need in order to import a score, and MIDI is very limited in the type of information it can represent.

MusicXML is the recommended format to use for import into other programs. To export a score to MusicXML or other formats, go to File〉Export. This displays a standard file dialog you can use to choose the file name for the exported file, as well as a drop-down menu to select the file type.

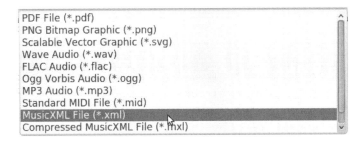

As we have already seen in the chapter on *Printing and Graphic Output*, MuseScore also provides a command File〉Export Parts to export the score and all parts individually. In addition to the various audio and graphic formats, you can choose MusicXML, or you can choose *.mscz* or *.mscx*. This can be useful if you wish to have non-linked versions of the parts in your score.

Chapter 33

Customization

One of the strengths of MuseScore is the degree of flexibility it offers through customization. We have already seen throughout this book how the appearance and behavior of most score elements can be altered through style settings and properties set in the *Inspector*. In this chapter, we will look at customizing the appearance and behavior of MuseScore itself. For instance, the location of the toolbars and windows, the contents of the palettes, the color of the background, the default style settings applied to new scores and to imported scores, the devices used for audio output, and keyboard shortcuts – all of these and more can be personalized to suit your needs.

User Interface

In the chapter on *Finding Your Way Around*, we looked at the various toolbars and windows within MuseScore. In this section, we will show how they can be customized.

Toolbars

The toolbars within the main window of MuseScore can be enabled or disabled individually by right-clicking an empty area of any toolbar and checking or unchecking the corresponding options in the context menu that appears.

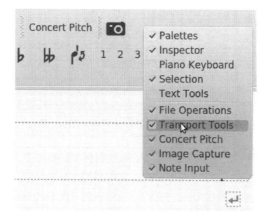

In addition, toolbars can be undocked so they float above the main window.

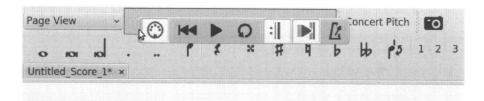

Once undocked, you can also re-dock a toolbar in another location.

Windows

As discussed in *Finding Your Way Around*, windows can be enabled or disabled via the View menu or by keyboard shortcuts. The *Inspector*, *Palettes*, *Selection Filter*, and *Piano Keyboard* can also be undocked and re-docked in the same manner as toolbars.

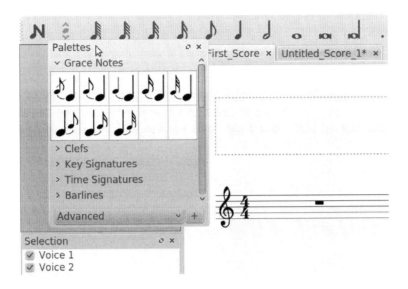

You can resize most windows in MuseScore whether docked or undocked.

Language

The MuseScore interface has been translated in whole or in part into over 50 languages, with more being added regularly. To select the language for your installation, go to `Edit` ⟩ `Preferences` ⟩ `General` and select from the *Language* drop-down menu. Clicking the `Update translations` button displays a dialog that allows you to download updated translations where available.

Language	Filename	File Size	Install/Update
English (US)	locale_en_U...	6.07 KB	No update
Afrikaans	locale_af.zip	23.76 KB	Update
العربية	locale_ar.zip	86.70 KB	Update
Asturianu	locale_ast.zip	99.29 KB	Update
Беларуская...	locale_be.zip	36.55 KB	Update
български	locale_bg.zip	131.92 KB	Update
Català	locale_ca.zip	315.53 KB	Update
Valencià	locale_ca@v...	454.14 KB	Update
Čeština	locale_cs.zip	457.36 KB	Update
Dansk	locale_da.zip	436.42 KB	Update
Deutsch	locale_de.zip	455.68 KB	Update
ελληνικά	locale_el.zip	429.68 KB	Update

Palettes

A particularly powerful feature of MuseScore is the ability to customize your palettes. This includes the ability to add and remove palettes as well as the ability to add and remove elements from palettes. So if there are symbols from the master *Symbols* palette (see *Miscellaneous Symbols* in the chapter on *Articulations and Other Symbols*) that you intend to use in many places within a score, you can copy these from the master *Symbols* palette to a custom palette in order to make them easier to find. Or, if there are particular text markings – perhaps with playback semantics defined (see the chapter on *Text*) – that you use often, you can copy them from your score to a custom palette in order to make them easier to apply. This can also be useful if you have a collection of fret diagrams (see *Fretboard Diagrams*) or bends (*Articulations and Other Symbols*) that you have created.

In this section, I will show you how to customize your palettes.

Workspaces

As mentioned in *Finding Your Way Around*, MuseScore provides two workspaces by default: *Basic* and *Advanced*. The workspace controls the contents of the *Palettes* window. The *Basic* workspace omits certain palettes that most users would not find useful, and includes only the most common elements on many of the remaining palettes. The *Advanced* workspace contains the full set of markings supported by MuseScore, with the exception of the special symbols found on the master *Symbols* palette.

In order to customize the palettes in MuseScore, you will need to create your own workspace first. Go to Edit ⟩ Workspaces ⟩ New or click the ⊞ button next to the workspace selection menu at the bottom of the *Palettes* window.

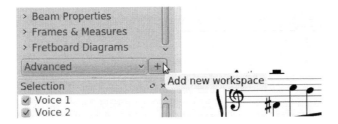

You will be prompted to give the workspace a name. After doing so, MuseScore will set up your new workspace as a copy of the workspace you were using at the time. If you were in the *Basic* workspace when you pressed the ⊞, your new workspace will contain the same limited set of palettes and elements as the *Basic* workspace. If you were in the *Advanced* workspace, however, your new workspace will contain the full set of palettes and elements.

Upon adding a new workspace, it is selected by default. You can switch between workspaces using the Edit ≫ Workspaces menu or the drop-down menu at the bottom of the *Palettes* window.

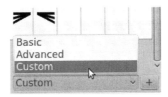

To delete the current workspace, use Edit ≫ Workspaces ≫ Delete .

Adding, removing, and arranging palettes

Once you have created a workspace, you can begin customizing the palettes for that workspace. You can add or remove palettes, rearrange them, and most importantly, add new elements to palettes. The latter feature is discussed in the next section, but first, I will discuss operations performed on palettes as a whole.

To add a new palette to your workspace, right-click a palette name and select Insert New Palette from the resulting palette context menu.

The *Palette Properties* dialog then appears, allowing you to type a name and change other settings.

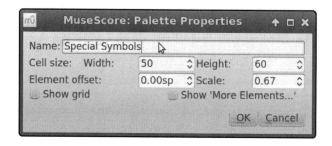

The settings in this dialog are:

Name – name displayed in *Palettes* window
Width – width of each cell in pixels
Height – height of each cell in pixels
Element offset – vertical position of elements within cells
Scale – size of palette items relative to actual size of elements in score
Show grid – display grid lines between palette cells

When you press OK, the new palette is inserted.

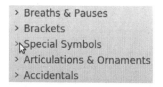

To rearrange the palettes within the *Palettes* window, use the Move Palette Up and Move Palette Down commands in the palette context menu.

You can save and load palettes individually using the Save Palette and Load Palette commands in the palette context menu. However, palettes are saved automatically, so it is not necessary to save them explicitly unless you wish to share a custom palette between different workspaces.

To delete a palette, use the Delete Palette command in the palette context menu.

Customizing palette contents

If you wish to customize the contents of a palette, first be sure you are in a custom workspace, then right-click the palette name and enable the Enable Editing option.

To add elements to a palette, you can drag an element either from the *Master Palette* or from your score to the desired palette, while holding Ctrl + Shift. The element will appear in the first empty cell.

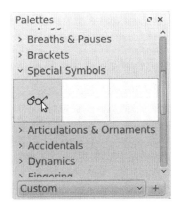

An element added to a palette as described in this section can then be added to scores in the usual fashion – either by dragging it to an element in your score, or, for elements types that support it, by selecting one or more elements in your score and then double-clicking the palette icon.

You can further customize the appearance of the element within the palette by right-clicking it and selecting Properties from the resulting cell context menu. This displays the *Cell Properties* dialog box.

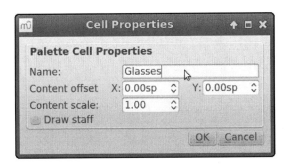

Name – name to display in tooltip when hovering mouse over palette cell
Content offset – position of element within cell
Content scale – size of palette item relative to actual size of element in score
Draw staff – display element on a staff within palette

You can remove an element from a palette by selecting Clear from the cell context menu.

Style

Another powerful customization available in MuseScore is the ability to not only define style settings for a given score, but to save those settings to a file, load them into other scores, and to set the default styles to be used for new scores, for imported scores, and for parts. In this section, we will look at how you can save and load style files. Later, you will see how to specify the styles to be used by default (see *Score* and *Import* below).

To save the style settings for the current score to a file, go to Style Save Style . A standard file dialog will appear, allowing you to specify a file name and location. The file extension *.mss* will be used, and the default location is the *Styles* folder MuseScore created for you (see *Folders* in the chapter on *File Operations*).

To load a previously saved *.mss* file into a score, go to Style Load Style . A standard file dialog will appear, allowing you to select a style to load.

Plugins

One of the great things about open source software is the sense of community it fosters, encouraging people to participate in the development of the software. There are many users of MuseScore who are also programmers, and while some of them have helped with the development of MuseScore, others still have found it more appropriate to contribute in other ways. MuseScore supports a plugin framework that allows programmers to write code that you can download to extend the capabilities of MuseScore.

There are plugins available to automate the performance of a number of tasks that might otherwise require many manual steps. Some of these are quite sophisticated. For example, one plugin can automatically add courtesy accidentals as required throughout your score. Another can analyze a four-part chorale and identify voice leading errors such as parallel fifths. Another can convert a score to shape notation.

It is beyond the scope of this book to teach you how to write your own plugins – for more information on that topic, consult `musescore.org`. However, you do not have to be a programmer to download and use the various plugins that are already provided on that web site. In this section, we will look at how to download and use a plugin.

Pre-installed plugins

MuseScore comes with a number of plugins already pre-installed, but they may still need to be enabled as described in *Enabling and disabling plugins* below. Some of the pre-installed plugins are intended for programmers only, to serve as a model for creating new plugins, but a few are useful as is:

abc_import – uses a web service to convert a score in the text-based ABC notation into a
    MusicXML file which is then imported into MuseScore
colornotes – colors notes in the current score according to pitch
notenames – adds text above each note in the current score, naming the pitches

Downloading plugins

To find plugins to download, go to musescore.org and browse the plugins menu. When you find a plugin you would like to try, download and save it to your Plugins folder (see *Folders* in the chapter on *File Operations*). Most plugins will be in *.zip* format, so you will need to use an appropriate program on your system to extract the contents of the archive into a new folder within the Plugins folder.

Once you have downloaded the plugin, you will need to enable it for use in MuseScore as described below.

Enabling and disabling plugins

To enable and disable plugins, go to Plugins ≫ Plugin Manager. The *Plugin Manager* lists the currently installed plugins (pre-installed as well as ones you have downloaded to your Plugins folder).

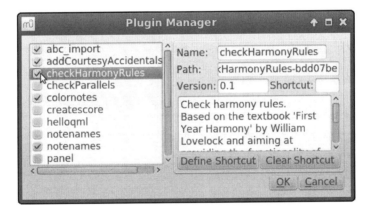

To enable or disable a particular plugin, select it from the list and check or uncheck the box to the left of its name.

On the right side of the dialog you will see a description of the plugin as well as buttons Define Shortcut and Clear Shortcut. These allow you to assign shortcuts for plugins in the same manner as described in *Shortcuts*.

Using plugins

To run a plugin, be sure it it is enabled (see above), and then you can run it from the Plugins menu. If you defined a keyboard shortcut for the plugin, you can also invoke it that way. Some plugins work on the current score as a whole; others work on a selection; others do not interact with the current score at all but instead load new ones or perform other tasks. Consult the documentation for the particular plugin you wish to use for more information.

Preferences

MuseScore allows you to control many aspects of its behavior via $\boxed{\text{Edit}} \rangle \boxed{\text{Preferences}}$. The resulting *Preferences* dialog is divided into a number of tabs.

General

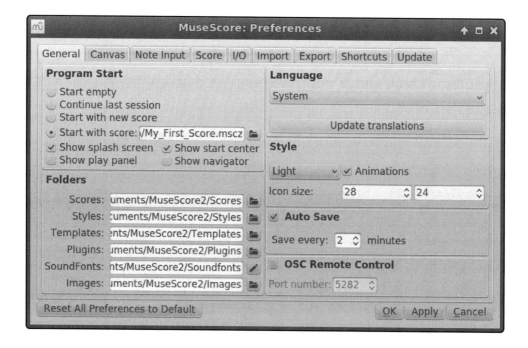

Program Start – select what scores and windows MuseScore displays when it is started

Folders – select location of the folders used by default when saving or loading different types of files

Language – select language to use for menus, dialogs, buttons, and other user interface elements

Style – colors and icon sizes for user interface

Auto Save – interval at which to automatically save a copy of current score to be used for recovery in the event of a crash

OSC Remote Control – enable certain operations in MuseScore to be controlled by other applications that use the Open Sound Control (OSC) standard

Canvas

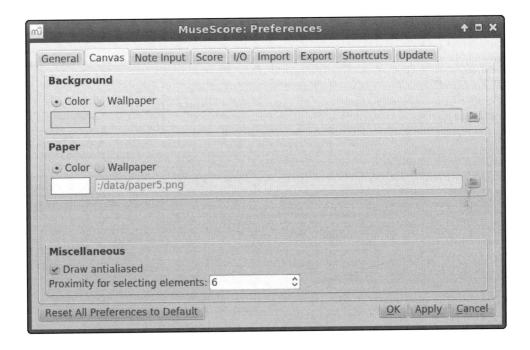

Background – appearance of the background behind the pages of your scores (on screen only)
Paper – appearance of the virtual paper on which your scores are displayed (on screen display)

Note Input

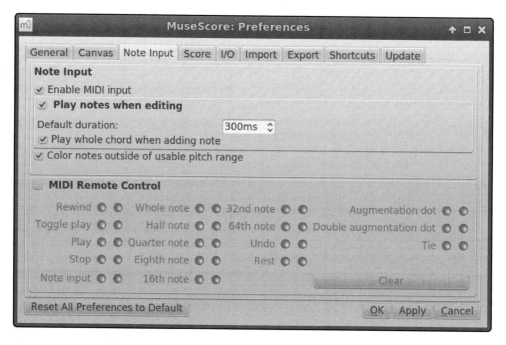

Note Input

Enable MIDI Input – allow MuseScore to respond to MIDI input

Play notes while editing – play each note when you select or edit it

Default duration – length to play each note while editing

Play whole chord when adding note – during note entry, when adding a note to an existing chord, play the whole chord rather than just the note being added

Color notes outside usable range – display notes in dark yellow or red if they are outside the amateur or professional ranges for the instrument as set in *Staff Properties*

MIDI Remote Control – assign keys on a MIDI device to perform various functions within MuseScore

The *MIDI Remote Control* section allows you to assign specific keys on your MIDI device to perform functions within MuseScore, such as changing duration. This can help you enter music using your MIDI keyboard alone with less need for the mouse or computer keyboard.

To assign a key on your MIDI device to perform a function, first enable the *MIDI Remote Control* option if it is not already. Then, press the second (rightmost) button next to the command to which you want to assign a key. The button will highlight in red, indicating that it is waiting for you to press the key you wish to use as shortcut. Press a key on your MIDI device and the first button will highlight in green, indicating a shortcut has been assigned.

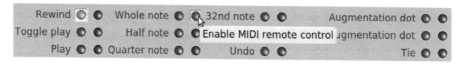

From now on, pressing that key on your MIDI device will perform the assigned command. You can temporarily disable these shortcuts – so the keys will enter notes as usual – by unchecking the *MIDI Remote Control* option. You can clear these shortcuts permanently using the [Clear] button.

Score

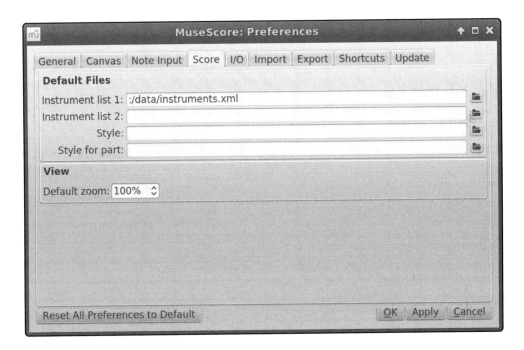

Instrument list 1 / 2 – specify files containing instrument definitions
Style – style file to be used when creating a new score from scratch
Style for part – style file to be used when generating parts
Default zoom – initial zoom setting when loading a score

Instrument list

The instrument list – used when creating new scores or adding instruments via [Edit ⟩ Instruments] – is built in to MuseScore. In this dialog, you can specify an alternate or additional instrument list. A full description of the syntax of this file is beyond the scope of this book, but you can get started by examining the file provided in the `instruments` folder within your MuseScore installation.

Style

You can customize the default styles used for new scores. First, create a style (*.mss*) file as described above in *Style*. You can then set this style to be used by default in this dialog. You can have separate defaults for scores created from scratch and for parts generated via File ⟩ Parts.

I/O

Most of the settings on this tab are platform-dependent. They allow you to select the audio output method used by MuseScore.

The JACK settings should be present on all platforms, but they will only be useful if you have JACK installed. A full discussion of JACK is beyond the scope of this book.

Import

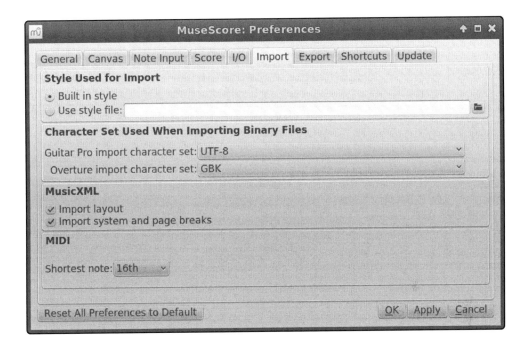

Style Used For Import – style file to apply when importing scores in other formats

Character Set Used When Importing Binary Files – select how non-ASCII text is interpreted in Guitar Pro and Overture files

MusicXML – control the import of formatting information

MIDI – select defaults to use when importing MIDI files

The *Style Used For Import* settings allow you to specify a style (*.mss*) file defining the default settings to apply when importing files in other formats.

Export

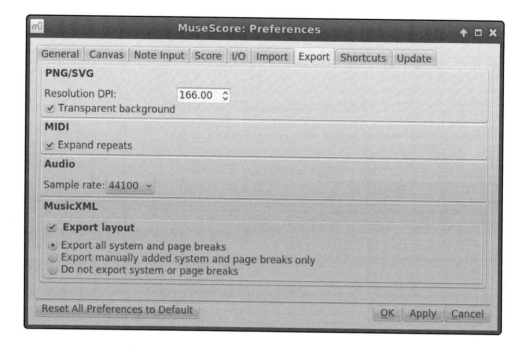

PNG/SVG
Resolution – DPI to use for graphic output
Transparent background – represent paper as transparent for graphic output
MIDI
Expand repeats – expand repeated section within exported MIDI file
Audio
Sample rate – sample rate to use for audio formats that support this setting
MusicXML
Export layout – control the export of formatting information

Shortcuts

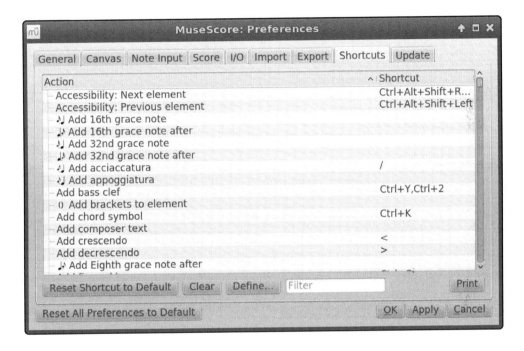

As have seen throughout this book, MuseScore provides keyboard shortcuts for many commands. There are also a number of commands that could be performed by keyboard, but there is no shortcut assigned by default – there are, after all, only so many keys available. MuseScore allows you to customize the keyboard shortcut assignments, so you can change which commands are performed by which keys. Commands can have multiple shortcuts, and shortcuts can consist of a sequence of keys pressed one after another, not just keys pressed simultaneously. For example, the command to insert a bass clef during note input is Ctrl + Y followed by Ctrl + 2 .

To customize the shortcut for a given command, first find the command in the list. To make this easier, there is a filter that allows you to type a word and find all commands that include it.

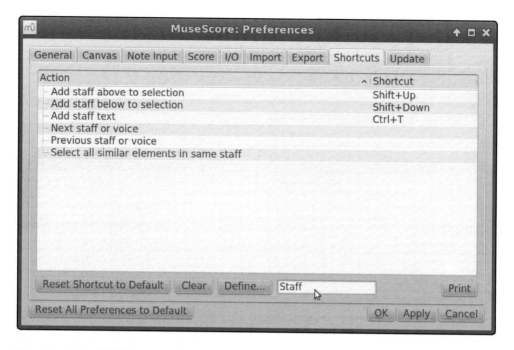

There is also a $\boxed{\text{Print}}$ button to allow you to print the full list.

Once you have found the command you wish to customize, select the command in the list and click the $\boxed{\text{Define}}$ button. A dialog box is displayed to allow you to define a new shortcut for the command.

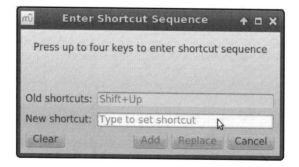

The existing shortcuts, if any, will be displayed. To define a new shortcut, simply press the combination of keys you wish to use. If the shortcut conflicts with a command already in use, you will be informed of the conflict. The $\boxed{\text{Clear}}$ button allows you to start over and try again, or you can cancel out of the dialog, find the command with the conflict, and clear or change its shortcut.

Once you have entered a new shortcut that does not conflict with any others, click the $\boxed{\text{Add}}$ button to add the new shortcut to the list of shortcuts for this command, or $\boxed{\text{Replace}}$ to replace the existing shortcut(s) with the new one. This will set the shortcut and close the dialog.

To restore the default shortcut for a command, select it from the list and click the $\boxed{\text{Reset Shortcut to Default}}$ button. To remove all shortcuts from a command, click the $\boxed{\text{Clear}}$

button.

Update

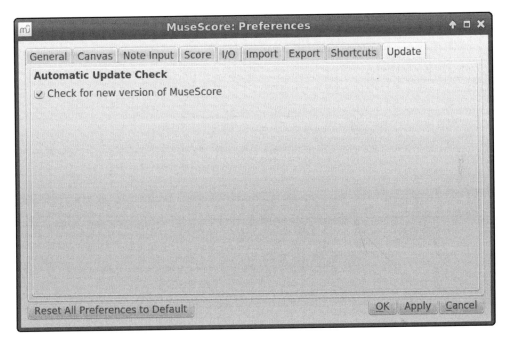

Check for new version of MuseScore – enable automatic check for updates

Index

13516640R00230

Printed in Great Britain
by Amazon.co.uk, Ltd.,
Marston Gate.